IMAGES
of America

HAWKINSVILLE

On the Cover: Pictured is one of the many steamboats that plied the waters of the Ocmulgee River during the late 19th century. (Courtesy of Georgia Archives, Vanishing Georgia, pul 003.)

IMAGES
of America

HAWKINSVILLE

Phillip A. Gibbs and Tracie L. Provost with
The Hawkinsville–Pulaski County
Historical Society

ARCADIA
PUBLISHING

ISBN 978-0-7385-5359-7

Published by Arcadia Publishing
Charleston SC, Chicago IL, Portsmouth NH, San Francisco CA

Printed in the United States of America

Library of Congress Catalog Card Number: 2007939592

For all general information contact Arcadia Publishing at:
Telephone 843-853-2070
Fax 843-853-0044
E-mail sales@arcadiapublishing.com
For customer service and orders:
Toll-Free 1-888-313-2665

Visit us on the Internet at www.arcadiapublishing.com

This book is dedicated to the people of Hawkinsville,
past, present, and future.

CONTENTS

ACKNOWLEDGMENTS

We would like to acknowledge the following people for their support for this project: Karen Bailey, Lucille Bennett, Emma Jean Bowen, Robert Bowen, Gwen Brown, Niki and Linda Cabero, Ted Coleman, Mary Colson, Evelyn Herrington, Tom and Karen Hunt, Pat Keller, Sammy Kershaw, Hugh and Barbara Lawson, Frankie Snow, John Sparrow, Julie Stewart, Charles and Irene Stone, Chuck Sutherland, Ramsey "Bub" Way, Sam Way, and Josh Wilcox.

Special recognition should go to Gail DeLoach and the staff of the Georgia Archives for both their assistance and hard work in locating and reproducing the many photographs for this project.

And to our friends and family, thank you for your support and patience over the past several months. You have been invaluable to the making of this book.

INTRODUCTION

Situated along the west banks of the Ocmulgee River and named for the federal Indian agent Benjamin Hawkins, the town of Hawkinsville has been the seat of government for Pulaski County, Georgia, for over 150 years. This same location, coincidentally, was, some suspect, an important religious and social center for the Swift Creek Indians, a people whom we now know maintained extensive trade and cultural relations with other native peoples in the region. But the Creek people's ancient claims to the land were not recognized by either white Georgians or the federal government. And after a series of wars in the early 1800s, the Creek people in Middle Georgia were relocated to the Oklahoma territory. After their removal in the early 1820s, white Georgians, Carolinians, and Virginians established settlements on both the east and west sides of the Ocmulgee River. Although the eastern settlement of Hartford flourished in the early 1820s and was seriously considered as the future location of the state's capital, the western settlement of Hawkinsville developed rapidly. By the eve of the Civil War, the town was fast becoming an important commercial center.

Hawkinsville's development stemmed from both its location on the river and its proximity to some of the South's richest cotton lands. From the mid-1800s to the 1920s, cotton farmers from Pulaski and surrounding counties came to Hawkinsville to load their cotton onto paddle wheelers. From Hawkinsville, these boats journeyed down the Ocmulgee and Altamaha Rivers to Darien, Georgia. There cotton was transported to the textile mills of New England and the British Isles. The growth of this cotton economy attracted not only farmers looking for good, arable land, but also bankers, grocers, blacksmiths, tanners, and horse and carriage traders.

But Hawkinsville was not only tied to the river; it was also tied to the institution of slavery, so much so that by the eve of the Civil War, Pulaski County and Hawkinsville had the highest concentration of slaves of any other area in Middle Georgia. Concerned about the future of their "peculiar institution," as well as their ability to govern their own affairs, the town and county's citizens voted overwhelmingly for Georgia's secession from the Union in 1861. After news arrived that Abraham Lincoln fully intended to put down the Southern rebellion, farmers, tradesmen, and members of the city's planter-merchant elite organized regiments that would later fight in some of the Civil War's bloodiest battles.

The South's defeat brought freedom for Hawkinsville's black residents, but it was a freedom not without its challenges. Few former slaves had knowledge of the world beyond the plantation, and most had little or no ability to read or write. Although many received some help from the federal government, Northern philanthropists, and even their former masters, it was not enough to prevent the city and county's whites from reestablishing a system that would subordinate blacks to white rule. Yet despite these obstacles, the city's black citizens established churches, schools, civic organizations, and businesses. Many during the early 1900s became respected and highly valued members of the community.

Although the city and region suffered an economic decline during and after the Civil War, the migration of Northern families to the area in the 1880s helped revitalize the local economy.

Many of the families joined hands with enterprising native Georgians and invested in banks, steamboats, gins, oil mills, railroads, and a telephone company. Magnificent new homes graced the city's tree-lined streets, new schools were established, an opera house was constructed, and Northern harness racers built stables and a track for the winter training of their horses. The city not only flourished but bustled with commercial and cultural activity. By the early 1900s, the people of Hawkinsville could claim with some justification that their city was the "Queen of the Wiregrass."

Apart from the great loss of life in World War I and the social and economic disruptions in the United States during the 1920s and 1930s, Hawkinsville's citizens had every reason to be optimistic as they approached the 100-year anniversary of their town. The increasing number of automobiles on the city's streets, together with the construction of new roads and the electrification of homes, convinced its citizens that the city was outdistancing many of its neighbors

Hawkinsville never became the bustling metropolis that many envisioned. On the contrary, it remains today a small town with quiet, wooded streets and friendly people. But to walk down one of the city's streets is to step back in time. Its elegant homes, some of which date to the 1820s and 1830s, and its historic business district are a reminder of how people full of hope and promise built not just a city but a community. The images and narrative that follow are their story.

One

A River and a Town

Hawkinsville sits 46 miles south of Macon on the Ocmulgee River. On the opposite bank sits the site of Old Hartford, once a thriving settlement that vied for being named state capital. This area has been under continual habitation for thousands of years. The Swift Creek Indians built mounds in what is now Old Hartford around 500 CE. This culture was later replaced by the Mississippian culture, which was supplanted by the Creek Confederacy by the 1700s. The Creeks were forced out by Americans in the 1800s.

Named for Col. Benjamin Hawkins, a Creek Indian agent, Hawkinsville started as a trading post. During Andrew Jackson's march to Florida during the Seminole Wars, it served as a temporary military camp. By the time Hawkinsville was incorporated in 1830, it had become a thriving commercial hub. Cotton and other agricultural goods moved via steamboat up and down the Ocmulgee River. Hawkinsville also served as a hub for overland travel. Two important Native American trails crossed here. These later became important trade routes and are today part of the U.S. highway system.

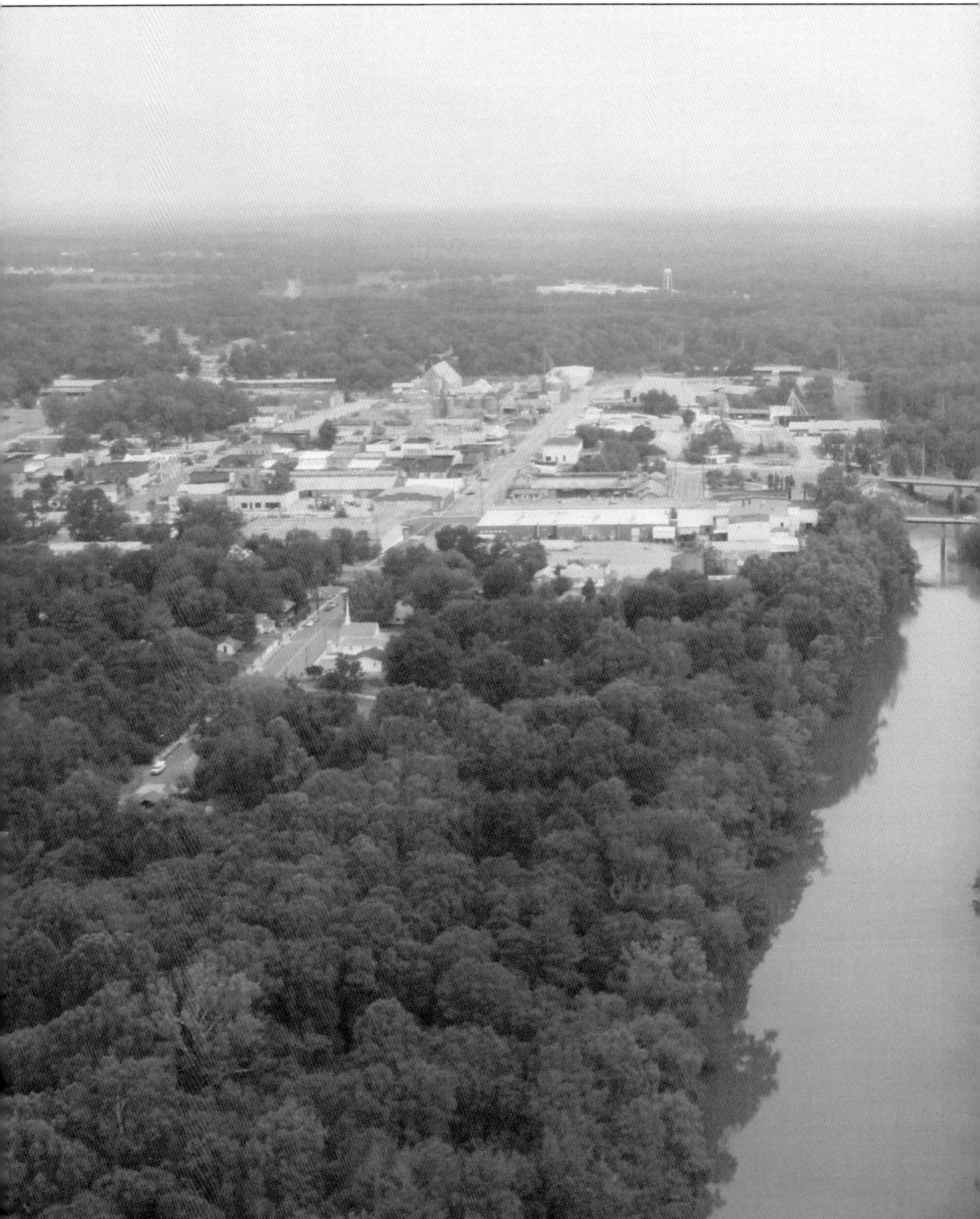

Hawkinsville is situated on the left bank of the Ocmulgee River. Old Hartford at one time sat on the right bank. Old Hartford was the original white settlement. The area has previously been

inhabited by the Creek nation and before that the Swift Creek Mound Builders. The Creeks set their capital here. (Courtesy of John Sparrow.)

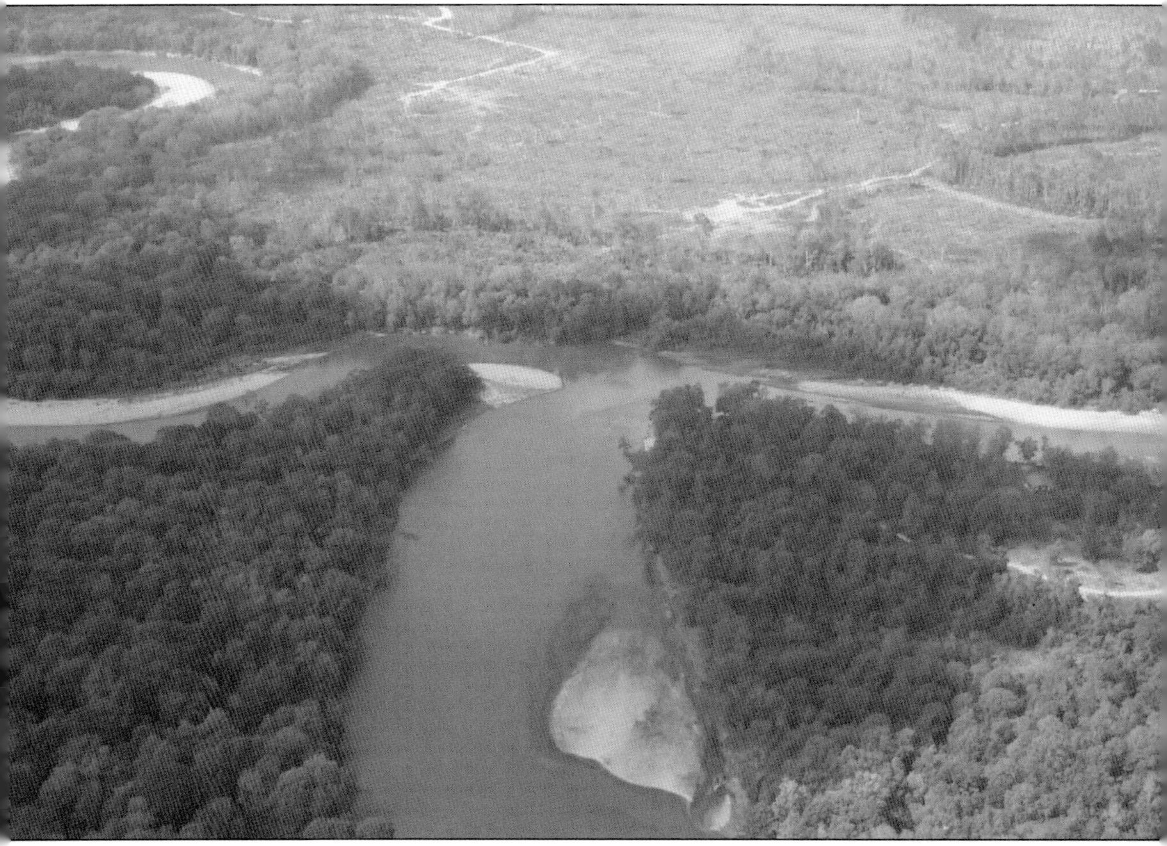

The Ocmulgee River runs 241 miles from the confluence of the Yellow, South, and Alcovy Rivers to where it joins the Oconee River to form the Altamaha River. It is believed that the name of the river comes from the Hitchiti Indian phrase *ok mulgis*, which translates to "bubbling water." The Altamaha River runs all the way to Darien. (Courtesy of John Sparrow.)

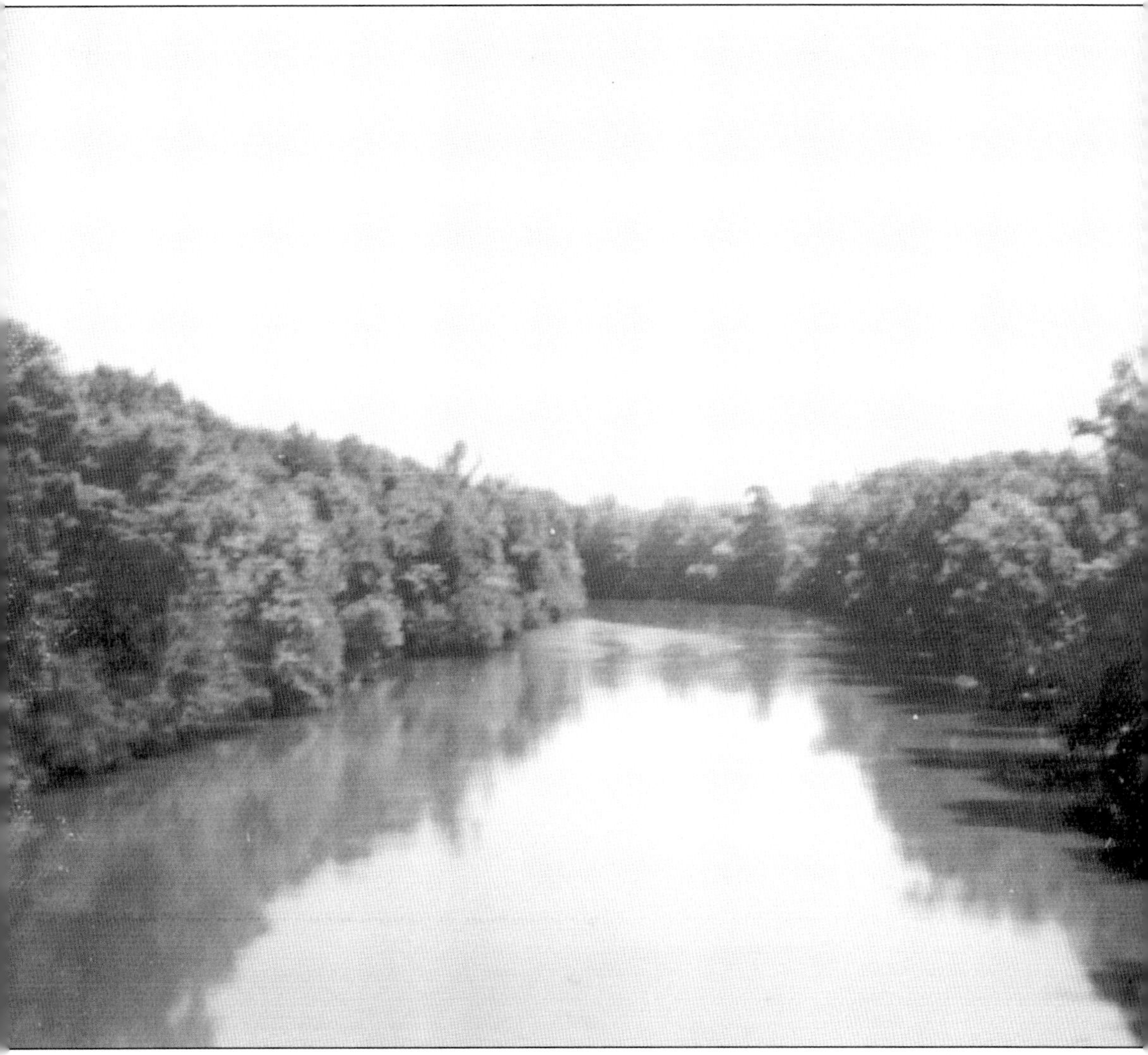

The Ocmulgee River near Hawkinsville is rather wide, nearly three miles in some places. It is also more shallow here than farther north. Over 1,000 years ago, mound builders settled along its shores. Mounds from the Swift Creek culture have been excavated near the site of Old Hartford, across the river from present-day Hawkinsville. (Courtesy of Emma Jean and Robert Bowen.)

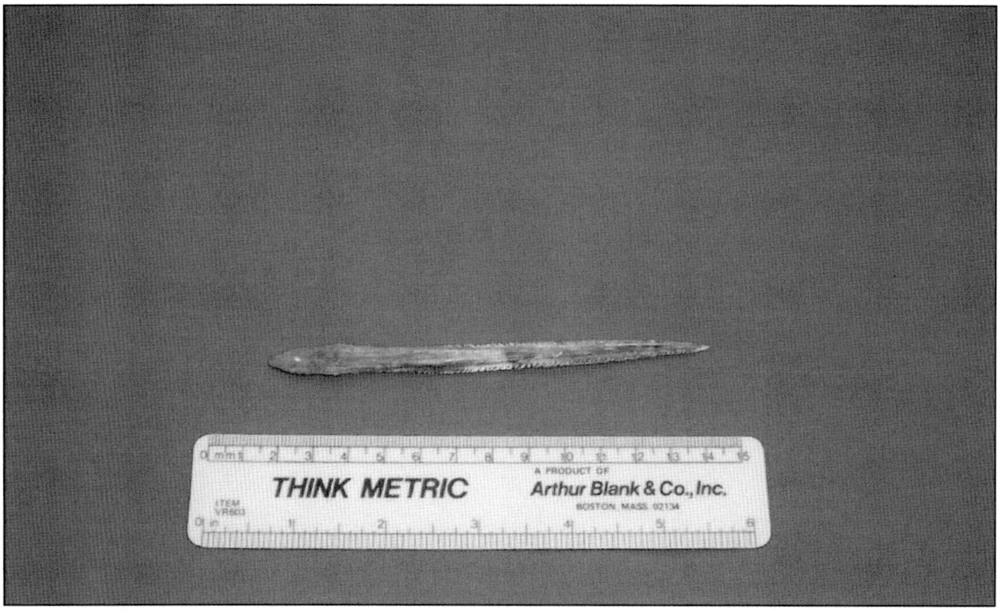

This stingray spine was found at the Hartford mound site in the ceremonial house. This was brought in from the coast and used as a tattooing needle. The Swift Creek Indians and later Creeks were known for their tattoos. (Courtesy of Phillip A. Gibbs and Frankie Snow.)

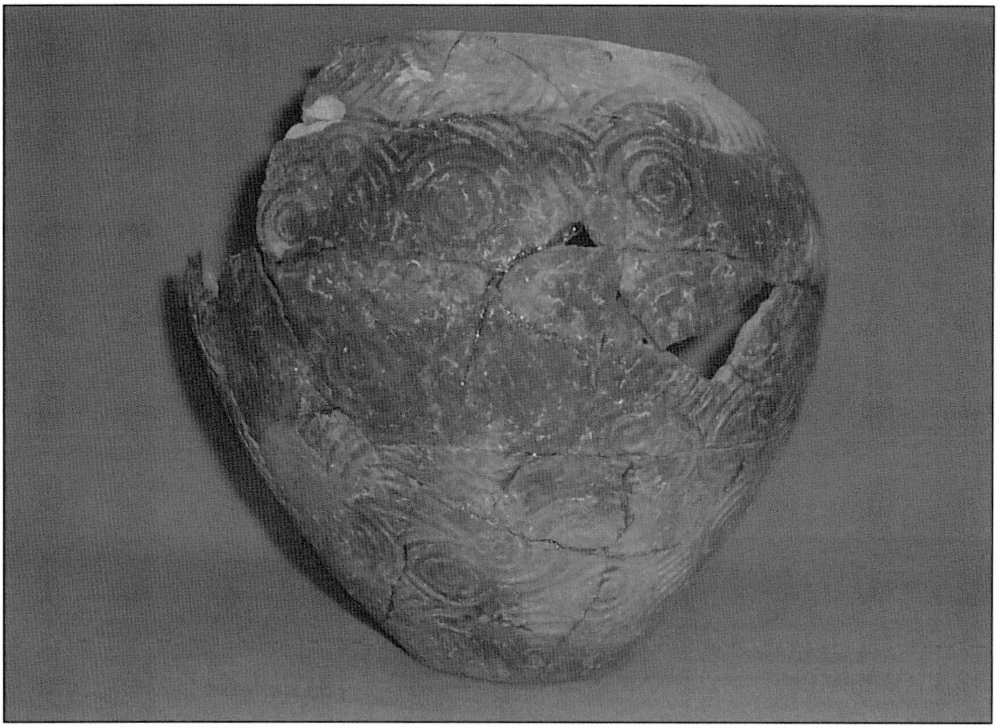

Found at the ceremonial house of the Hartford mound site, char marks on the outside indicate this vessel was used for cooking. It exhibits a traditional curvilinear, abstract, Swift Creek design. The vessel has been carbon-dated to 550–600 CE. (Courtesy of Phillip A. Gibbs and Frankie Snow.)

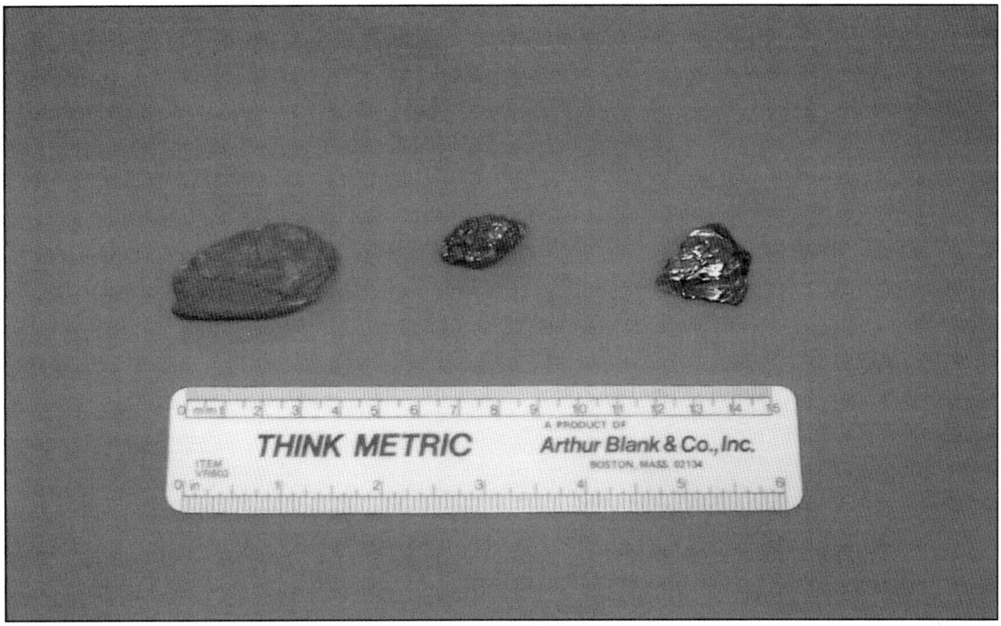

Swift Creek Indians traveled widely and had active trade routes. Among the artifacts found at the Hartford mound site were minerals not indigenous to the area. Shown here are a galena sample from the Mississippi Valley, graphite from the Piedmont, and pyrite. Also found at the site were copper and silver ear spools from the Lake Michigan region. (Courtesy of Phillip A. Gibbs and Frankie Snow.)

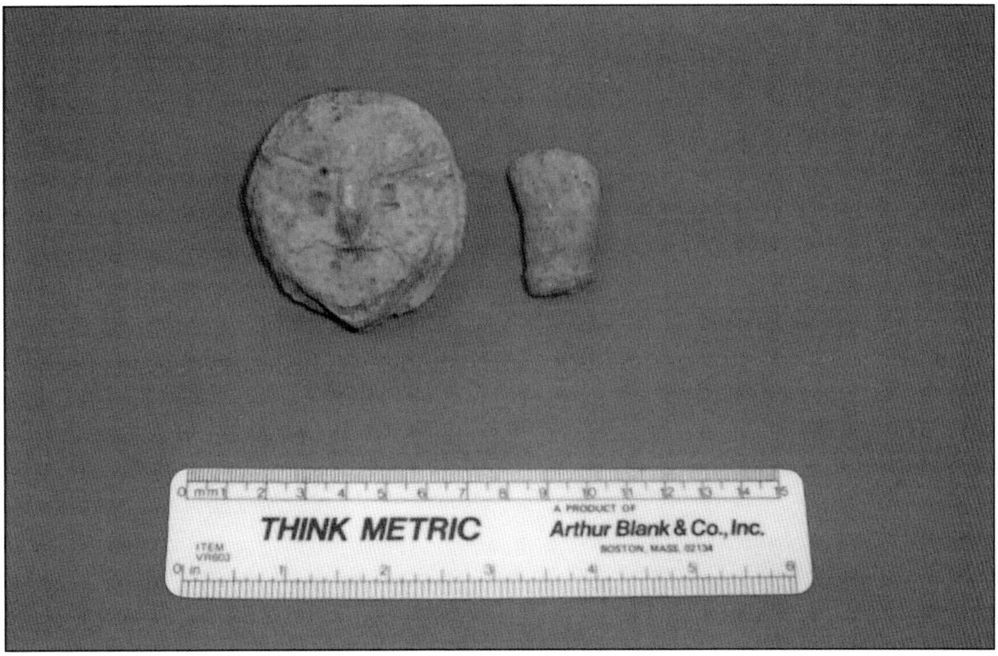

The Swift Creek Indians were master craftsmen, creating objects that were both useful and beautiful. On the left is an intricately carved face that was on a vessel handle. On the right is the leg of a figurine. Artifacts were taken from the Hartford mound site. (Courtesy of Phillip A. Gibbs and Frankie Snow.)

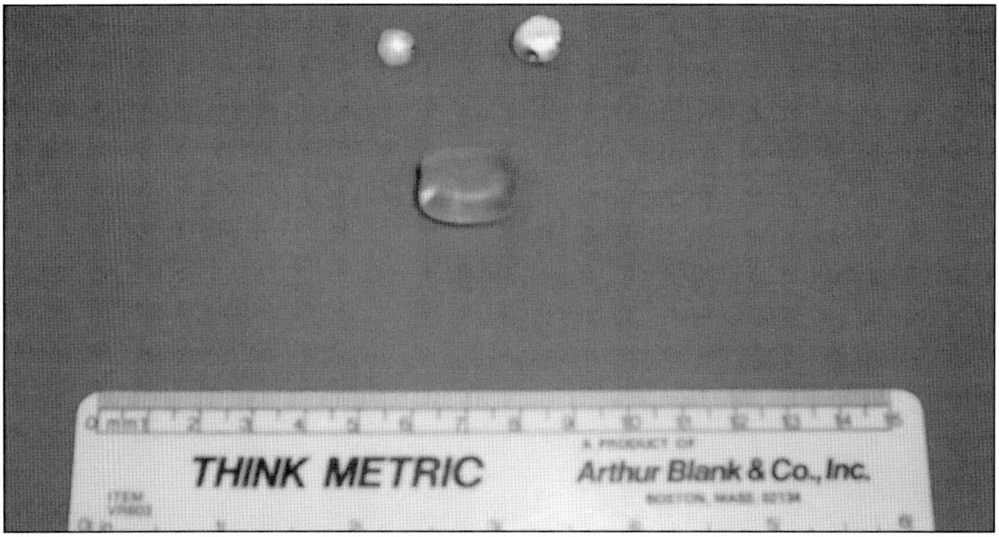

Jewelry was also important to the Swift Creek culture. Hundreds of beads were found in the ceremonial house at the Hartford mound site. Some of the beads were created from materials found close to Hartford; others were made from imported material. Pictured here are quartz and freshwater-pearl beads taken from the Hartford mound site. (Courtesy of Phillip A. Gibbs and Frankie Snow.)

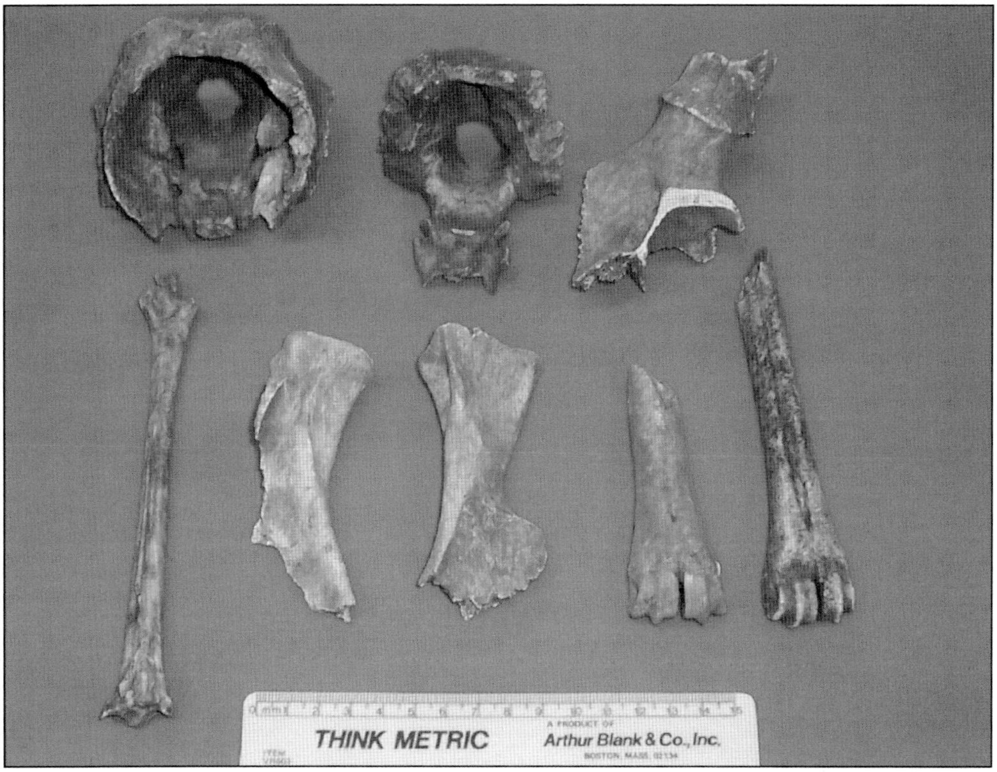

The ceremonial house at the Hartford mounds was used to hold great feasts. Bones from over 50 animals, mainly turkey and deer, were found there. (Courtesy of Phillip A. Gibbs and Frankie Snow.)

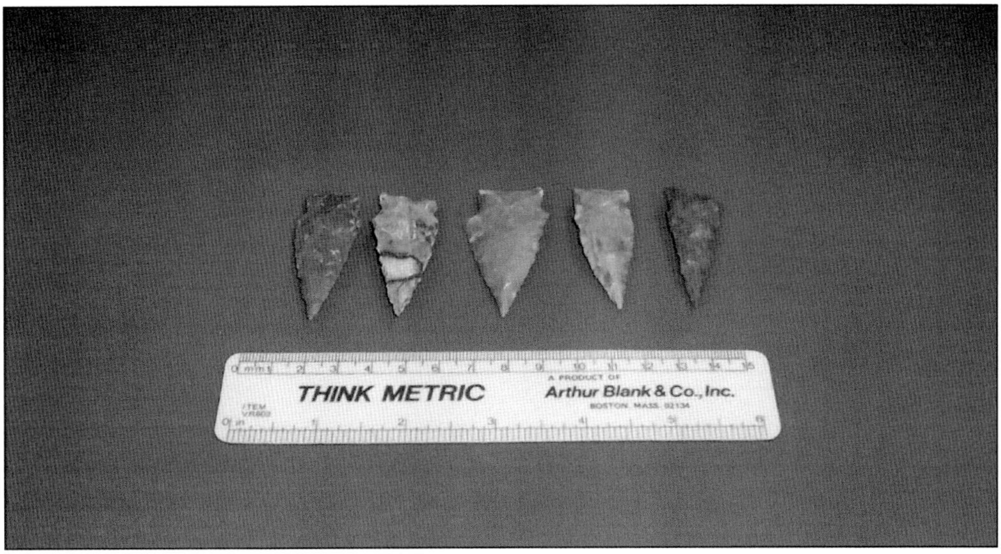

Over 300 projectiles were found on the floor of the Hartford mound ceremonial house. These would have been attached to either arrows or spears and used for hunting or warfare. (Courtesy of Phillip A. Gibbs and Frankie Snow.)

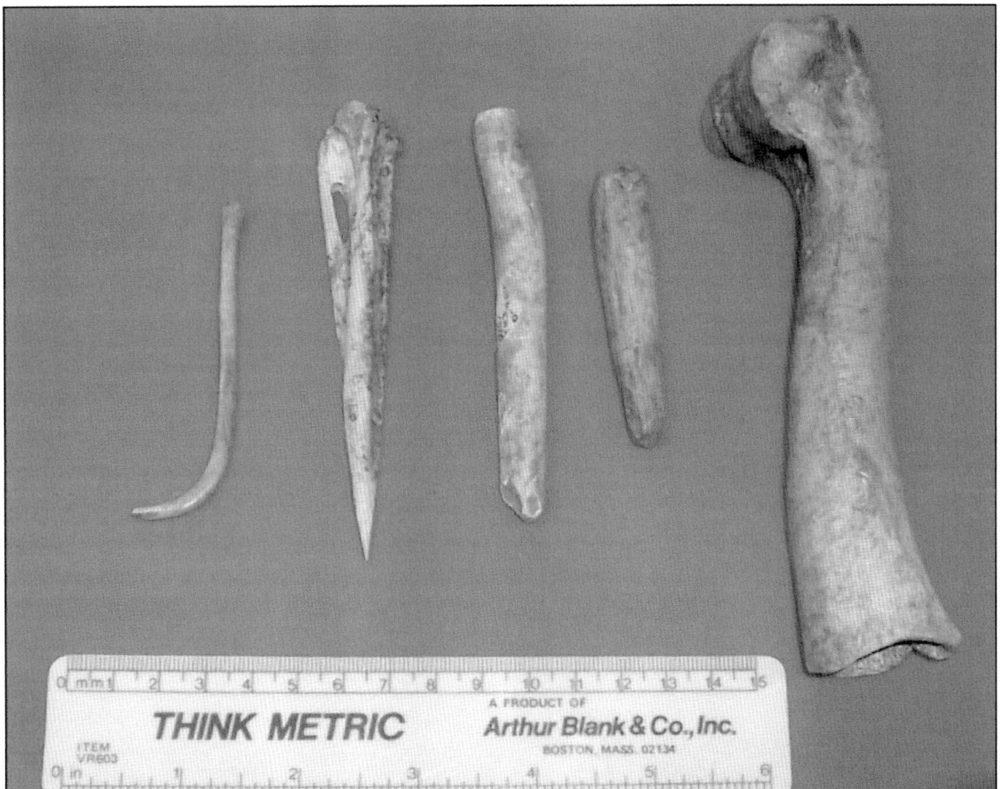

The Swift Creek Indians did not believe in waste and used every part of a killed animal. Here animal bones have been fashioned into various tools to be used by the tribe. (Courtesy of Phillip A. Gibbs and Frankie Snow.)

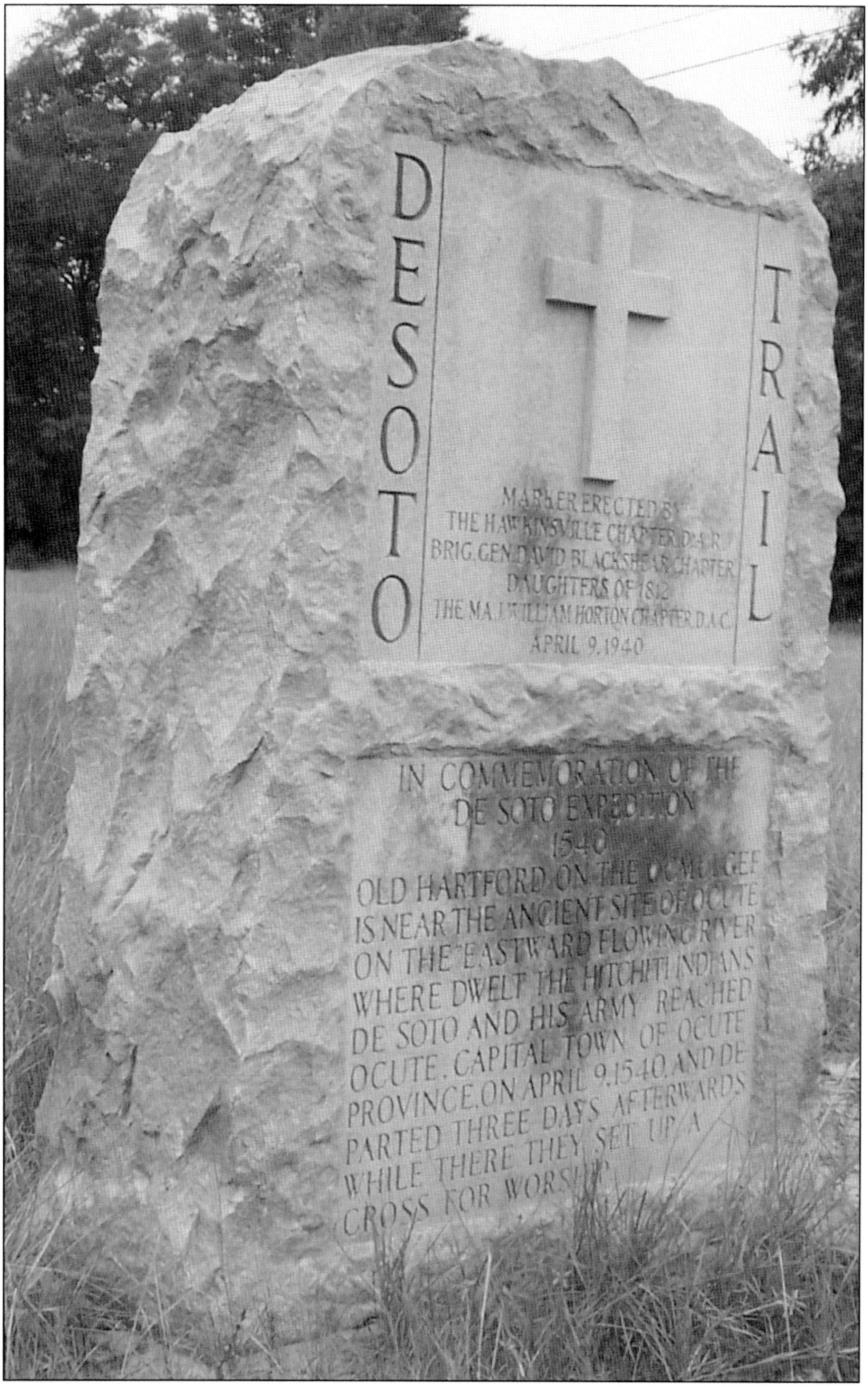

The Spanish explorer Hernando De Soto passed near Hawkinsville during 1540. Originally, it was believed that his trail was much closer to Old Hartford across the Ocmulgee River, but recent evidence has proven this incorrect. (Courtesy of Phillip A. Gibbs.)

William McIntosh (1775–1825) was a mixed-blood Creek who fought for Andrew Jackson during the Creek Indian War of 1813–1814. He led troops during the decisive Battle of Horseshoe Bend in Alabama. He had previously worked under Benjamin Hawkins to contain the problematic Creek leader Red Sticks. In his later life, he was one of nine Creek chiefs to sign the 1825 Treaty of Indian Springs, which ceded all Creek land in Georgia to the United States for $400,000. (Courtesy of Library of Congress.)

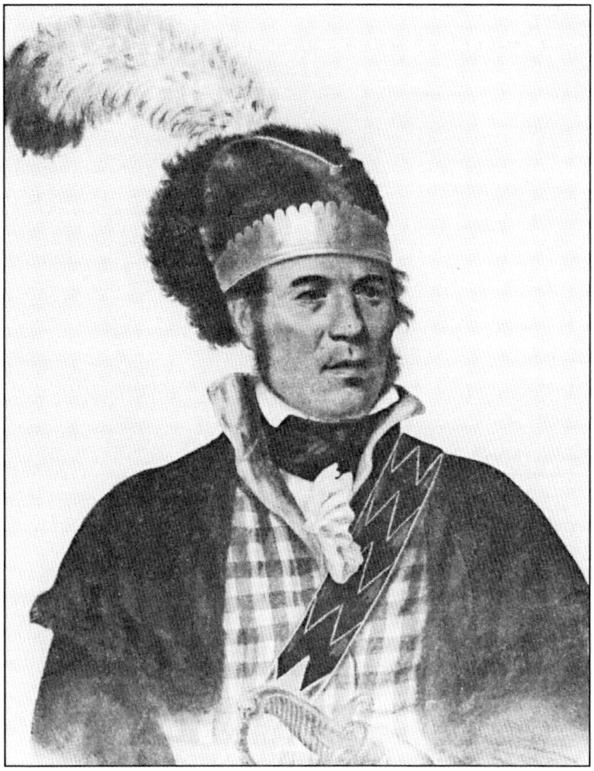

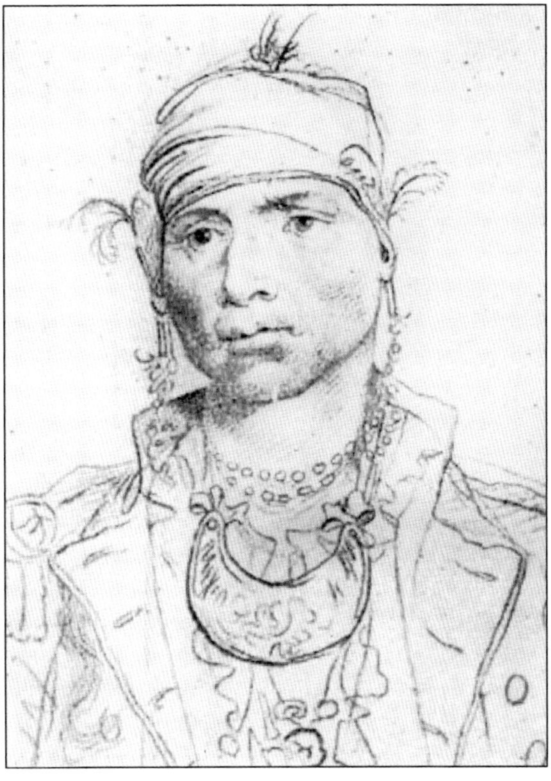

Alexander McGillivray (1750–1793) was a Creek leader in the late 18th century. Of mixed parentage, he received a European-style education in Charleston, South Carolina, that allowed him to gain considerable influence within the Creek nation during the American Revolution. His influence was key in centralizing power within the Creek Confederacy. McGillivray was one of the leaders in the fight to keep Creek lands out of the hands of white settlers in Georgia. (Courtesy of Library of Congress.)

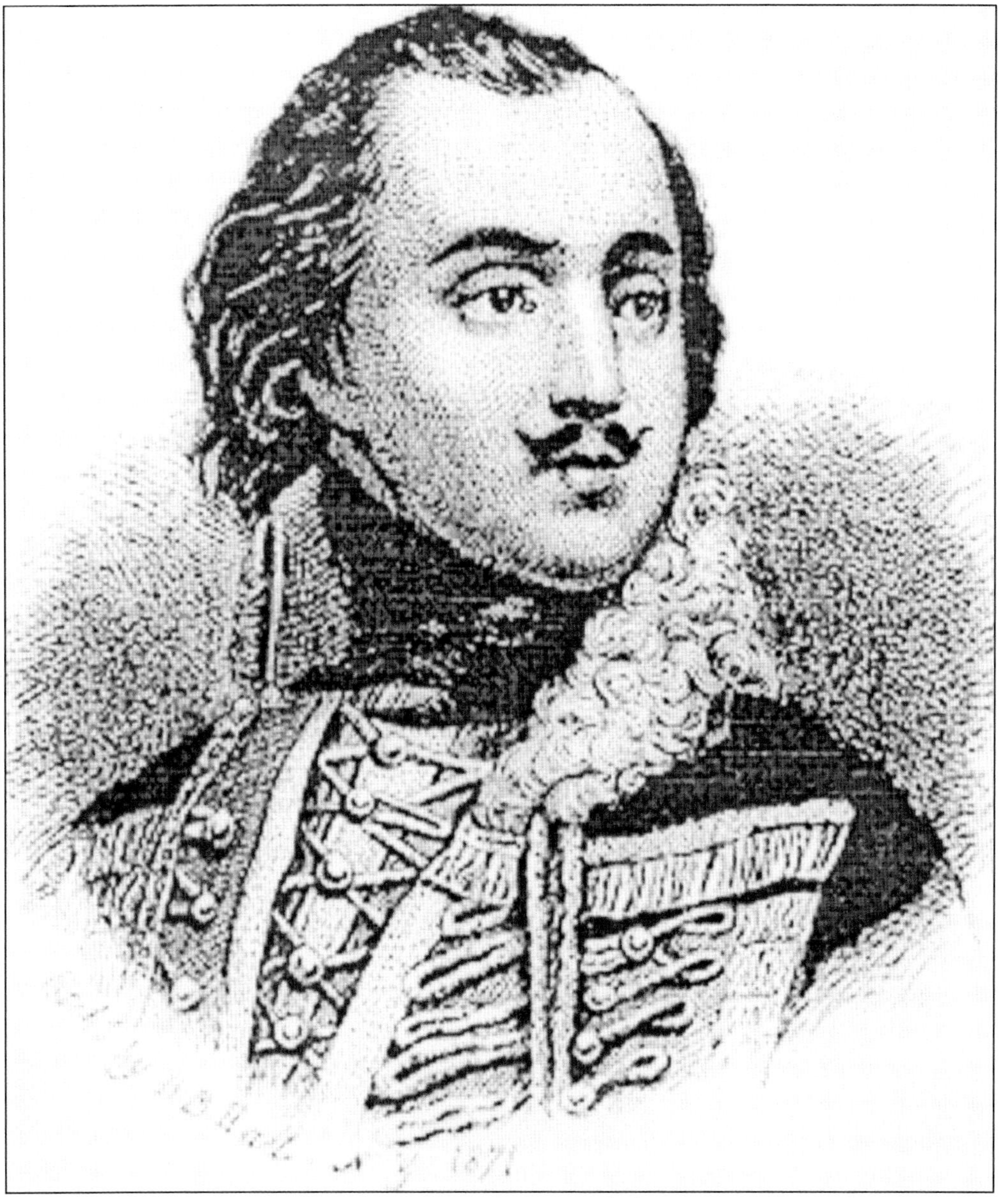

Kazimierz Pulaski (Casmir Pulaski, 1746–1779) was a Polish military commander who, after fighting the Russians, was recruited by the Marquis de Lafayette to fight for the Colonial side in the American Revolution. He created Pulaski's Legion and became known as the "Father of American Cavalry." During the Battle of Savannah, he was mortally wounded. In 1808, Pulaski County was created out of Laurens County and named after the Revolutionary War hero. (Courtesy of Pulaski County Clerk of Superior Court's Office.)

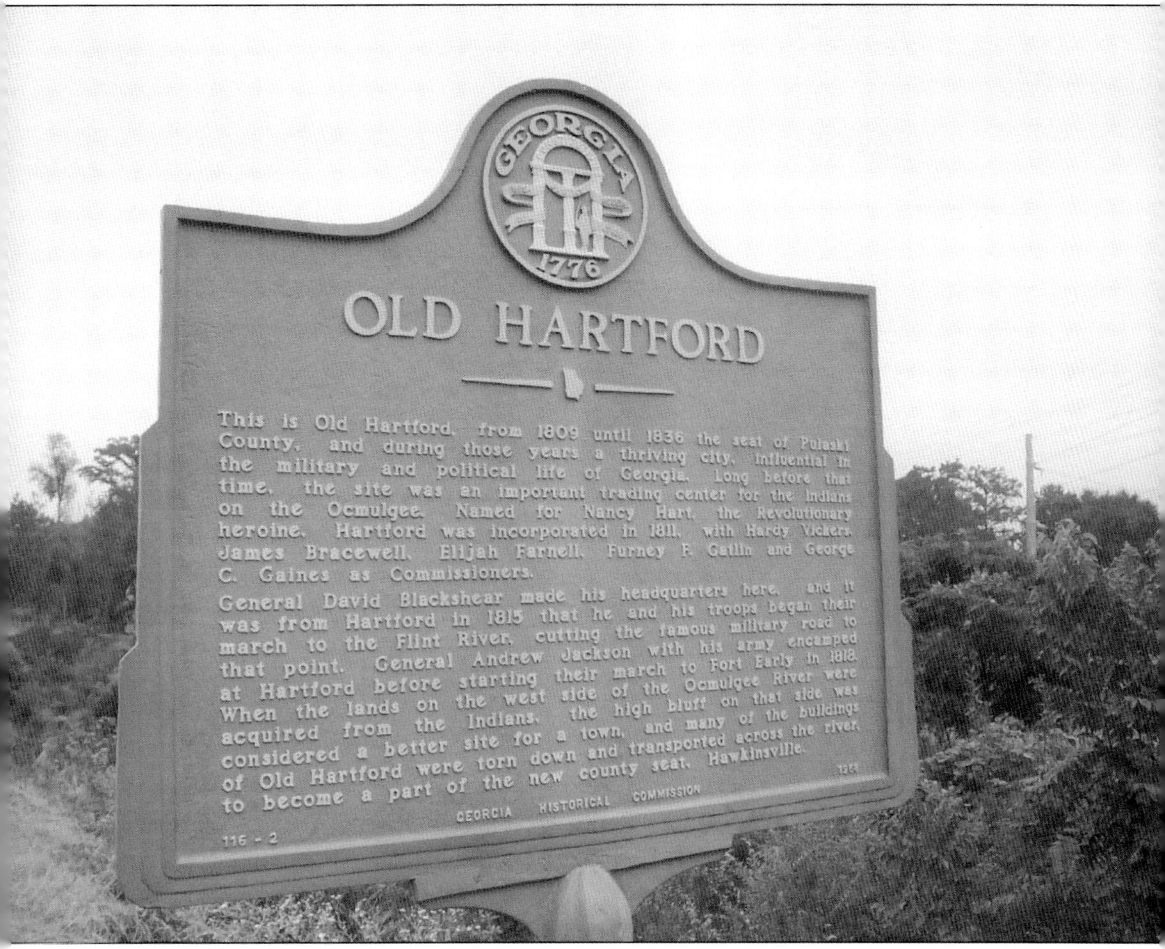

Old Hartford was the original white settlement along the Ocmulgee River. Named for the Revolutionary War heroine Nancy Hart, Hartford was incorporated in 1811. It served as the Pulaski County seat from 1809 until 1836. It came within a few votes of being named the state capital. The city fell into disuse after the Treaty of Indian Springs ceded land west of the Ocmulgee to Georgia. Hawkinsville was founded on the strategic bluff opposite Hartford and quickly eclipsed it. (Courtesy of Phillip A. Gibbs.)

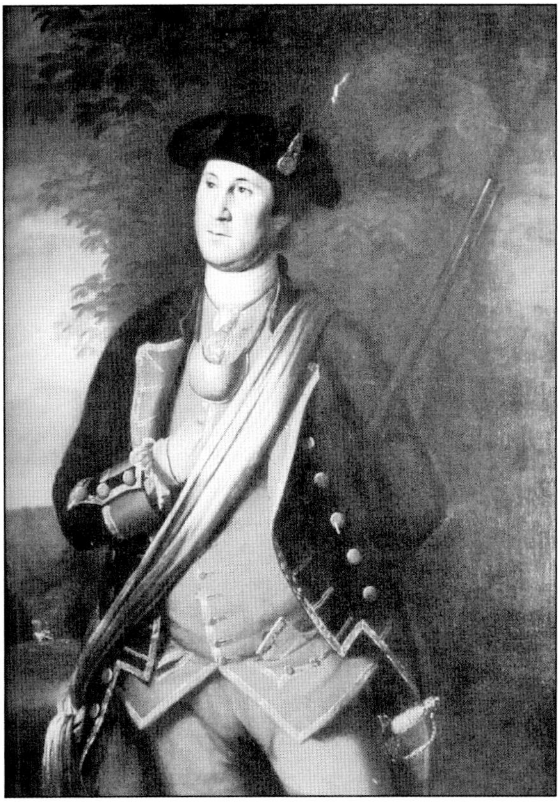

During his presidency, George Washington (1732–1799) appointed Col. Benjamin Hawkins as the general superintendent of all tribes south of the Ohio River. Washington also relied heavily on Hawkins's advice during the negotiations with Creek leaders that culminated in the Treaty of New York in 1790, which ceded some Creek lands in Georgia to the United States. (Courtesy of Library of Congress.)

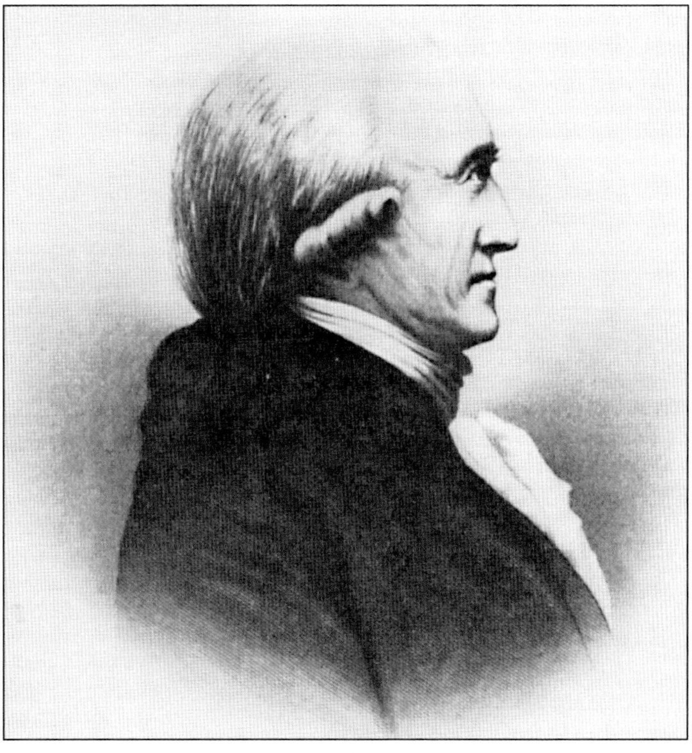

Col. Benjamin Hawkins (1754–1816) served as Gen. George Washington's interpreter for the first two years of the Revolutionary War and in 1785 became the Continental Congress's representative in negotiations with the Creek Indians. Beginning in 1796, Hawkins again served Washington, now president, as the superintendent of Indian affairs. He moved to Crawford County, Georgia, and became the principal agent to the Creek tribe. Both Fort Hawkins in Macon and Hawkinsville are named in honor of him. (Courtesy of Washington Library, Macon, Georgia.)

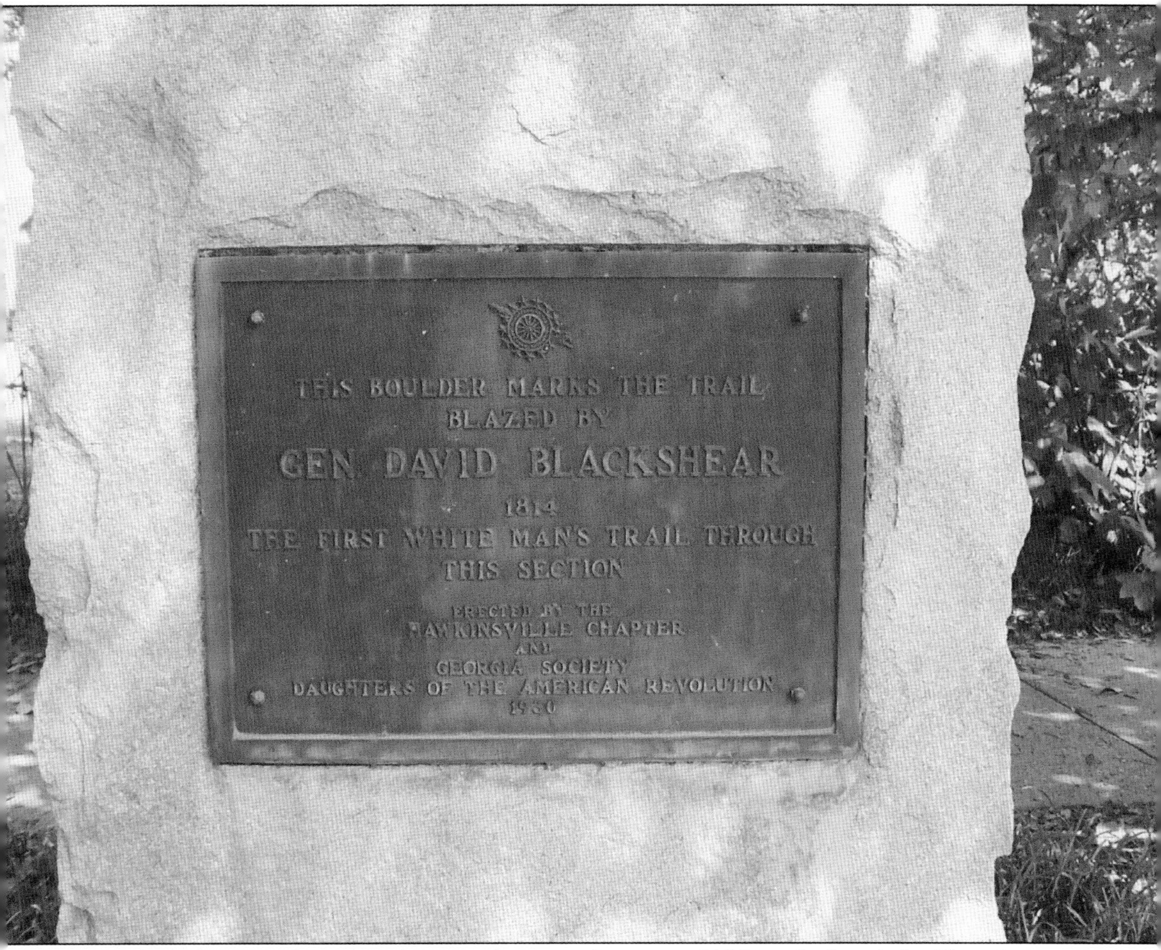

This Blackshear Trail marker denotes the route between Old Hartford and the Flint River. Originally an old Creek Indian trail, it was found useful by white settlers who made it their own. Gen. David Blackshear was in charge of troops that constructed a permanent road using the old trail that is commonly known as the Blackshear Road. (Courtesy of Phillip A. Gibbs.)

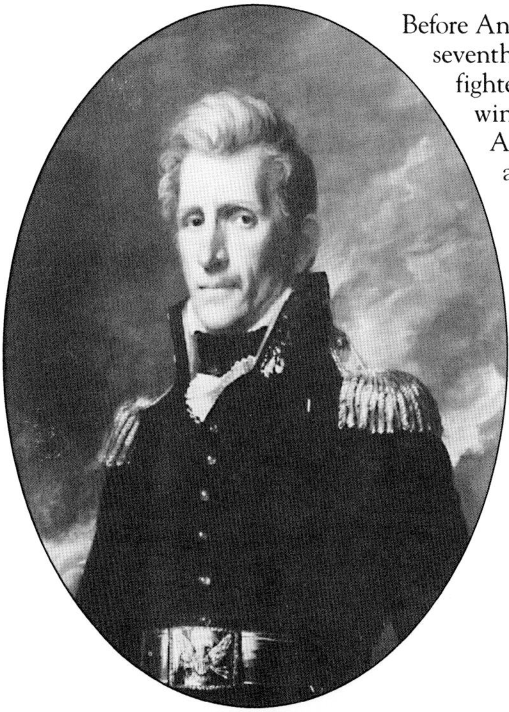

Before Andrew Jackson (1767–1845) became America's seventh president, he was known as a fierce Indian fighter. He led troops during the Creek War, winning the Battle of Horseshoe Bend in Alabama in 1814. "Old Hickory" led a campaign against the Creek and Seminole Indians in Georgia during the First Seminole War. He also led an invasion of Spanish-held Florida to prevent it from becoming a refuge for runaway slaves and a haven for rebellious Native Americans. (Courtesy of Addison Gallery, Phillips Academy.)

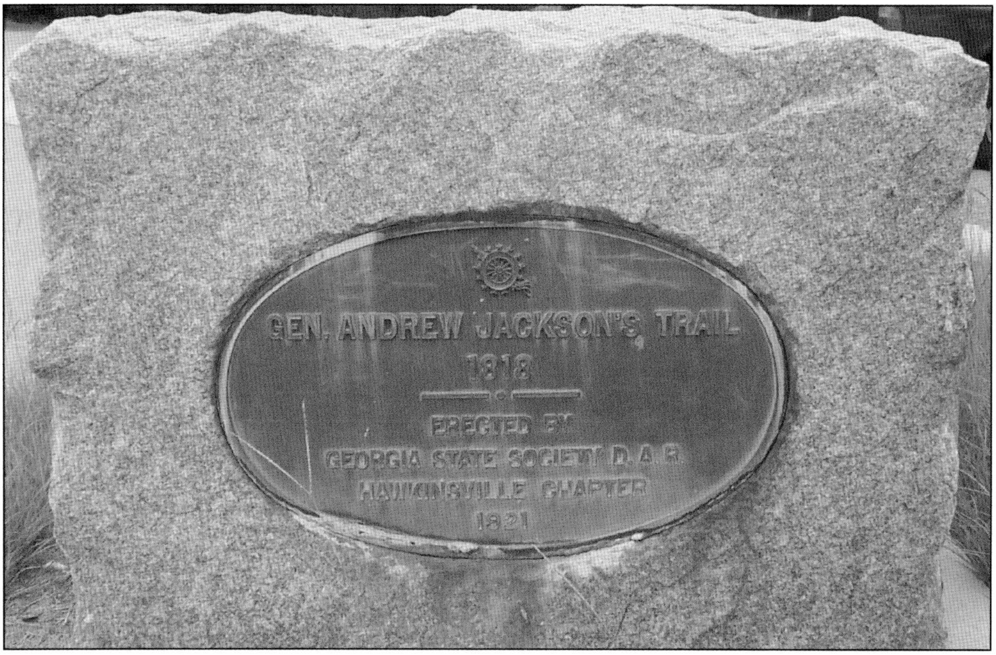

Gen. Andrew Jackson was placed in charge of American troops at Fort Scott in 1818. In April of that year, he led 800 U.S Army regulars, 1,000 Tennessee Volunteers, 1,000 Georgia Volunteers, and 1,400 allied Lower Creek warriors on an invasion of Spanish Florida, which had become a haven for rebellious Native Americans and runaway slaves. During his march through Georgia, the troops stopped to camp outside of Hawkinsville before proceeding southward. (Courtesy of Phillip A. Gibbs.)

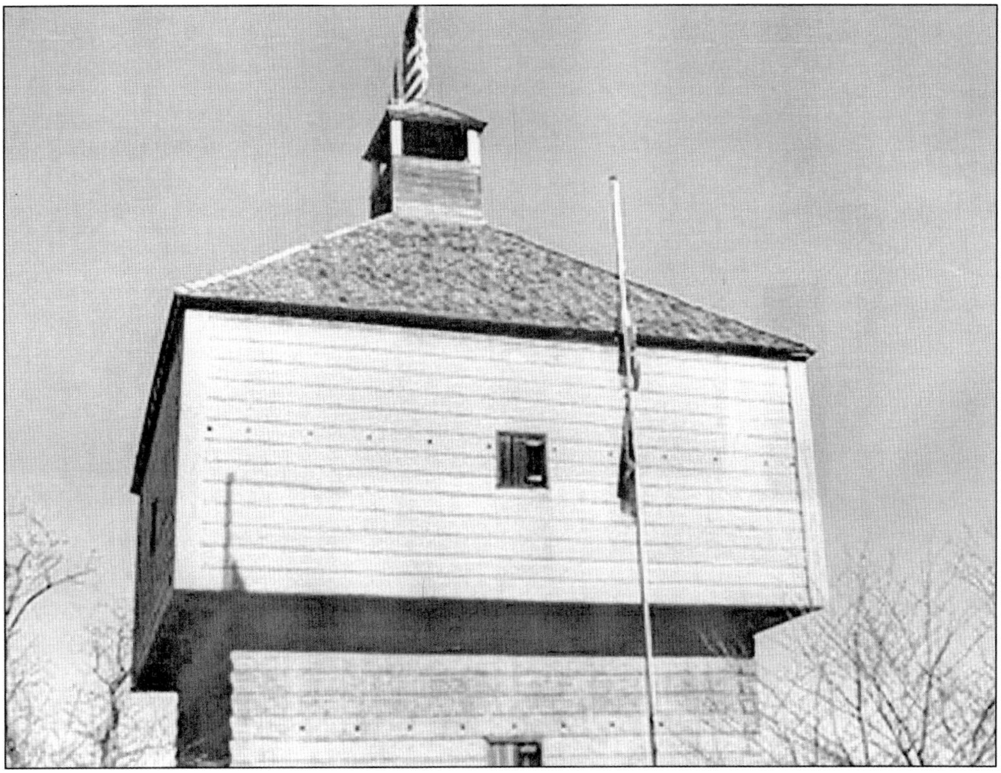

Fort Hawkins, located in Macon, Georgia, was one of a series of forts built to protect white settlers from angry Creek Indians trying to reclaim their land. Fort Mitchell in Hartford was another such fort and would have looked similar. (Courtesy of Washington Library, Macon, Georgia.)

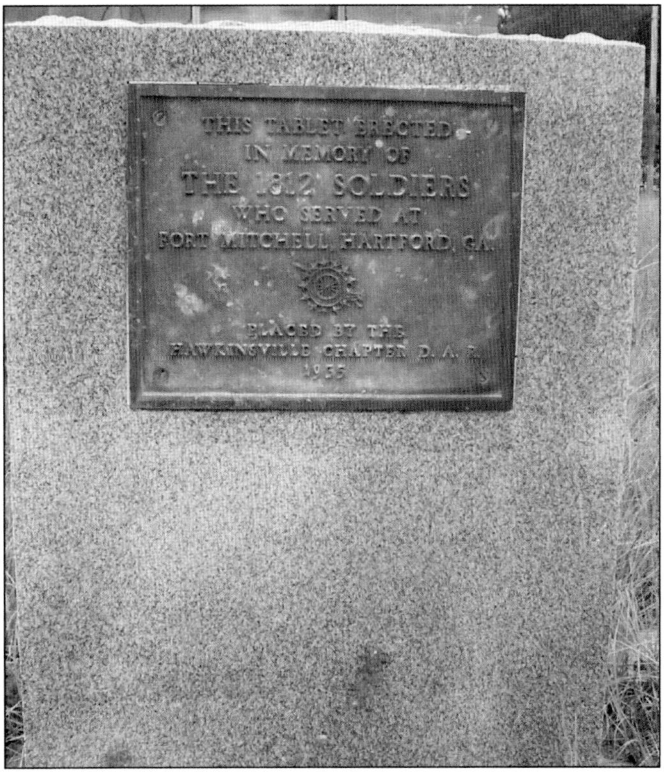

Fort Mitchell was one of four forts built in Pulaski County. Erected in 1812 about half a mile north of Hartford, the fort was about 100 feet square with two block houses situated at opposite ends of the stockade. The stockade itself was constructed of pine and was garrisoned by about 20 men. (Courtesy of Phillip A. Gibbs.)

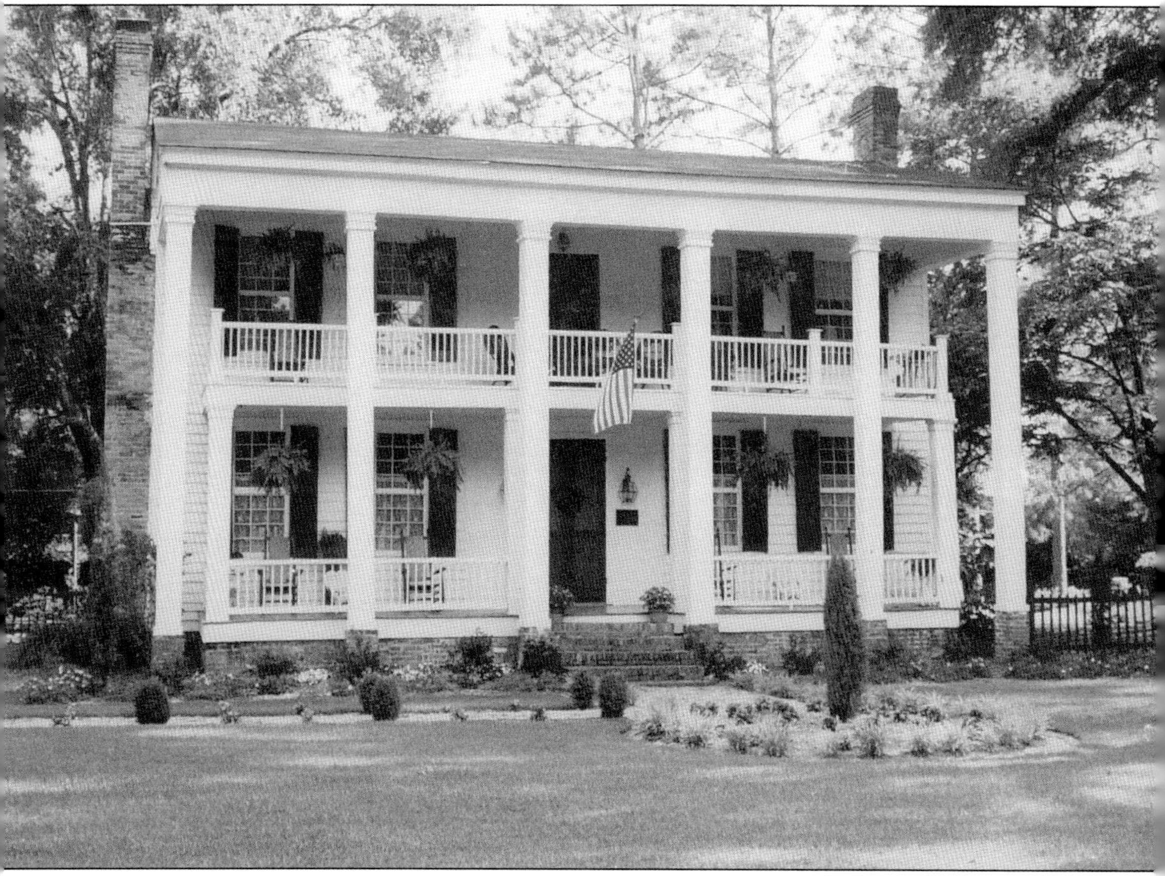

Taylor Hall was built in January 1825 by Dr. Robert Newsom Taylor. Originally situated in Old Hartford, it was dismantled board by board and reconstructed across the river in newly founded Hawkinsville by Creek labor in 1835. A guesthouse was added in 1899. Taylor Hall is the oldest house in the city. Dr. Taylor had a thriving medical practice and served as Hawkinsville's first mayor. (Courtesy of Pulaski Historical Society.)

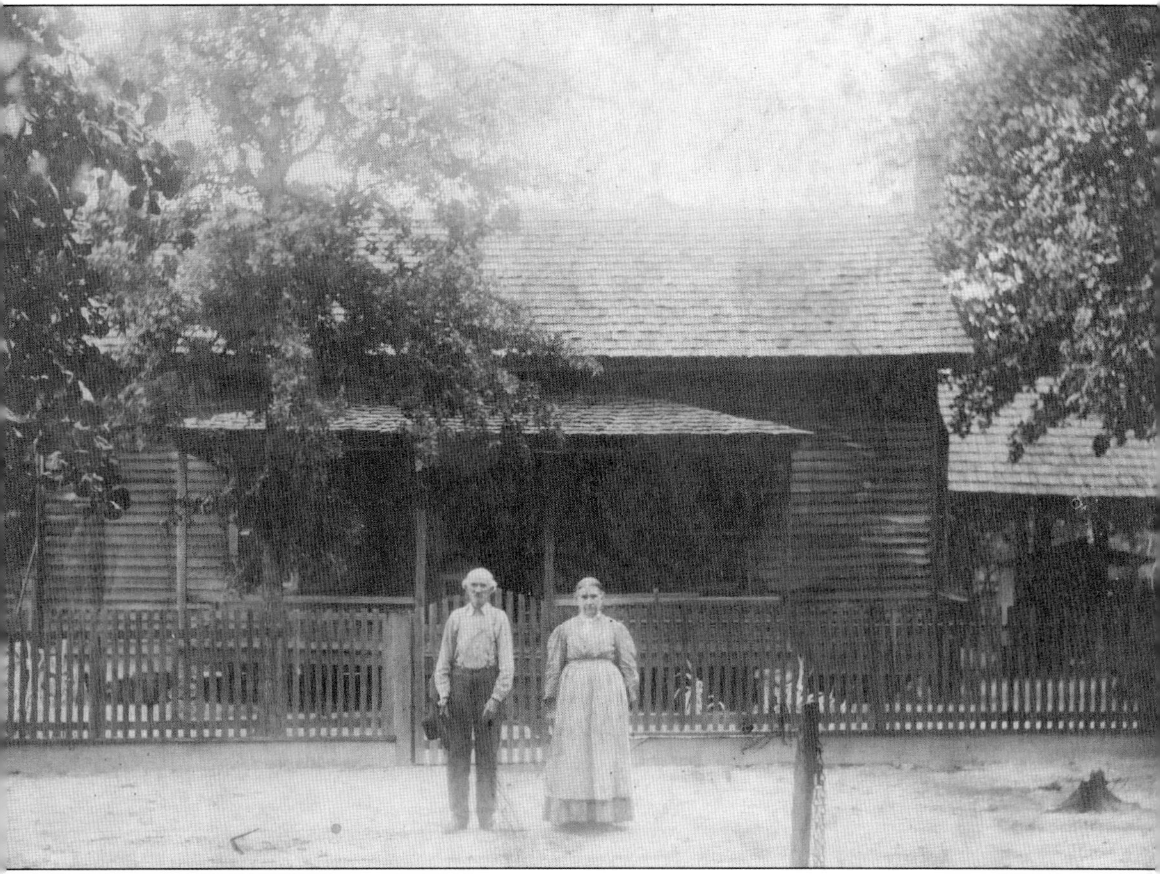

Most cotton growers in the Wiregrass region operated relatively small farms and owned less than five slaves. The majority of the work was done by the family. Contrary to the popular stereotype of large white mansions, most Wiregrass farmers lived in modest clapboard houses as seen here. While this picture of the Mashburn house was taken in the late 19th century, the style was found much earlier. (Courtesy of Josh Wilcox.)

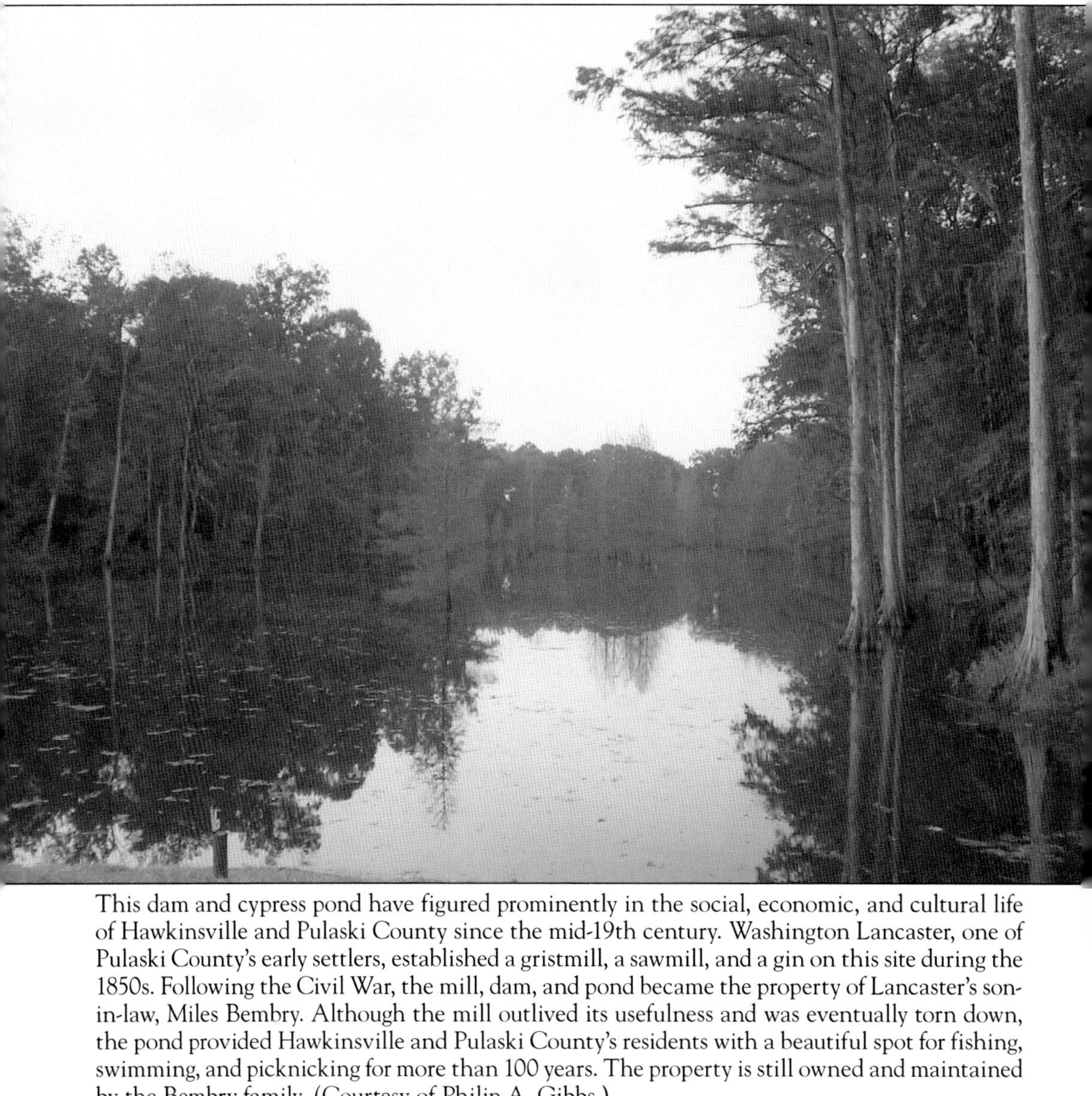

This dam and cypress pond have figured prominently in the social, economic, and cultural life of Hawkinsville and Pulaski County since the mid-19th century. Washington Lancaster, one of Pulaski County's early settlers, established a gristmill, a sawmill, and a gin on this site during the 1850s. Following the Civil War, the mill, dam, and pond became the property of Lancaster's son-in-law, Miles Bembry. Although the mill outlived its usefulness and was eventually torn down, the pond provided Hawkinsville and Pulaski County's residents with a beautiful spot for fishing, swimming, and picknicking for more than 100 years. The property is still owned and maintained by the Bembry family. (Courtesy of Philip A. Gibbs.)

Two

FROM OLD SOUTH TO NEW

Encouraged by the growing demand for cotton and the availability of fertile land, families from the Carolinas, Virginia, and some northeastern states migrated to the counties surrounding Hawkinsville. There they built houses, established cotton plantations, and began living the lifestyle of the planter elite. Hawkinsville benefited from the expansion of cotton agriculture. Its location on the Ocmulgee River made it an important center for the sale and transport of cotton and other crops.

The culture these planters created is visible in Hawkinsville and Pulaski County today. In many areas of the city, one can still see magnificent homes dating to the antebellum period. But one can also see the legacy of slavery in the community. A large percentage of the city's population is black, and many of these same citizens can trace their ancestry to slaves and sharecroppers who labored on the cotton plantations.

The war brought on by the South's secession from the Union also left its mark on the city. Orange Hill Cemetery, which dates to the 1830s, is the last resting place of numerous Hawkinsville citizens who served in the Confederate army during the Civil War. And not far from the cemetery is St. Thomas AME Church, established by former slaves during the period of congressional Reconstruction in the late 1860s.

The terrible loss of life and devastation caused by the war, however, did not prevent the city from enjoying a period of considerable prosperity. During the 1880s, Northern families worked with local planters and aspiring businessmen to establish mercantile firms, railroads, and banks. These same entrepreneurs built lovely homes and stately mansions that still grace the city's streets today.

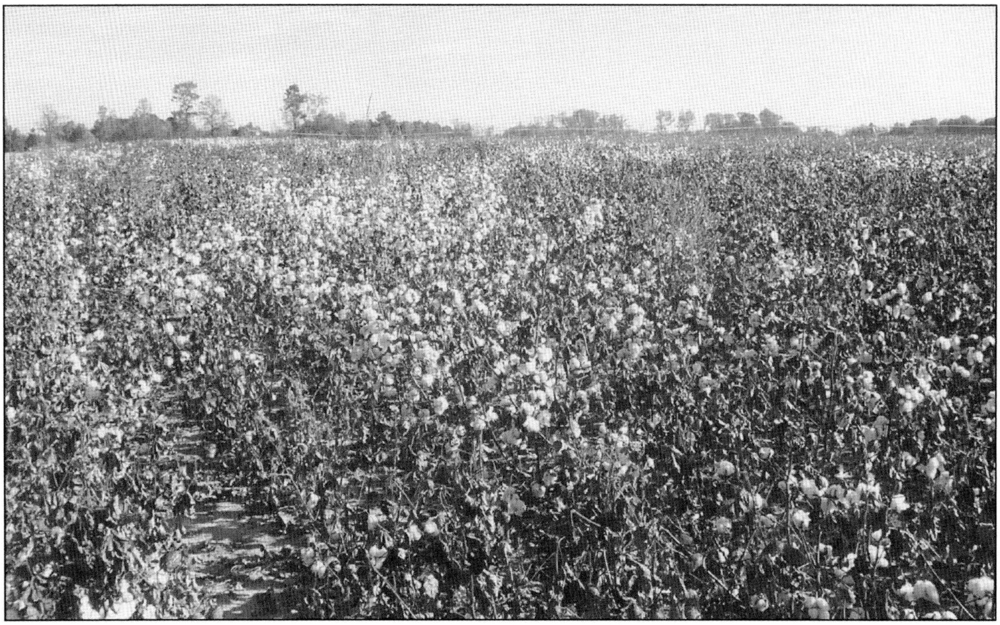

Cotton was not grown in Georgia to any large degree until the early 19th century. It was then that the demand for cotton increased in the growing textile industries of England and the northeastern United States. The introduction of inventions such as the jenny and the power loom during this period reduced the time and labor necessary for the spinning and weaving of cotton. This improvement in the production process, together with a population explosion in Europe, increased the demand for cotton cloth in the industrial regions of England and the northeast. Cotton requires a long growing season. Both the climate and soil of Middle Georgia are conducive to the growing of short-staple cotton. (Courtesy of Phillip A. Gibbs.)

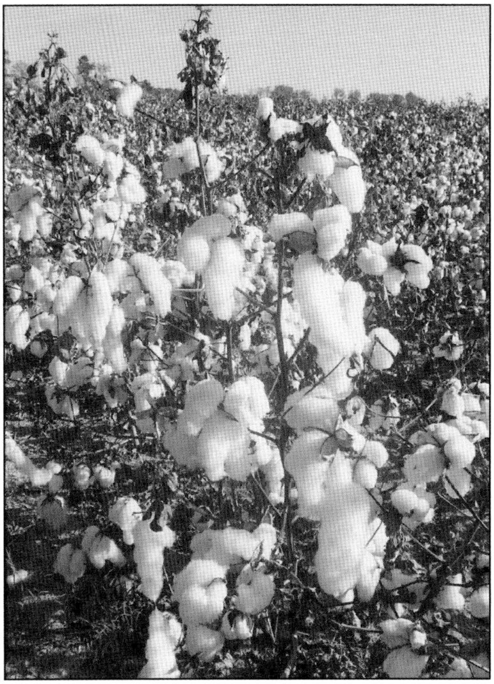

Short-staple cotton grew well in the climate and soil of Middle Georgia. But unlike the sea island variety, short-staple cotton had numerous seeds in the fiber. Without the invention of some device to remove the seeds, cotton was not profitable to grow in Middle Georgia or other parts of the South. (Courtesy of Phillip A. Gibbs.)

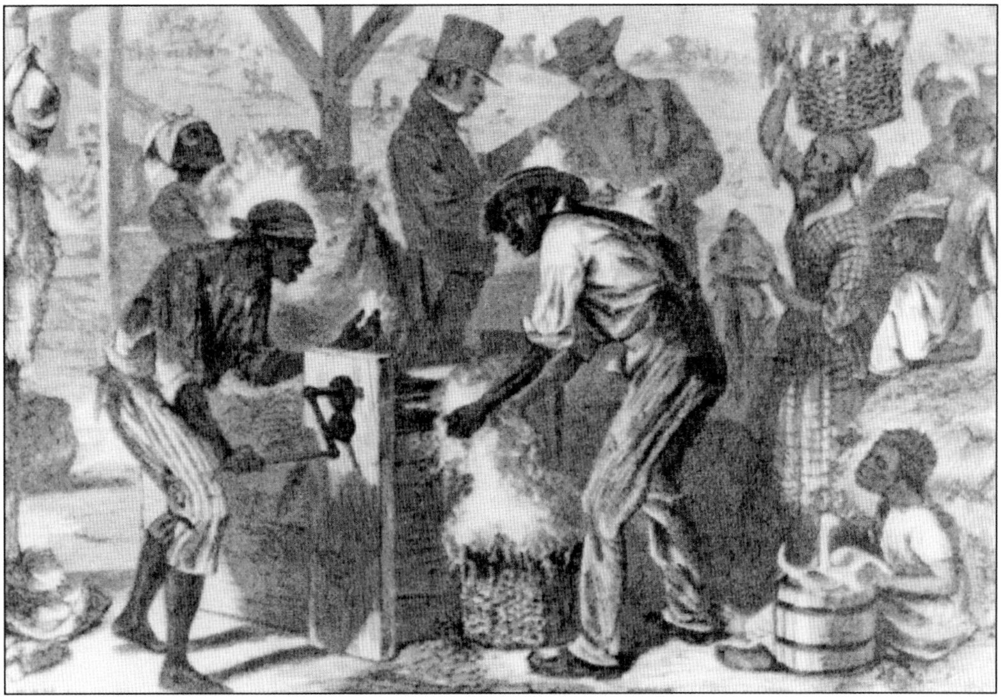

Eli Whitney's cotton gin, a simple device that used wire teeth attached to rollers to tear the cotton from the seed, led to the expansion of cotton farming in Pulaski County, Georgia. (Courtesy of Library of Congress.)

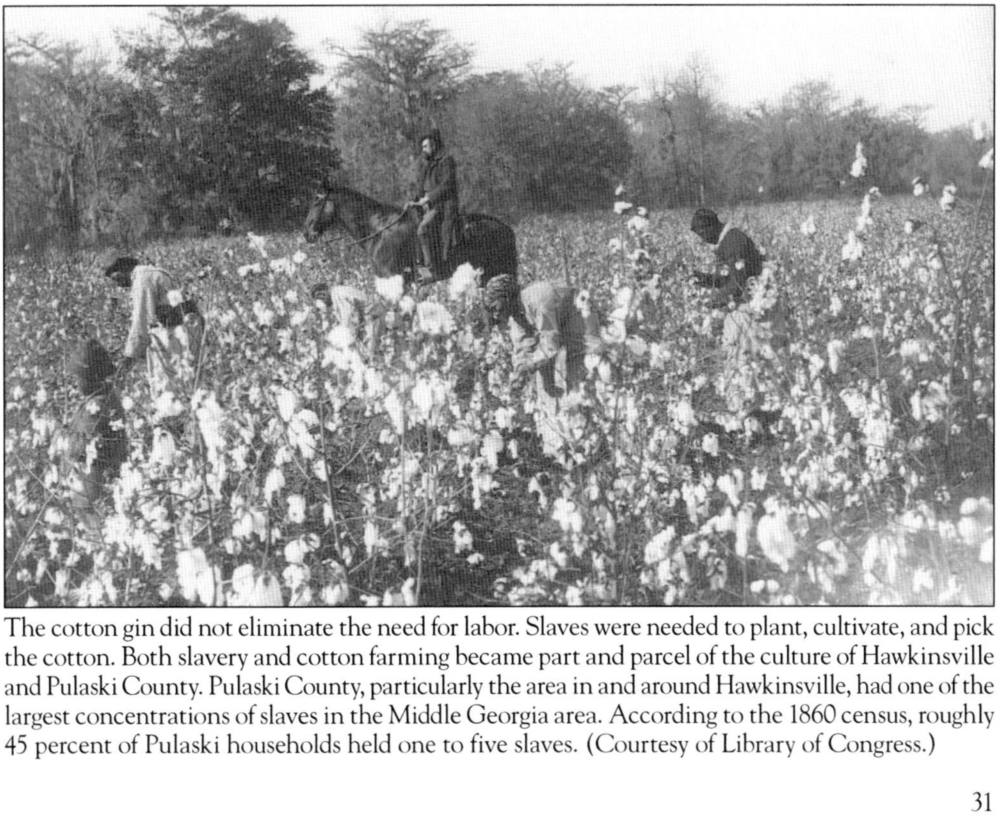

The cotton gin did not eliminate the need for labor. Slaves were needed to plant, cultivate, and pick the cotton. Both slavery and cotton farming became part and parcel of the culture of Hawkinsville and Pulaski County. Pulaski County, particularly the area in and around Hawkinsville, had one of the largest concentrations of slaves in the Middle Georgia area. According to the 1860 census, roughly 45 percent of Pulaski households held one to five slaves. (Courtesy of Library of Congress.)

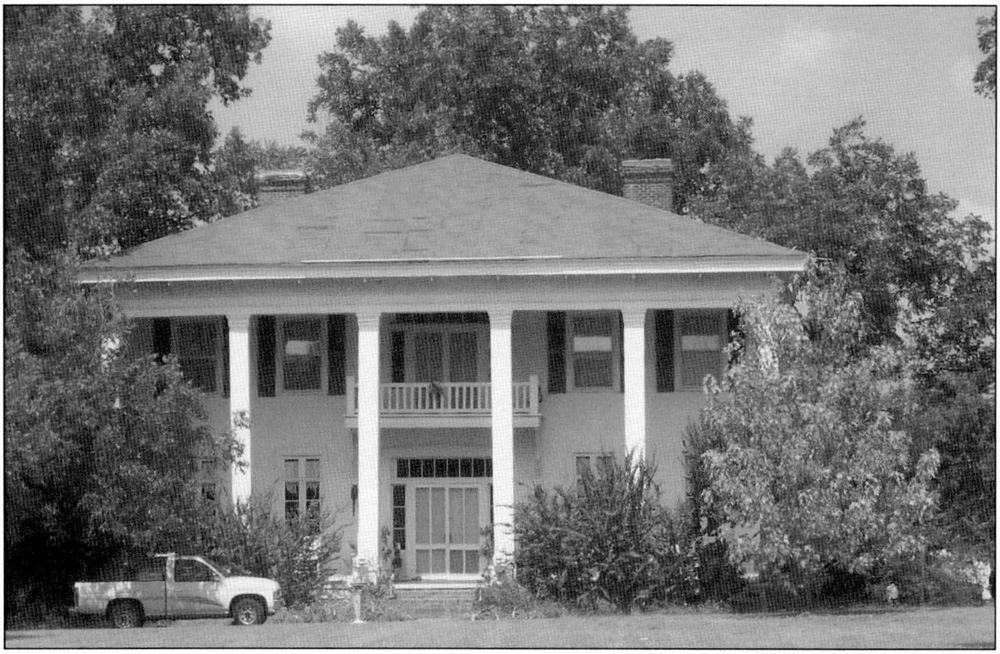

Profits from the sale of cotton afforded some planters, cotton brokers, bankers, and merchants in Pulaski County and Hawkinsville to live in grand style. The Richardson house, located three miles outside of Hawkinsville, was just one of many plantation homes that dominated the landscape of Pulaski County. (Courtesy of Phillip A. Gibbs.)

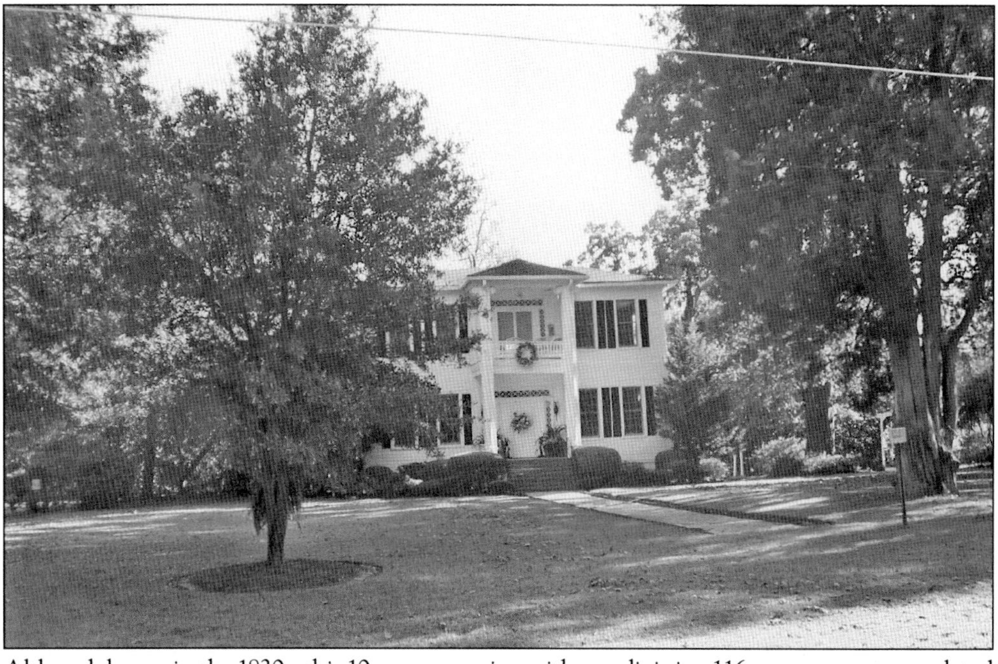

Although begun in the 1830s, this 10-room mansion with an adjoining 116 acres was not completed until the early 1850s. Just prior to the Civil War, it became the home of Seaborn Manning, a respected businessman and planter who died in battle in Virginia during the war. The house is said to be the oldest home in Hawkinsville on its original site. (Courtesy of Phillip A. Gibbs.)

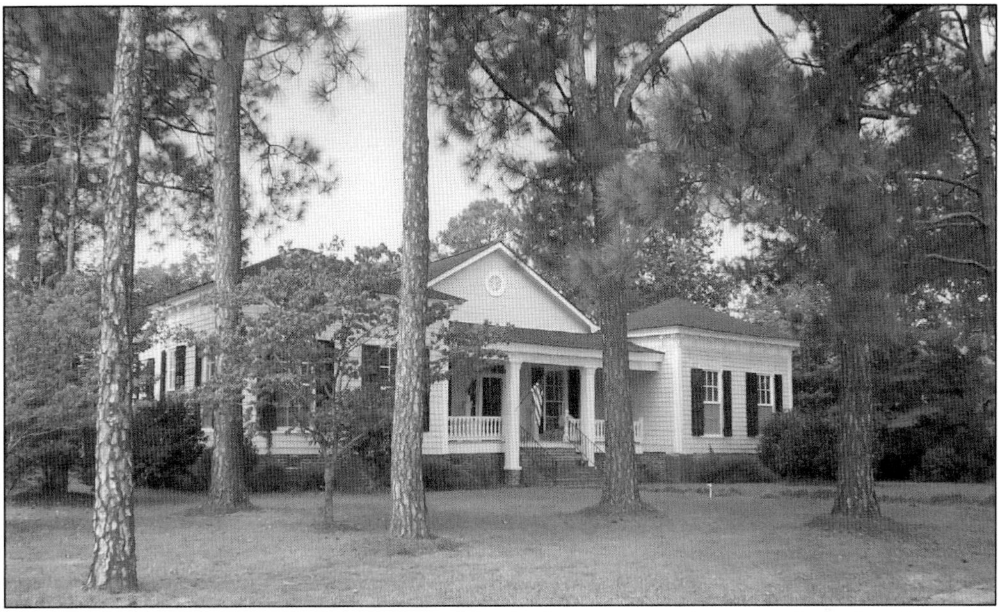

The Jelks family made their fortune in cotton warehouses, steamboats, and merchandising. In 1835, members of the James Oliver Jelks family built this simple but elegant home. When first constructed, it had four rooms, a central hall, a wraparound porch, and a detached kitchen. (Courtesy of Phillip A. Gibbs.)

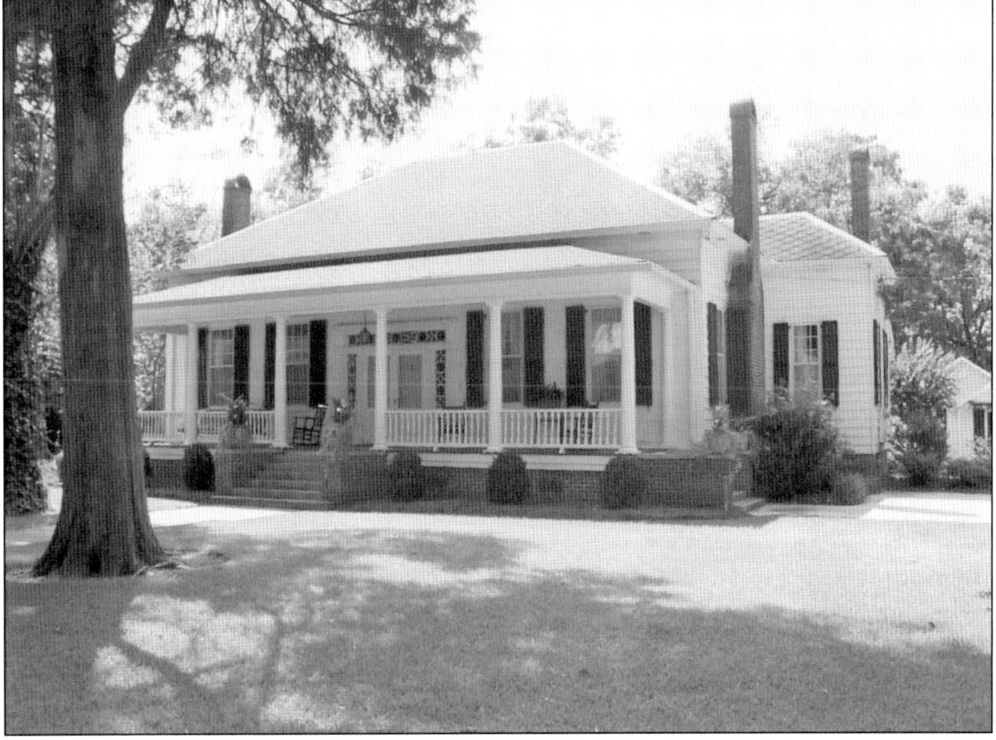

The McCormick family acquired this 1830s home in 1860. The home still has its original front and seven fireplaces. The 1830s smokehouse is also still intact. (Courtesy of Phillip A. Gibbs.)

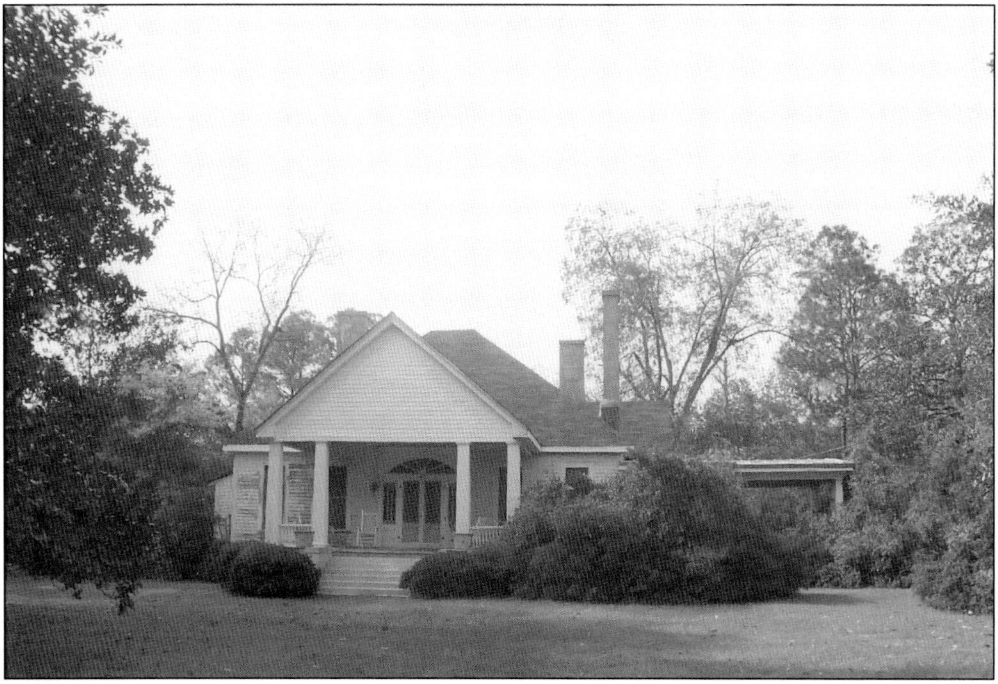

Built in 1837 and acquired by the Talton family a year later, this home has remained in the Talton family for five generations. Its large bay window in the parlor was the scene of many receptions and weddings in the 19th century. (Courtesy of Phillip A. Gibbs.)

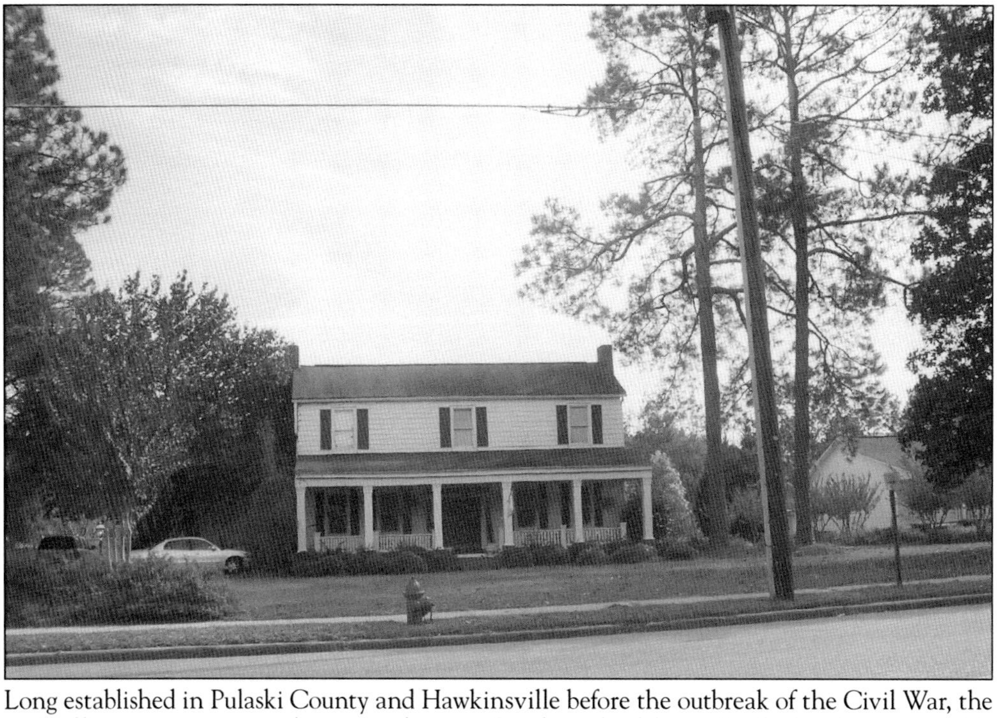

Long established in Pulaski County and Hawkinsville before the outbreak of the Civil War, the McDuffies were prominent planters in the area. One branch of the McDuffie family acquired this farmhouse and the surrounding land in the late 1830s. (Courtesy of Phillip A. Gibbs.)

The election of Abraham Lincoln to the presidency in 1860 convinced voters in Hawkinsville and Pulaski County to support secessionist delegates to the Georgia Convention on Secession in Milledgeville. Although Lincoln stated repeatedly that he would not interfere with the institution of slavery where it already existed, Hawkinsville and Pulaski County slaveholders found his opposition to the expansion of slavery a threat to both their property rights and their long-term economic interests. (Courtesy of Library of Congress.)

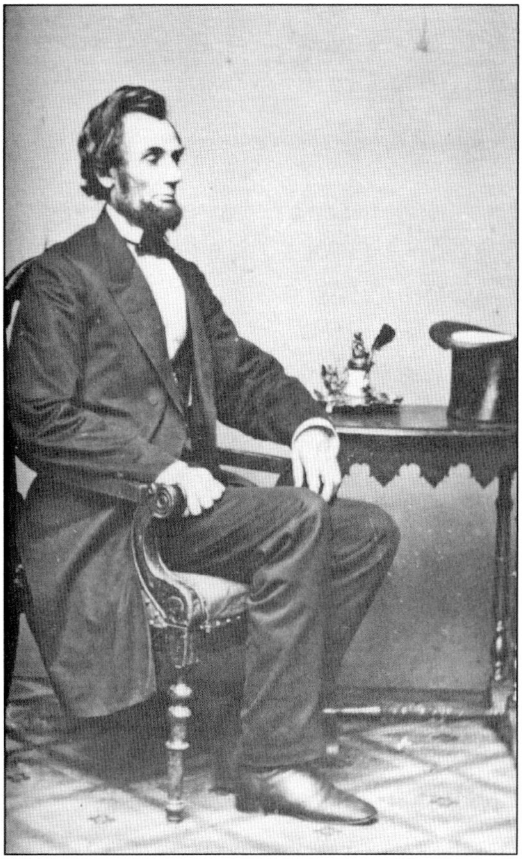

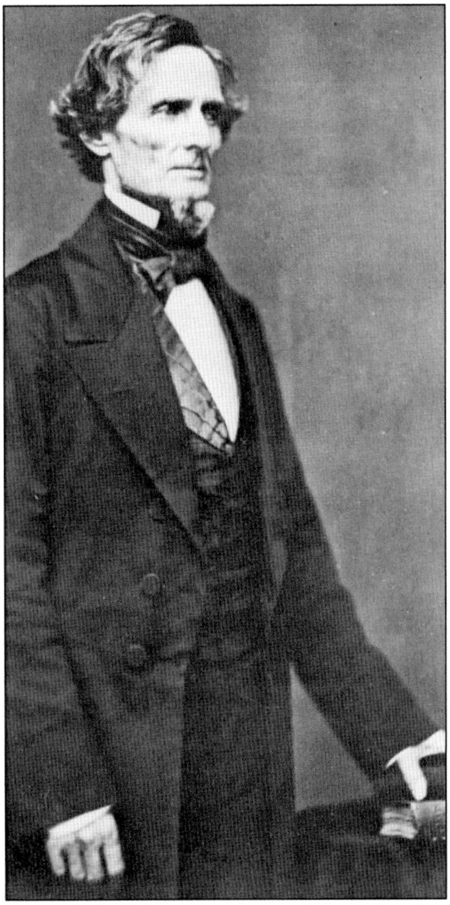

Following the secession convention's decision to take Georgia out of the Union, the state joined the Confederate States of America. The white citizens of Hawkinsville and the surrounding county pledged their loyalty to the Confederacy and its new president, Jefferson Davis. (Courtesy of Library of Congress.)

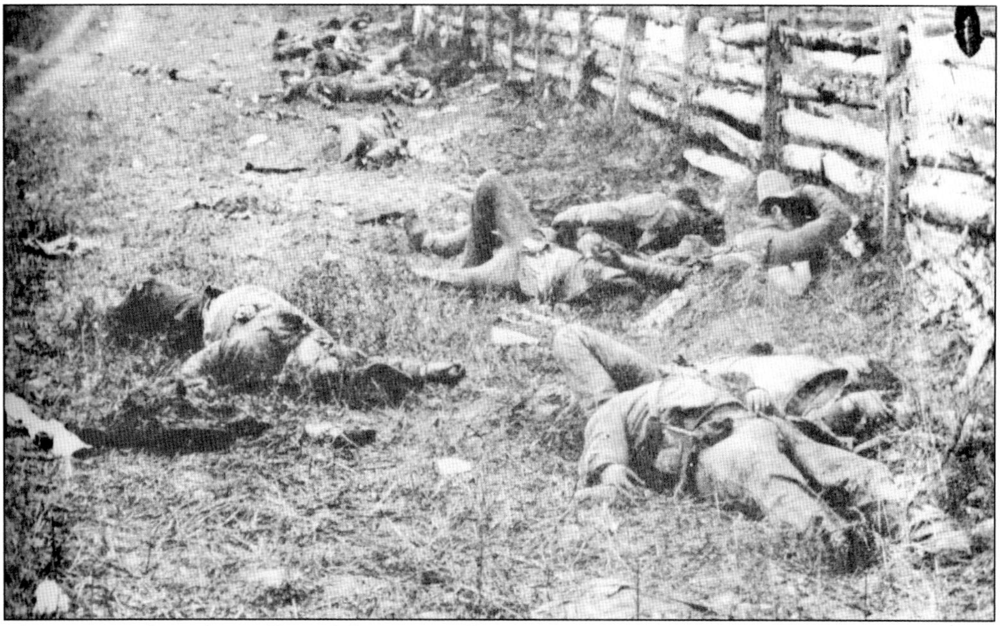

The citizens of Hawkinsville and the surrounding county sent hundreds of men into battle during the Civil War. Regiments such as the Pulaski Blues, Volunteers, Rangers, and Greys fought in some of the first major battles of the war. Many Hawkinsville and Pulaski soldiers were wounded, taken prisoner, or killed at such battles as First and Second Manassas, Cedar Mountain, Seven Pines, and Antietam, one of the bloodiest battles of the war. (Courtesy of Library of Congress.)

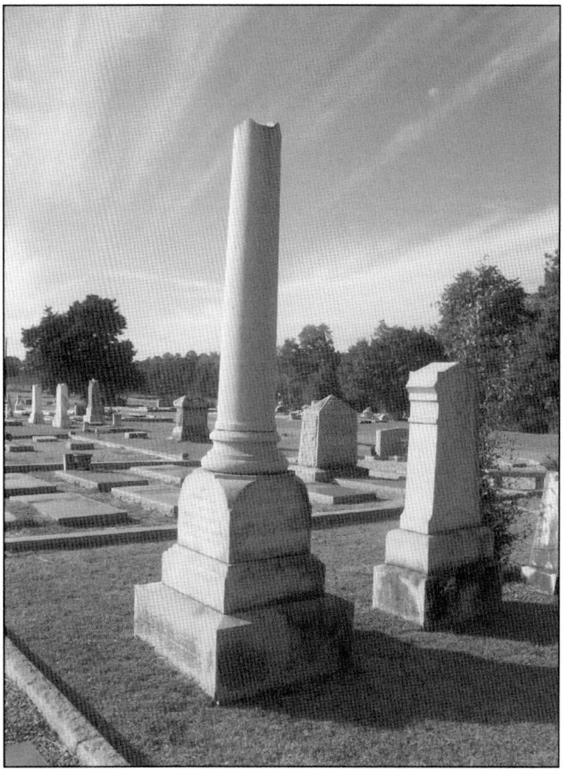

A wealthy Hawkinsville merchant and planter, Lt. Col. Seaborn Manning of the 49th Georgia Infantry died at the Battle of Cedar Mountain, Virginia, in 1862. According to historian Mark V. Wetherington, Manning's wife, Harriet, insisted that his body be laid to rest in Orange Hill Cemetery in Hawkinsville. (Courtesy of Phillip A. Gibbs.)

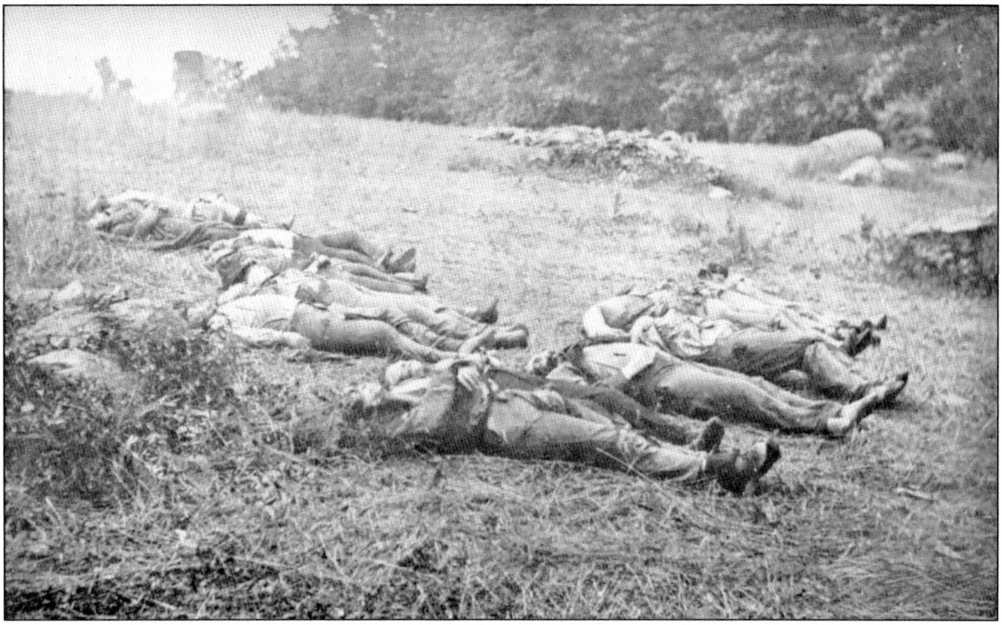

Young men from Hawkinsville and Pulaski County were with Robert E. Lee and the Army of Northern Virginia when Lee invaded Pennsylvania in the summer of 1863. Unfortunately, many of those same young men never returned home. (Courtesy of Library of Congress.)

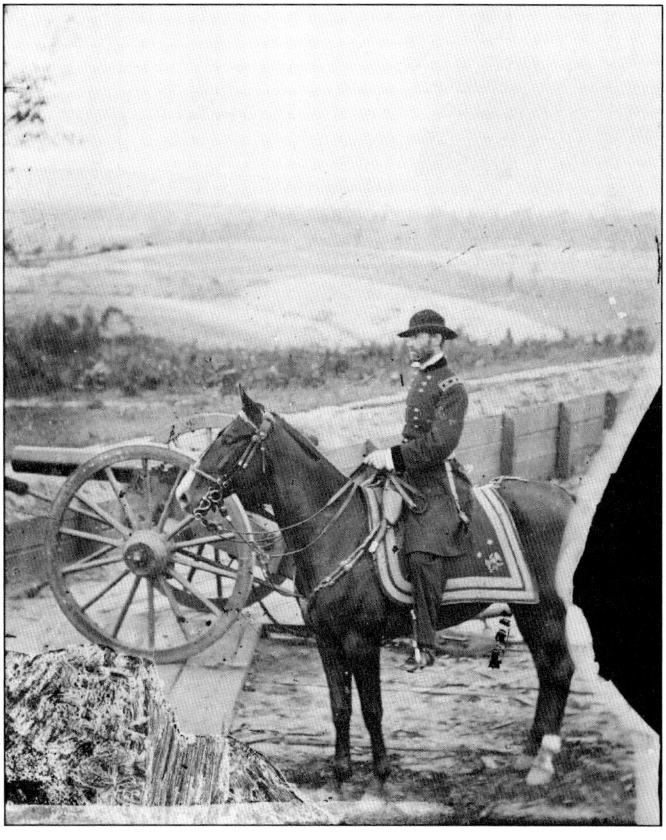

Soon after Gen. William Tecumseh Sherman occupied and burned Atlanta, he began his March to the Sea. Determined to rob the Confederacy of anything that could be used to continue the war, Sherman instructed his men to destroy railroads, gins, barns, and cotton fields. Although Sherman's troops never came close to Hawkinsville, young and old members of the city's militia did fight in several engagements against Sherman's troops in Jones County, approximately 65 miles north of Hawkinsville. (Courtesy of Library of Congress.)

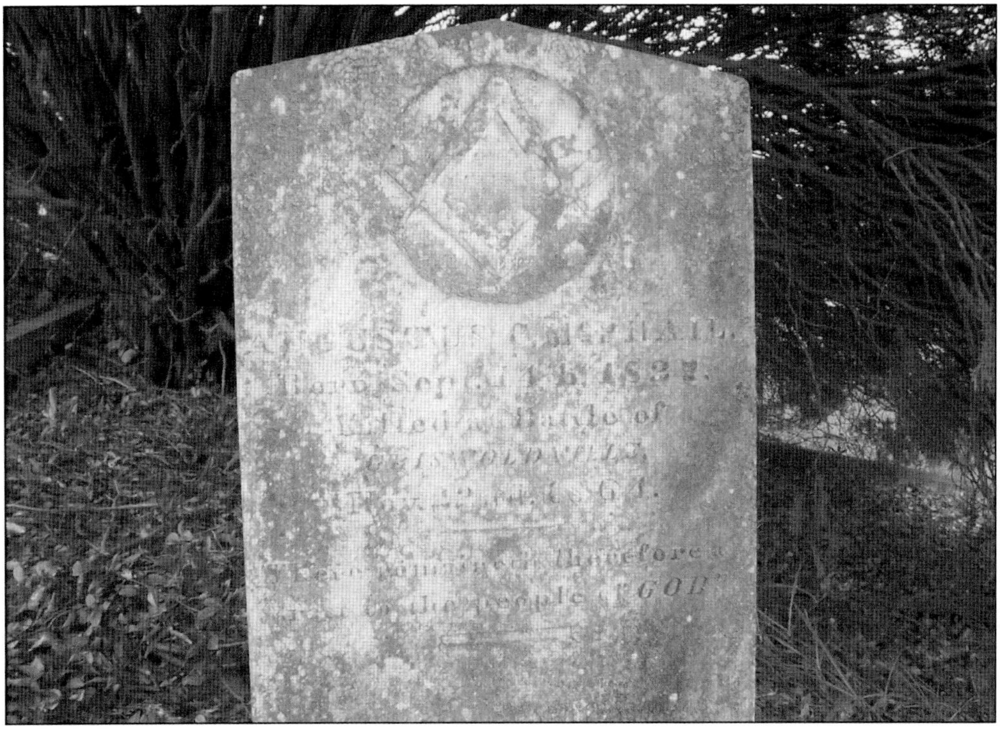

Augustus McPhall, who died in one of several futile assaults against Federal forces at Griswoldville in Jones County, Georgia, in November 1864, was returned home for burial in Hawkinsville's Orange Hill Cemetery. (Courtesy of Phillip A. Gibbs.)

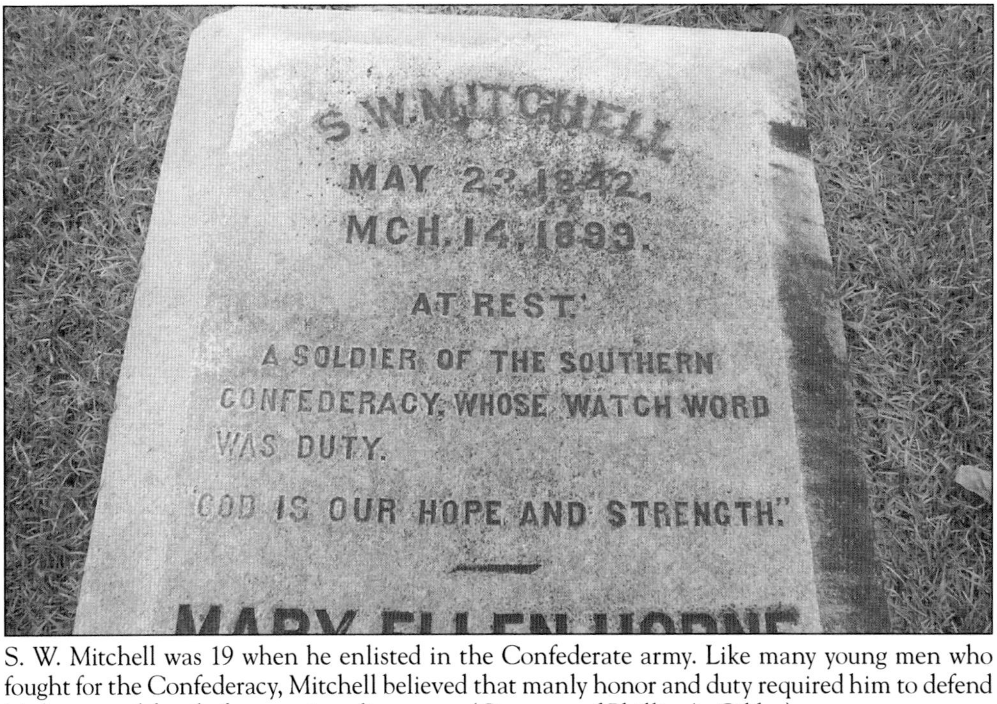

S. W. Mitchell was 19 when he enlisted in the Confederate army. Like many young men who fought for the Confederacy, Mitchell believed that manly honor and duty required him to defend his home and family from an invading army. (Courtesy of Phillip A. Gibbs.)

In 1908, the Hawkinsville Chapter of the United Daughters of the Confederacy erected this memorial to the city and county's Confederate veterans, living and dead. Originally, as seen here, the memorial was situated in the middle of Commerce Street. It now stands next to the Pulaski County Courthouse. (Courtesy of Hawkinsville *Dispatch and News*.)

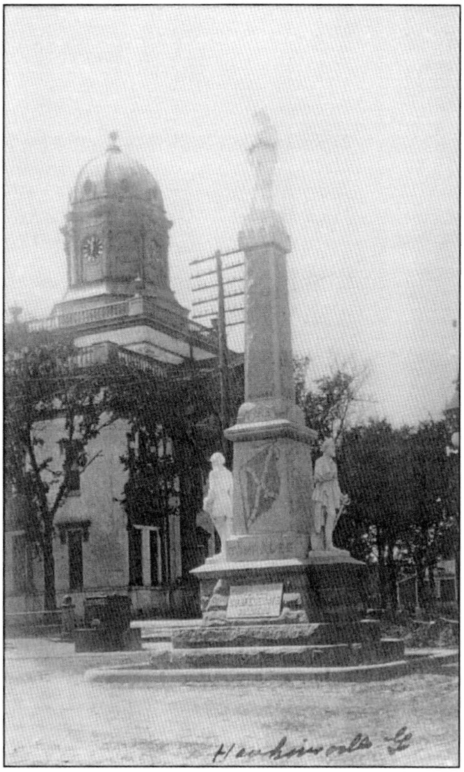

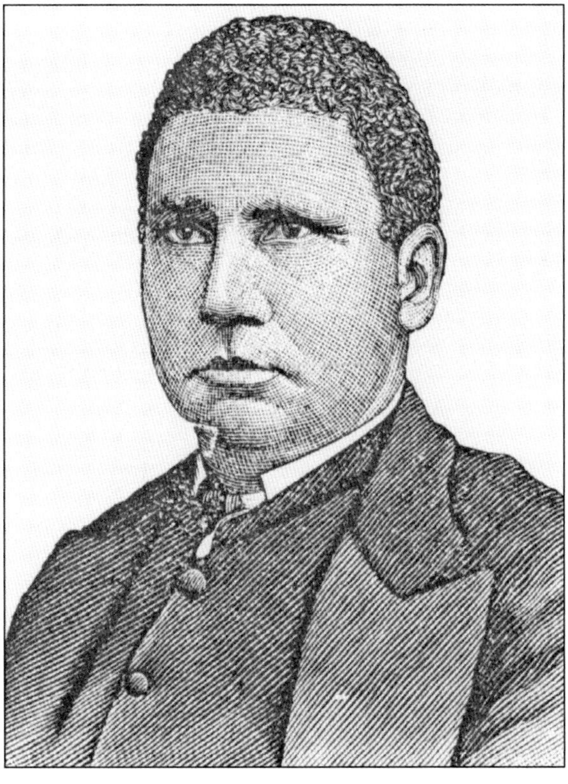

Following the 1865 Confederacy's defeat, Hawkinsville's freed slaves received assistance from Freedman's Bureaus, Northern philanthropists, and, in some cases, their former masters in starting their new lives. Ministers such as Henry McNeil Turner, the country's first African American to serve as chaplain to the U.S. Army, helped the city's black citizens establish St. Thomas African Methodist Episcopal (AME) Church. McNeil would leave Hawkinsville and found other churches in Georgia. Later in life, however, he became disillusioned with the refusal of both Northern and Southern whites to accept blacks as equal citizens. As a result, he called for blacks to return to Africa. (Courtesy of International Library of Afro-American Life and Culture.)

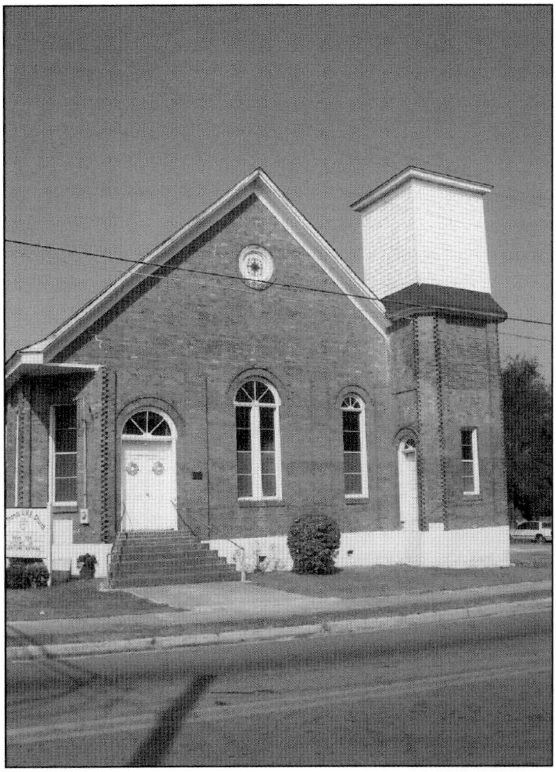

Shortly after the Civil War, Rev. Henry McNeal Turner organized St. Thomas AME Church. Although the present structure dates from 1908, there has been a church structure at the Dooly Street site since 1877. The present church, many believe, was constructed by skilled African American carpenters in the area. Crafted in the folk Victorian style of the period, St. Thomas features a side steeple, decorative brick buttresses, rounded brick arches, tongue-and-groove wainscoting, and decorative ironwork on the choir loft. Today the church serves as both a house of worship and a community meeting place for various groups and special events. Recognized as an integral part of Hawkinsville's history and culture, the church has received grants from the Georgia Historic Preservation Division to repair and maintain the roof and masonry work. (Courtesy of Phillip A. Gibbs.)

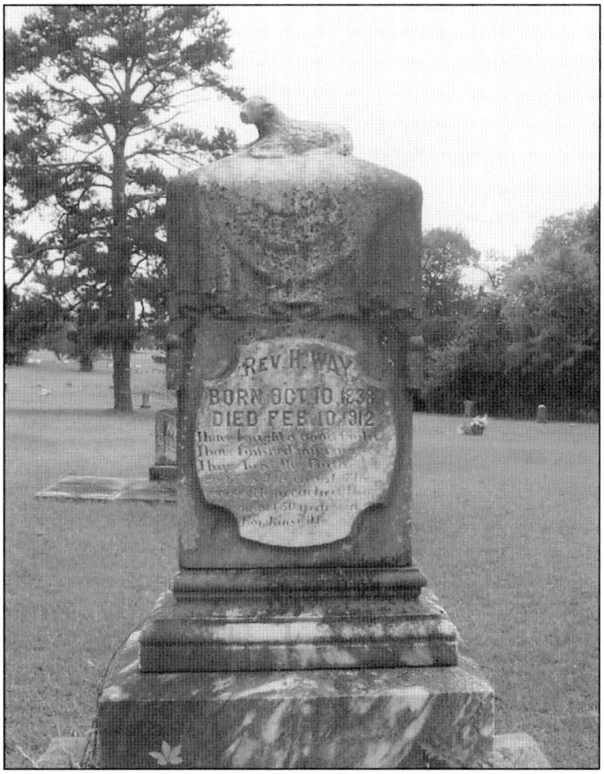

Henry Way, a former slave belonging to Dr. E. F. Way, was a minister at Springfield Baptist Church in the 1890s. He later assumed ministerial duties at Christian Hope Baptist Church. Today Henry Way Street bears the name of the good reverend. (Courtesy of Phillip A. Gibbs.)

Founded soon after the Civil War, Springfield Baptist Church is the oldest African American church in Hawkinsville. Although the facade and interior of the church have undergone alterations over the years, the original structure remains intact. Churches like Springfield and St. Thomas not only served as centers of worship, but also as schools for former slaves and their children. (Courtesy of Phillip A. Gibbs.)

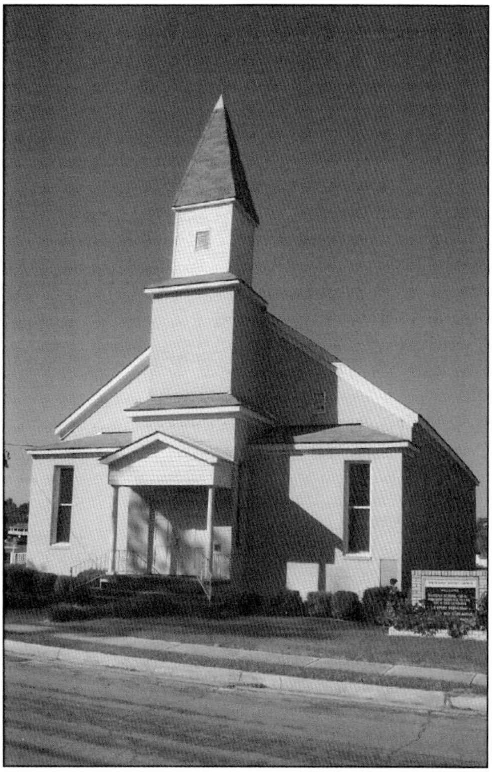

While many newly freed slaves and their children continued to work on plantations as free laborers, others started their own businesses. Russell Harris's great-grandfather opened a blacksmith shop in the 1890s near the present-day Hawkinsville Fire Department. Under his father's tutelage, Russell learned the trade and took over the present shop in the 1930s. But by the late 1950s, blacksmiths were in little demand. Undeterred, Harris put his knowledge of ironwork to good use and became a skilled welder. Proud of his heritage as a fourth-generation blacksmith, Harris still has his grandfather's anvil. (Courtesy of Phillip A. Gibbs.)

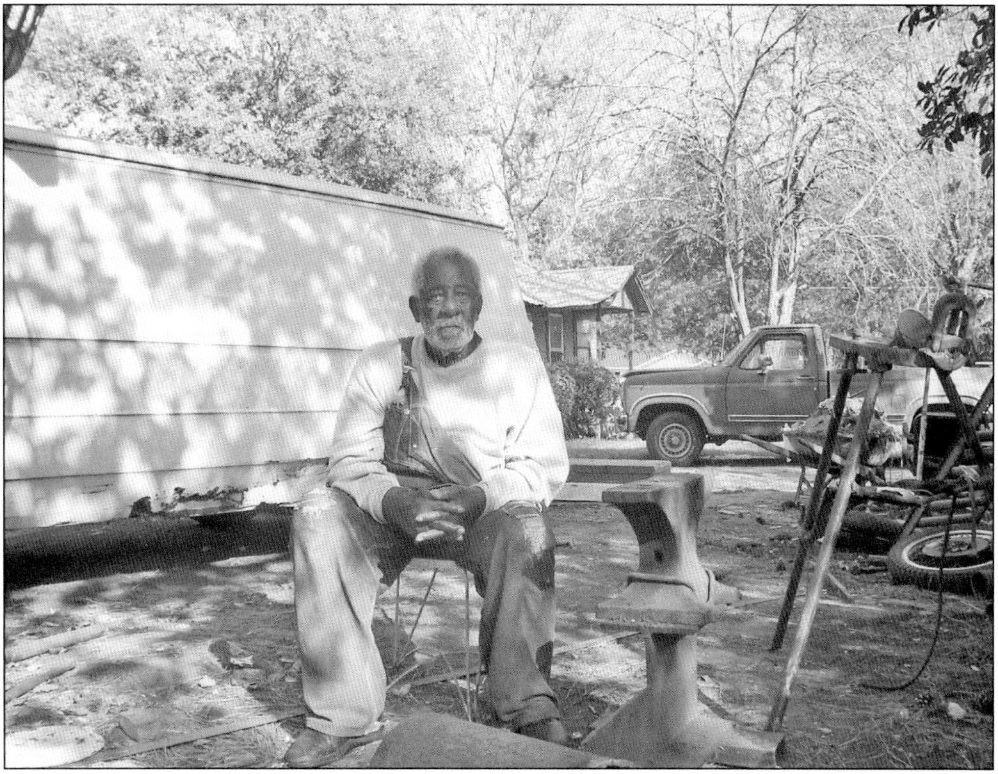

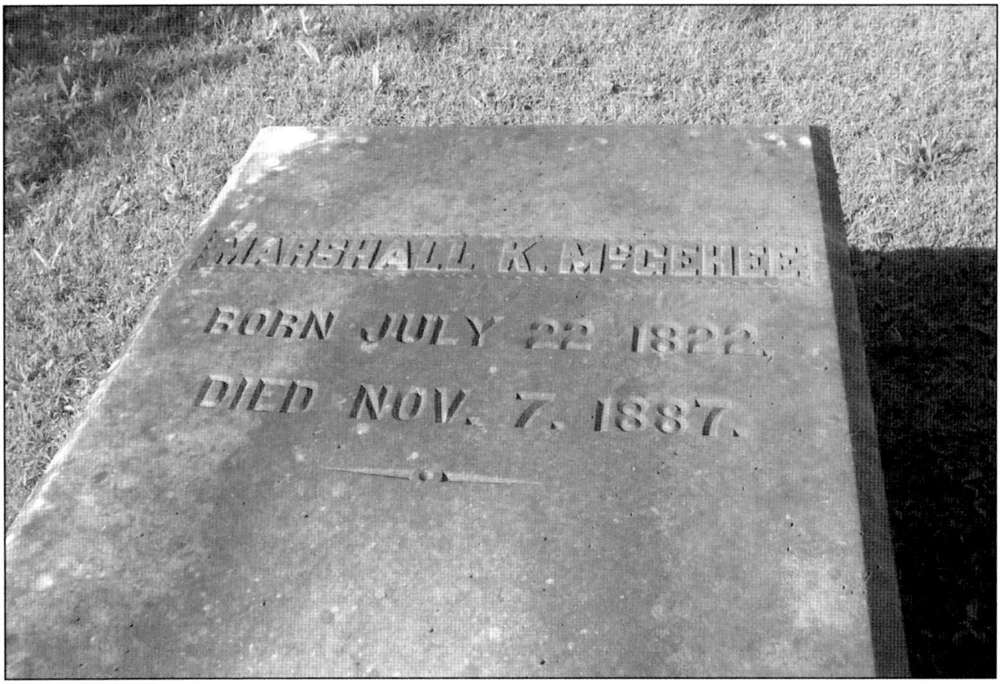

The McGhee brothers were skilled carpenters who lived in Hawkinsville during the period of slavery as free persons of color. After slavery, the brothers and their families prospered from the city's population growth and the subsequent demand for housing. The McGhees' affluence is evidenced by the design of their tombstones and the iron gate that surrounds their family plot. (Courtesy of Phillip A. Gibbs.)

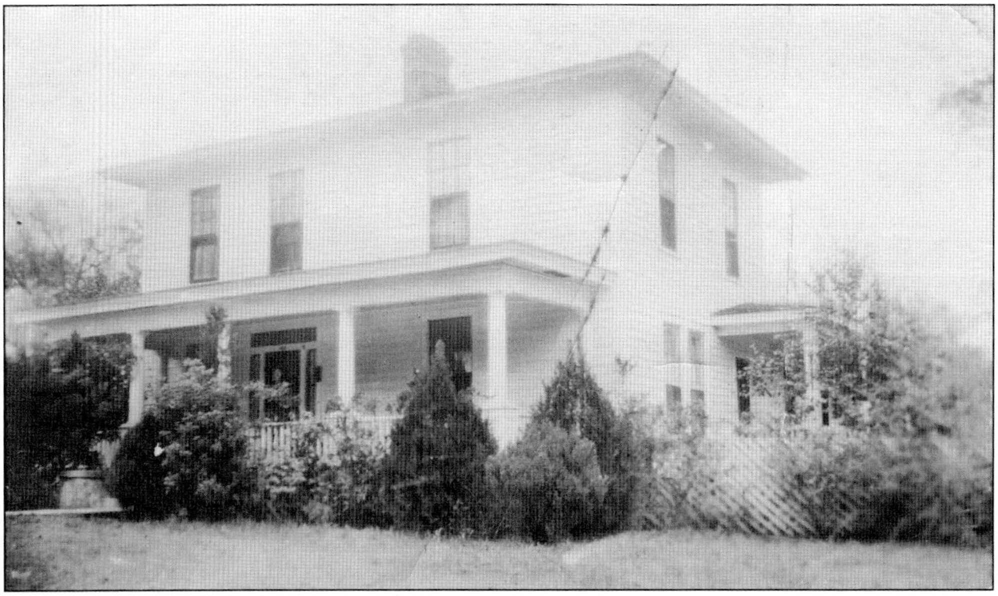

Following the Civil War, a number of Northern families moved to Middle Georgia seeking cheap land and economic opportunity. Benjamin F. Parsons, a Massachusetts merchant, relocated his family to Hawkinsville in 1878 and built this New England–style home. Unlike most Georgia homes, the house had a central chimney and an attached kitchen. (Courtesy of Phillip A. Gibbs.)

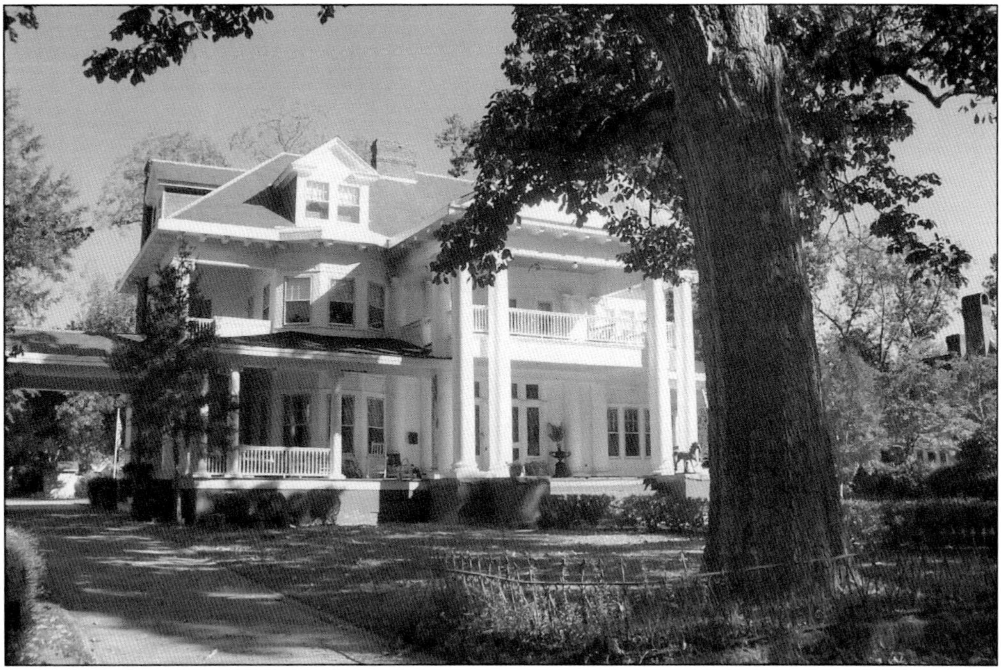

Benjamin Parsons's son, William Naramore Parsons, became a successful businessman in Hawkinsville, so successful that he constructed this neoclassical home in 1901 on Jackson Street. William N. Parsons contracted with J. L. Huggins to build the house using plans drawn by E. S. Childs, a New York architect. His house was the first in Hawkinsville to have indoor plumbing both upstairs and downstairs, and electric lights in every room. A windmill, the remains of which can still be seen in the yard, powered these lights. (Courtesy of Phillip A. Gibbs.)

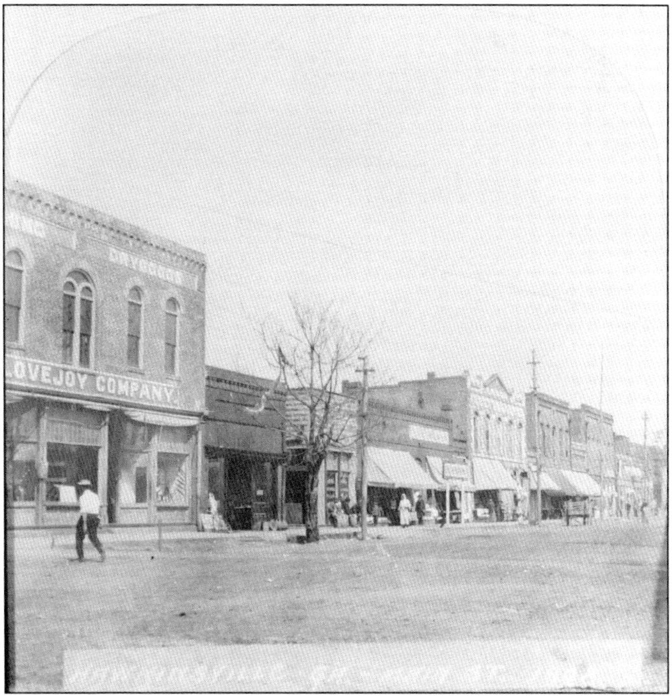

By the end of the 19th century, Hawkinsville's streets were dotted with numerous clothing, furniture, and produce stores. The city's thriving downtown attracted visitors from around the region. (Courtesy of Georgia Archives, Vanishing Georgia, pul 005.)

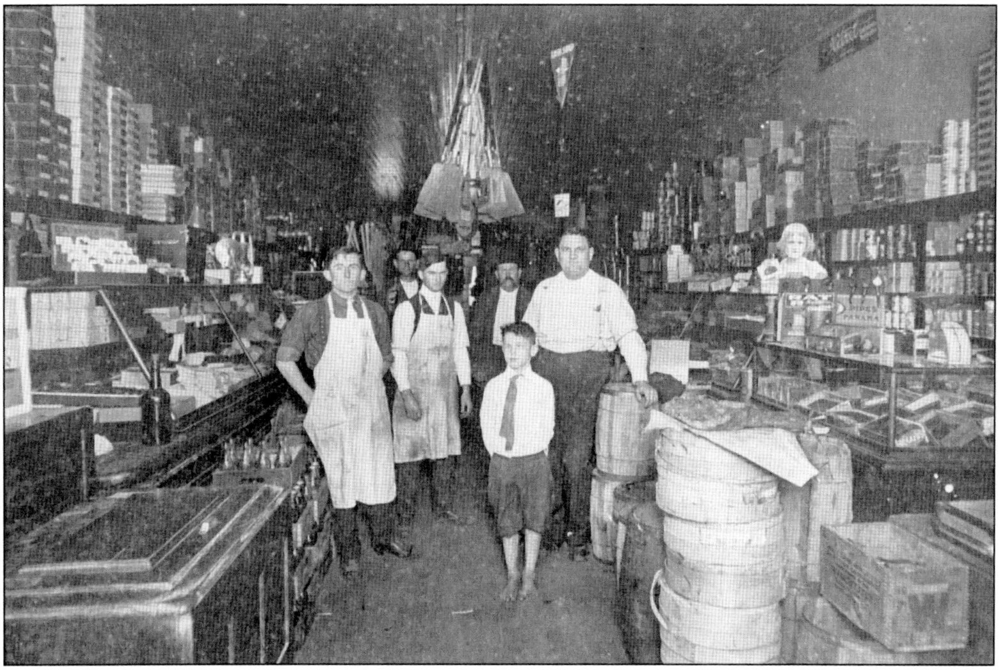

Ragan's Store was just one of several mercantile firms that sold a variety of goods, including hoop cheese, salt fish, and a mix of clothing and household items. Like many ambitious, young men in the region, L. C. Ragan, the proprietor of the store pictured above, left his family's plantation to open a business in Hawkinsville. (Courtesy of Georgia Archives, Vanishing Georgia, pul 096.)

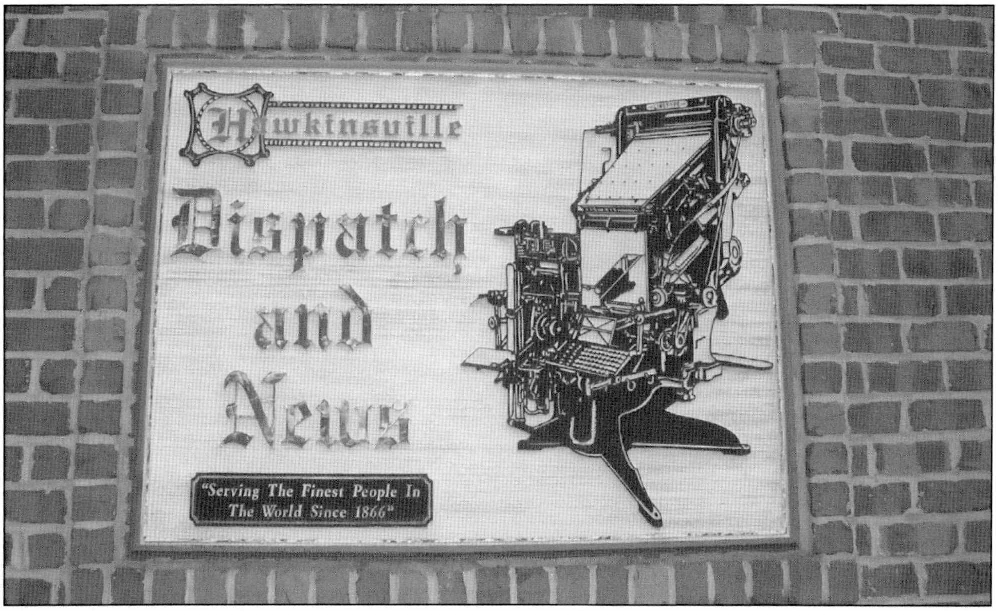

Prior to the Civil War, the *Pulaski Times* was the principal newspaper in Hawkinsville and Pulaski County. But with the outbreak of hostilities, the paper folded. Shortly after the war, a new paper, the *Hawkinsville Dispatch*, was established. In 1885, a rival newspaper, the *Hawkinsville News*, was published. In 1890, the two papers consolidated to create the *Hawkinsville Dispatch and News*. (Courtesy of Phillip A. Gibbs.)

W. N. Parsons joined hands with many of Hawkinsville's older families and established Planter's Bank in 1896. Today the bank has branches in several Middle Georgia cities. (Courtesy of Sam Way.)

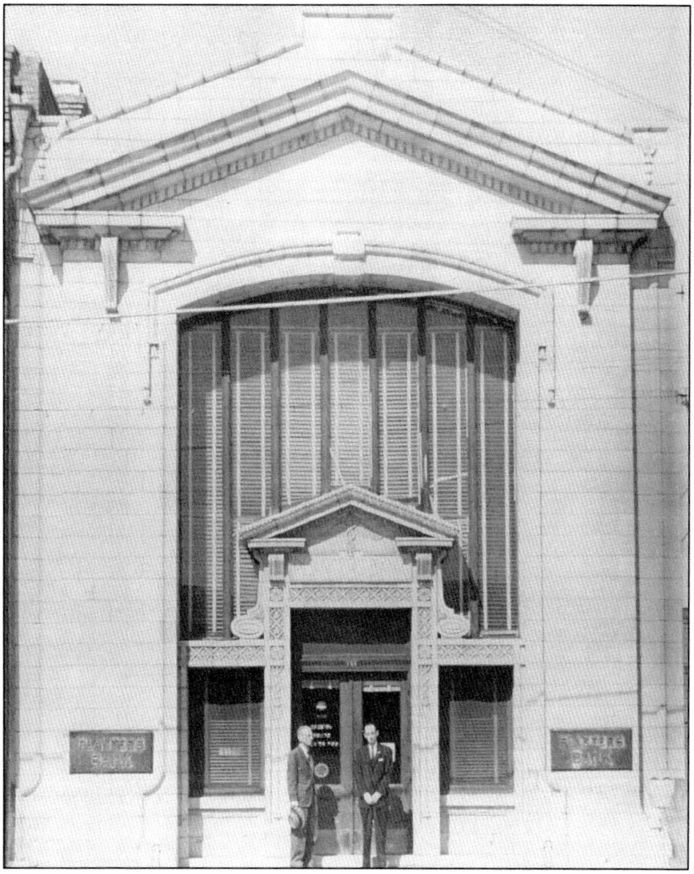

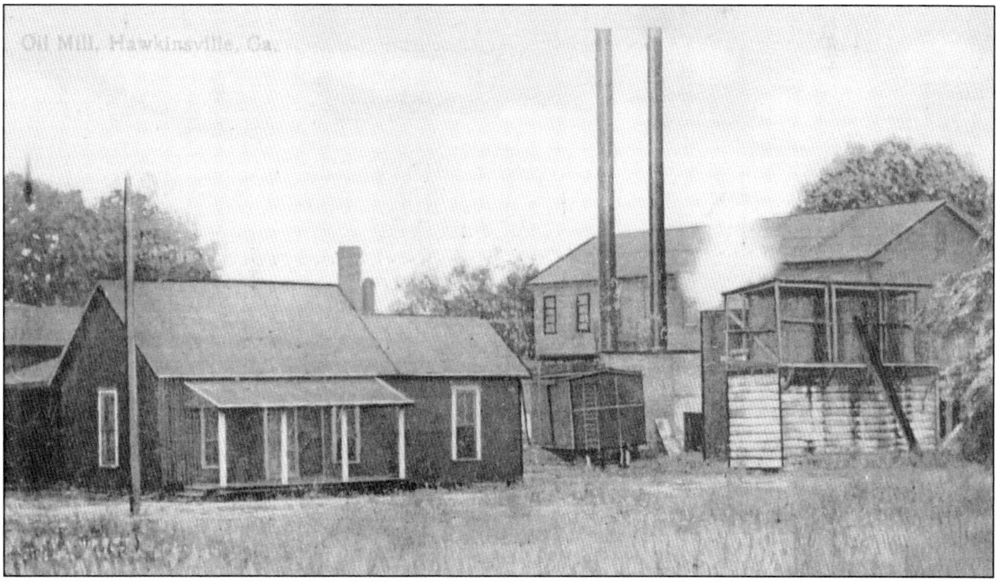

W. N. Parsons invested not only in banks, but also in cotton mills, gins, and oil companies. He was the manager and owner of Lathrop Oil Mill in Hawkinsville. (Courtesy of Georgia Archives, Vanishing Georgia, pul 006.)

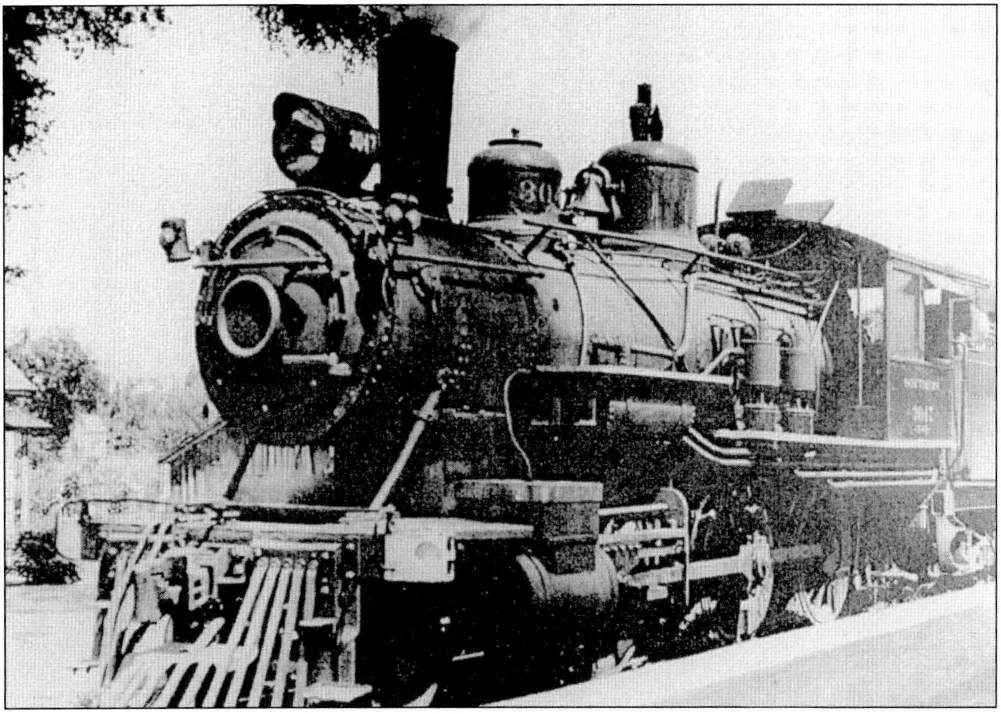

Before the Civil War, businessmen in the area had established the Central Railroad of Georgia. Following the war, local citizens and Northern businessmen established new rail companies and routes. The Macon and Brunswick, which was later acquired by the East Tennessee, Virginia, and Georgia Railroad, became a critical link between Macon, Hawkinsville, and the Georgia coast. The Wrightsville and Tennille connected the city with emerging cities like Dublin, Georgia. (Courtesy of Sam Way.)

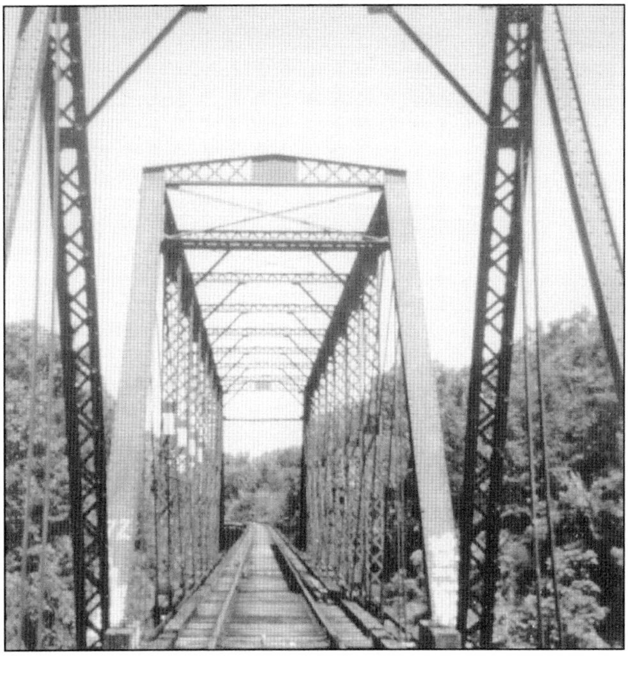

Linking Hawkinsville with cities in South Georgia necessitated the construction of railroad trestles across the Ocmulgee River. In an effort to promote economic development in the region, local governments, together with the state government, helped subsidize the laying of track and the building of trestles. (Courtesy of Emma Jean and Robert Bowen.)

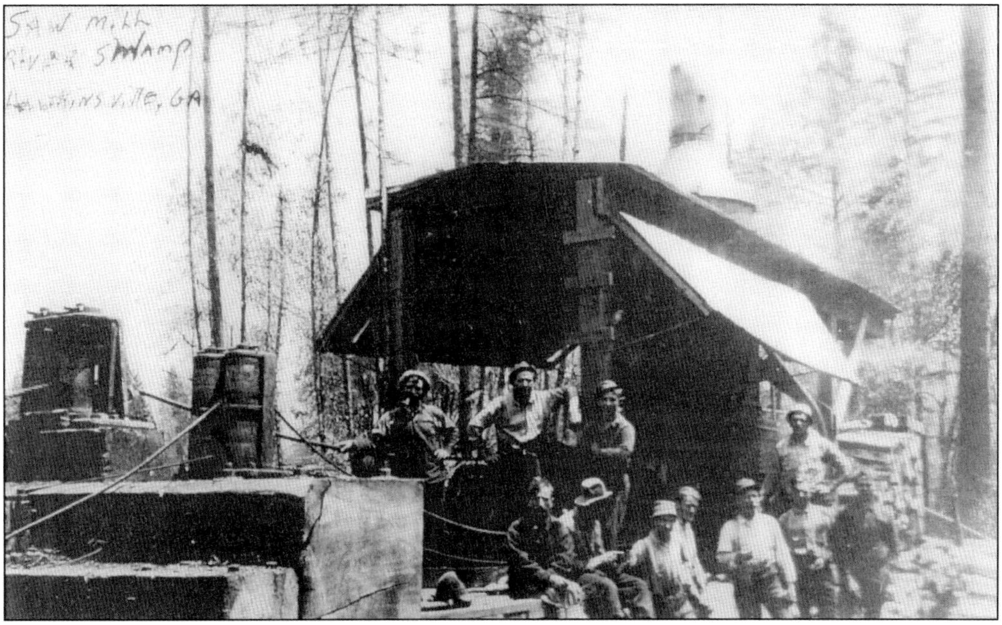

Soon after the Civil War, Northern businessmen became interested in the rich pine forests of the region. Many, such as New Yorker William E. Dodge and William P. Eastman of New Hampshire, purchased thousands of acres of land and set up sawmilling operations in neighboring counties. Not to be outdone, Hawkinsville and Pulaski County citizens also established sawmills like the one pictured above. (Courtesy of Hawkinsville *Dispatch and News*.)

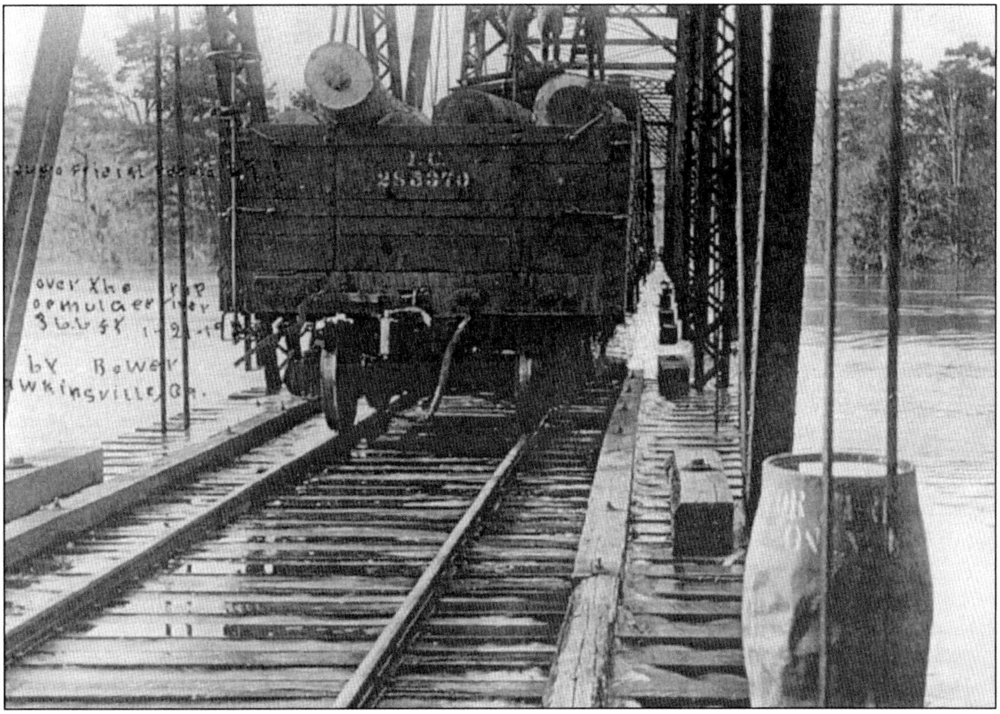

Railroads in the Middle Georgia area played a critical role in the logging industry. Trains like the one pictured here carried logs to pulp mills as well as sawmills. (Courtesy of Sam Way.)

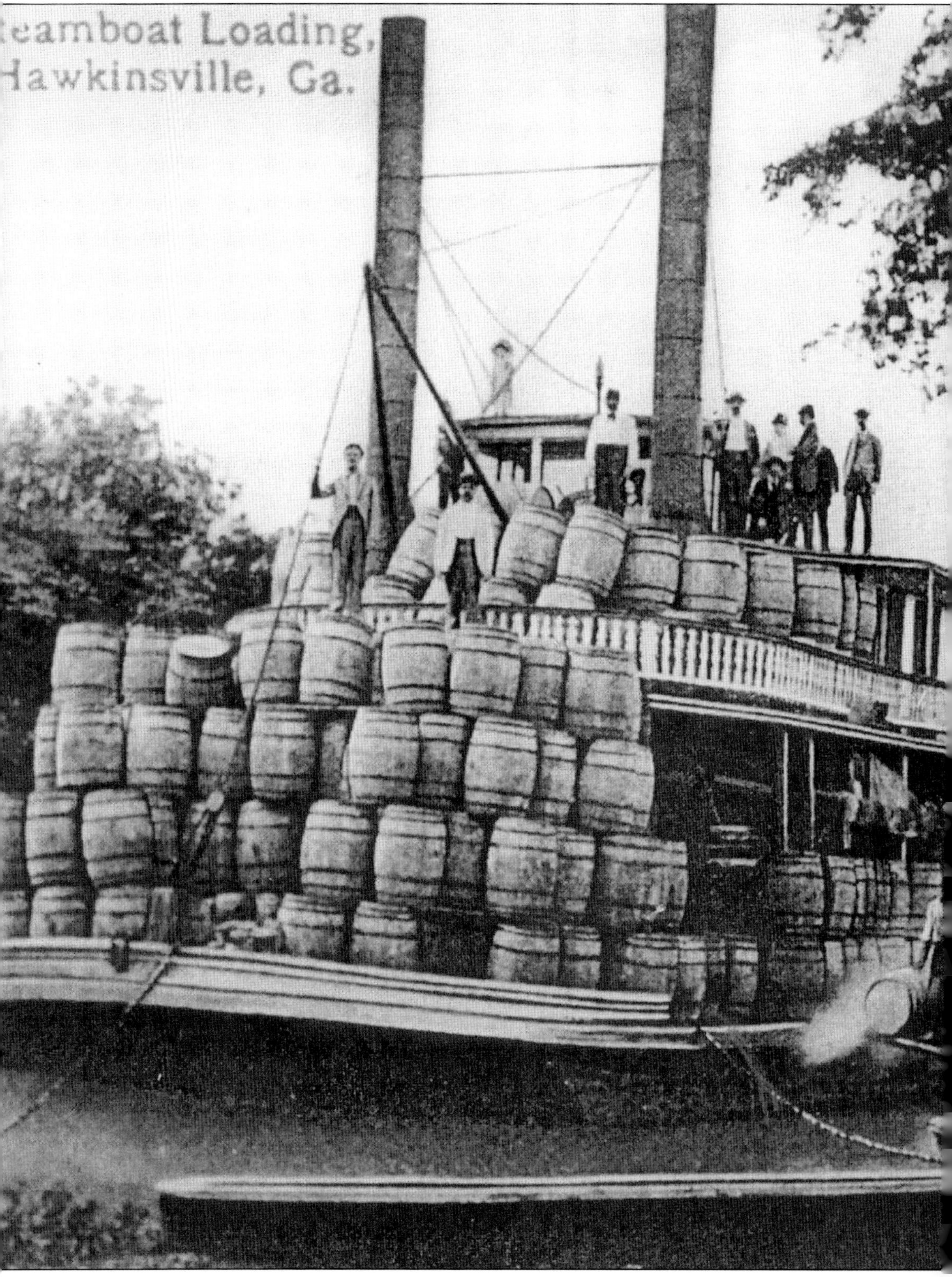

Steamboat Loading,
Hawkinsville, Ga.

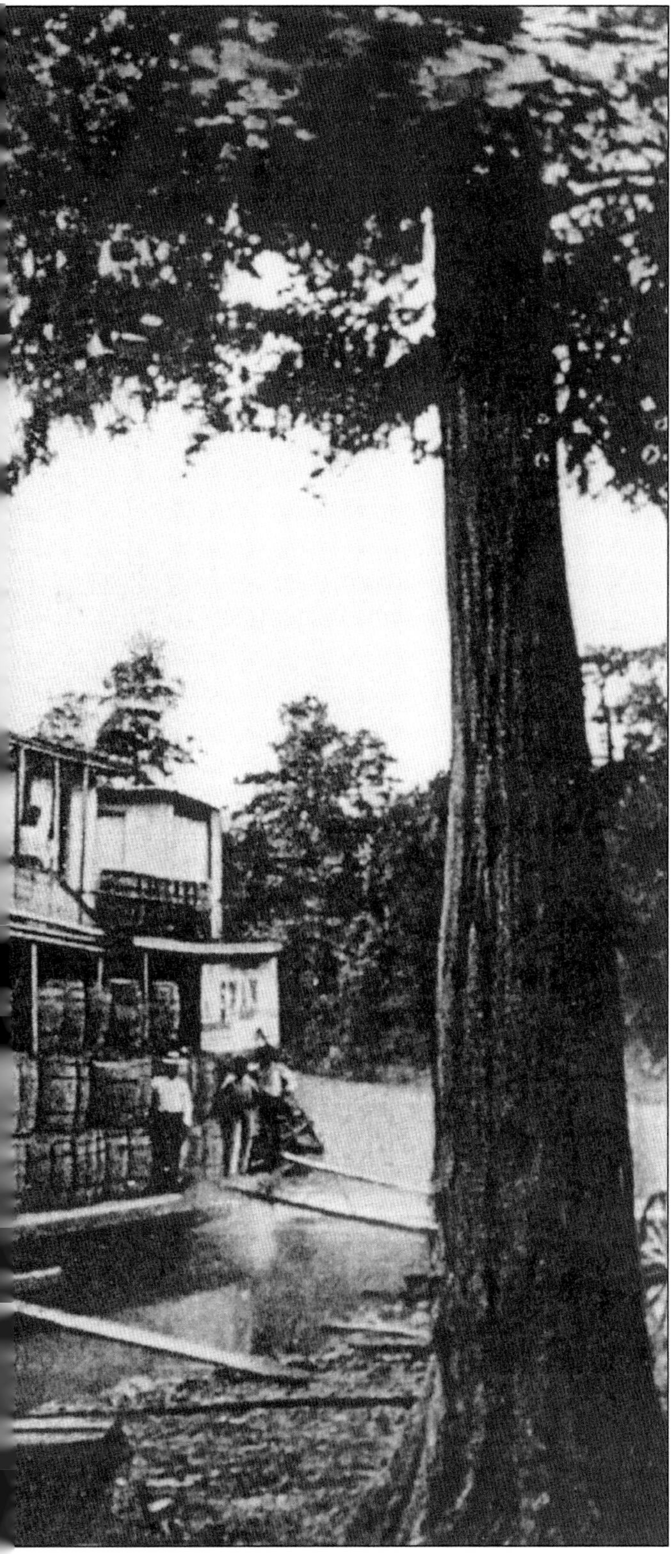

The pine forests in Pulaski and other neighboring counties were a source of turpentine, an important ingredient in oil, paper, and paint. Distilleries were established in Pulaski County and other areas for the processing of the pine rosin into turpentine. Barrels of turpentine were then loaded onto steamboats in Hawkinsville and transported down the Ocmulgee and Altamaha Rivers to Darien, Georgia. (Courtesy of Georgia Archives, Vanishing Georgia, pul 003.)

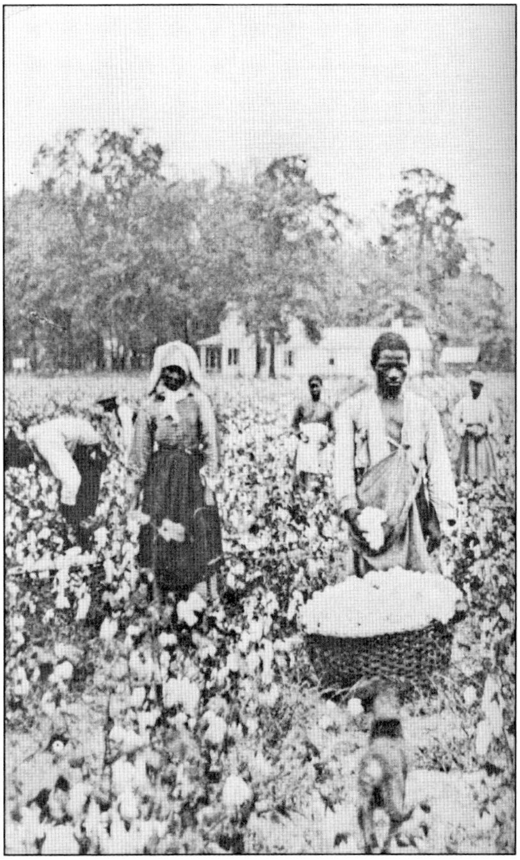

The establishment of new steamboat and railroad lines spurred the expansion of cotton growing in Middle and South Georgia. Many white and black Georgians in the area who had no land or capital had little choice but to work other people's land for a share of the cotton crop. (Courtesy of Library of Congress.)

Living conditions for sharecroppers were often quite stark. Having no money, housing, or implements of their own, they lived in small houses provided by the landowner. Most got their supplies from small stores that placed liens on their cotton crop. Unfortunately, interest rates were high and crop prices in the late 19th century were often very low. As a consequence, many sharecroppers became prisoners of debt. (Courtesy of James Davidson.)

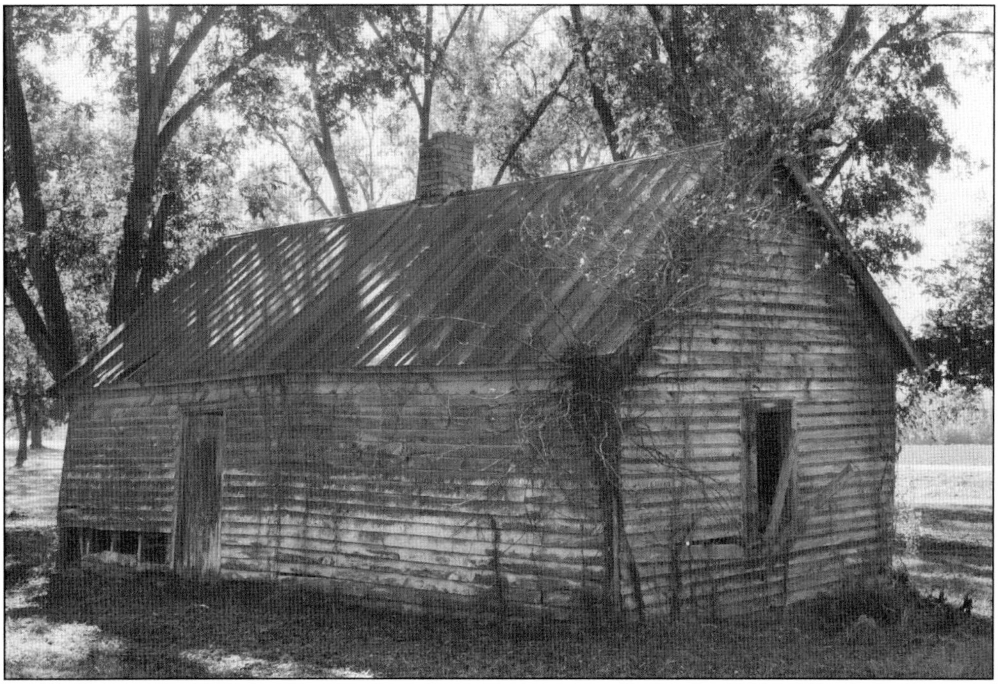

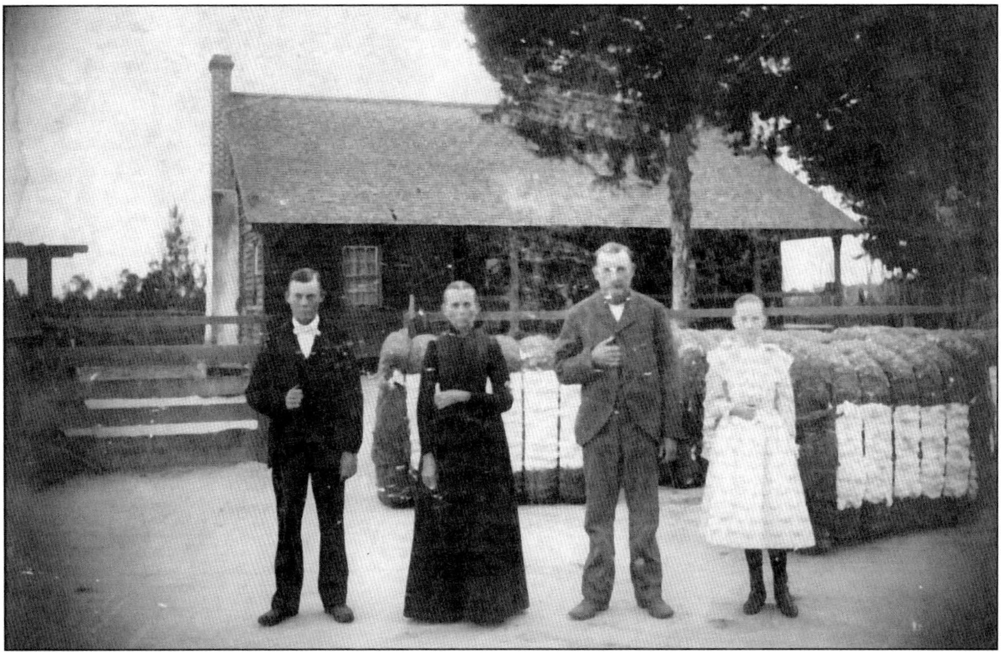

Despite the ups and downs of the cotton market, "King Cotton" had returned, and many land-owning families in the late 19th century and early 1900s were able to prosper. Pulaski County families, like the one pictured above, took their cotton to Hawkinsville to be ginned and then sold to cotton brokers. (Courtesy of Lucille Bennett.)

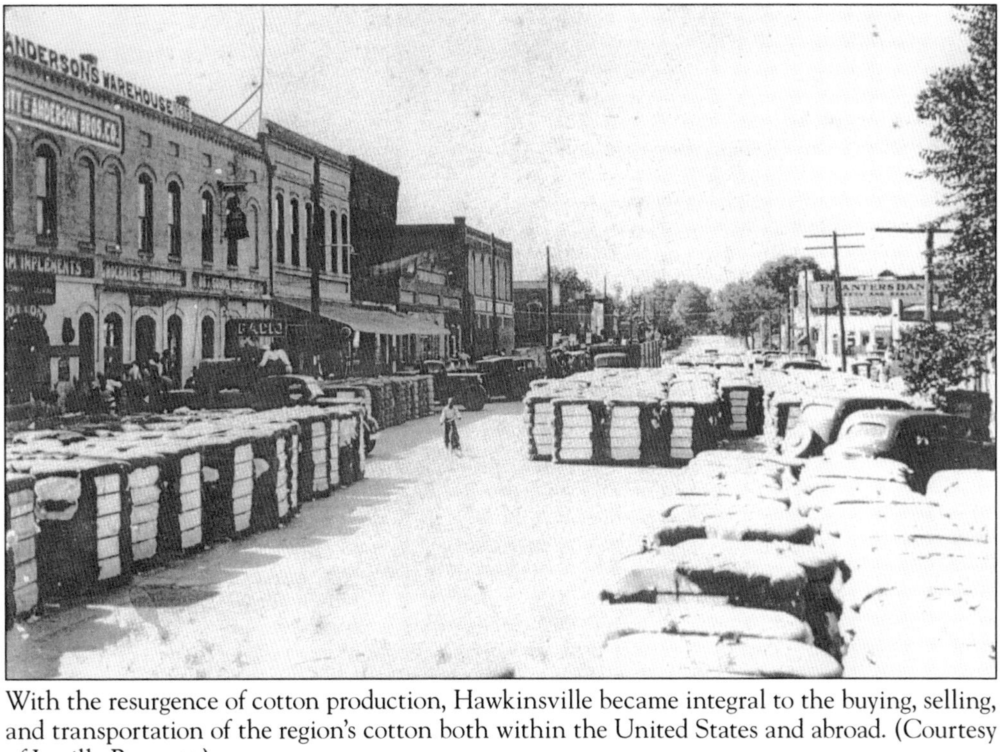

With the resurgence of cotton production, Hawkinsville became integral to the buying, selling, and transportation of the region's cotton both within the United States and abroad. (Courtesy of Lucille Bennett.)

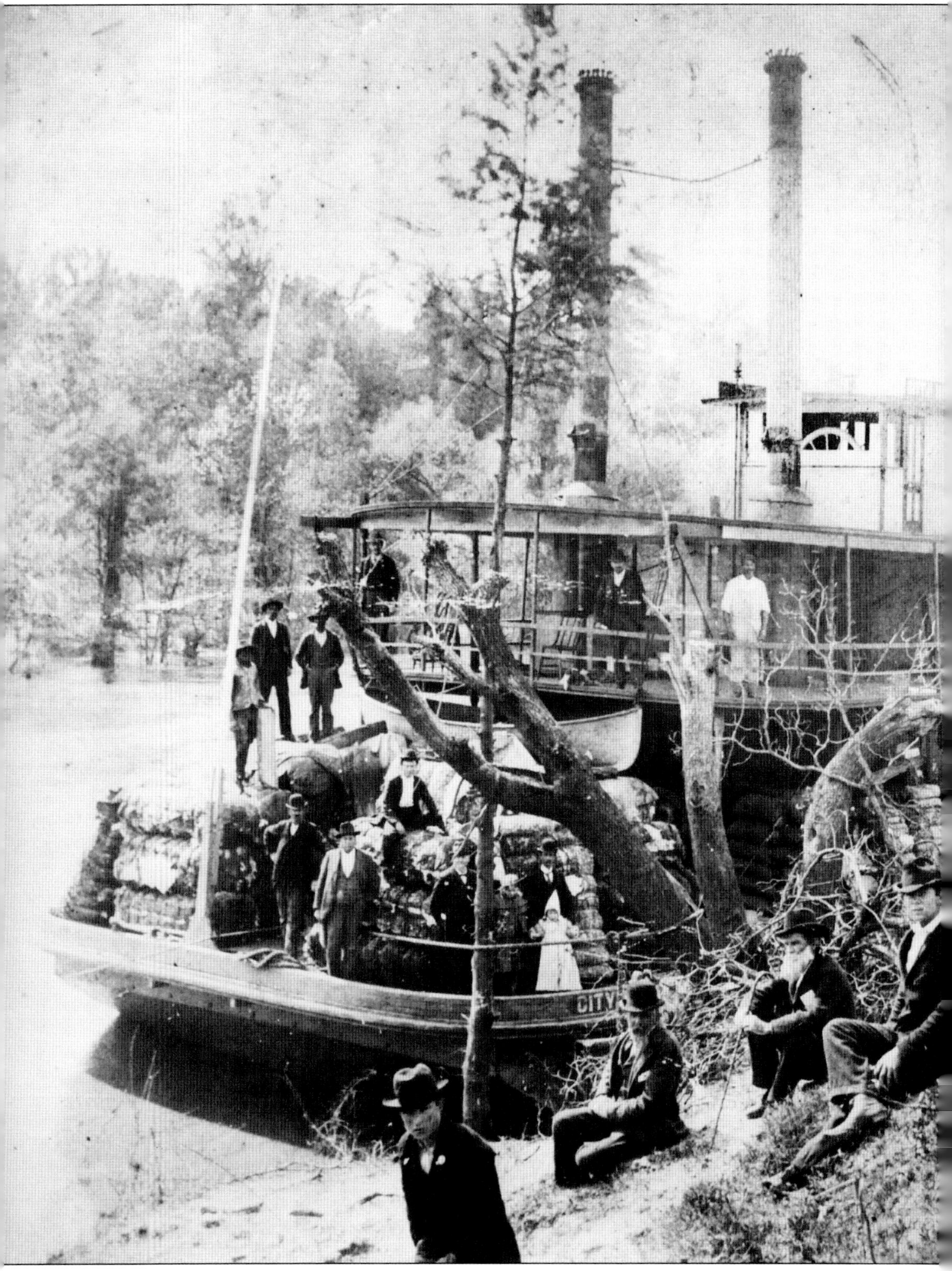
CITY

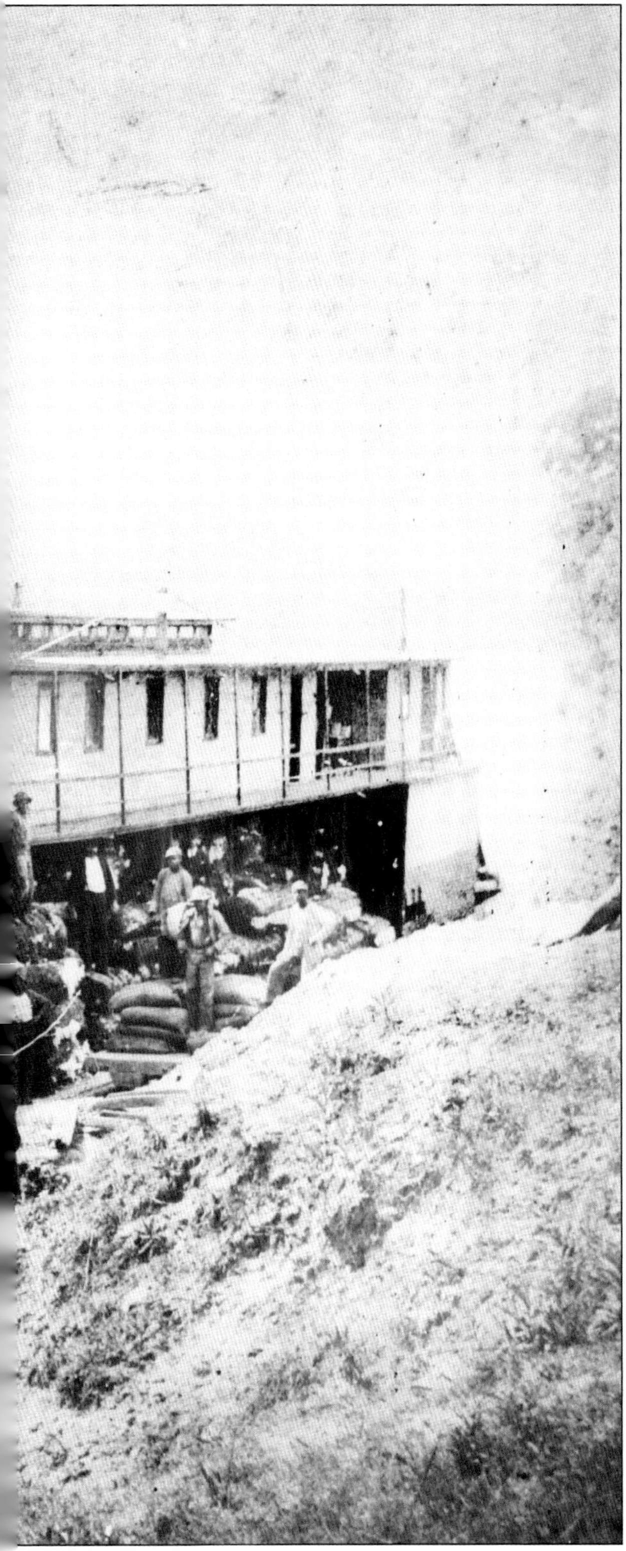

Financed by Hawkinsville merchants and constructed in nearby Abbeville, *The City of Hawkinsville* carried cotton and other Middle Georgia products up and down the Ocmulgee and Altamaha Rivers. (Courtesy of Georgia Archives, Vanishing Georgia, pul 071.)

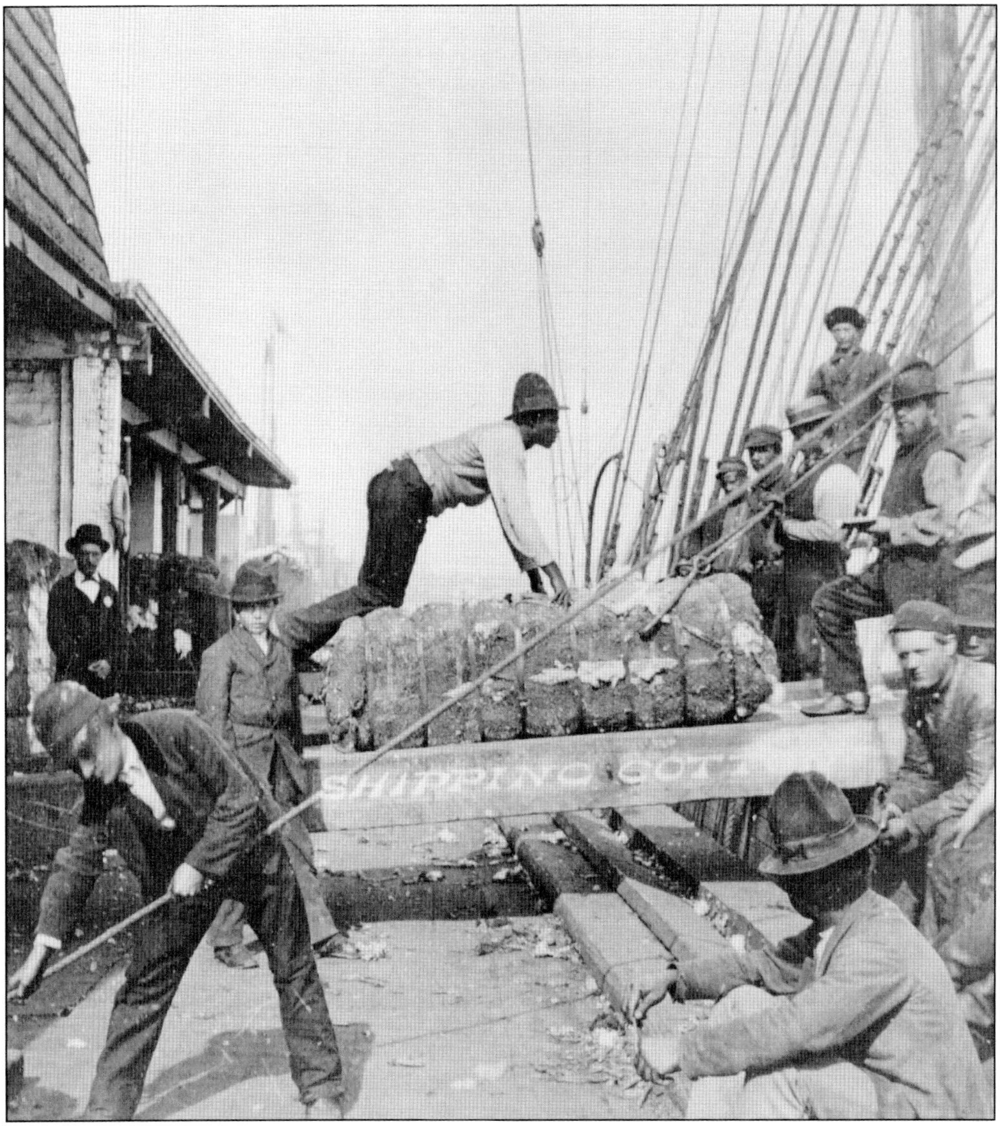

Both steamboats and railroads carried cotton from Pulaski County to Savannah. Here cotton from Middle Georgia is waiting to be loaded onto outbound ships. (Courtesy of Georgia Archives, Vanishing Georgia, ctm 084.)

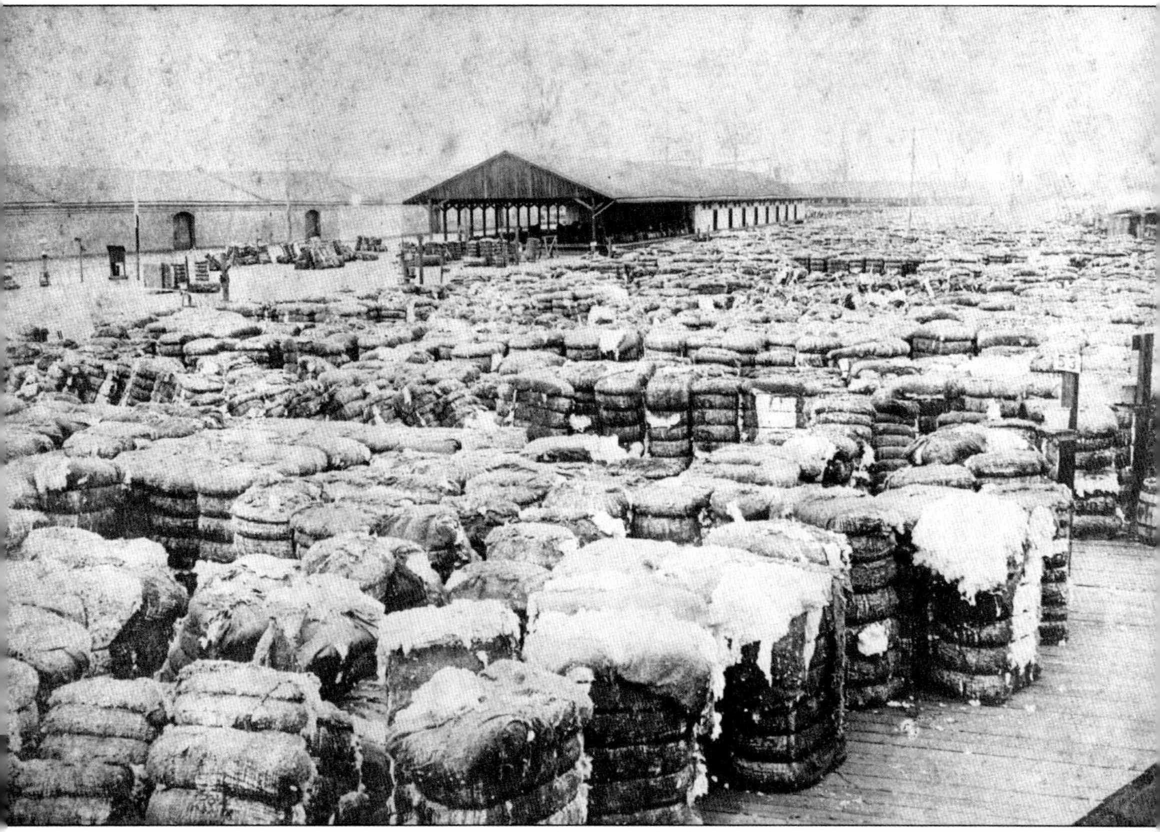

Pulaski County cotton farmers and Hawkinsville cotton brokers and gin owners had an intimate connection to not only Savannah, but also the larger world. The area's cotton was shipped to cities and cotton mills in Liverpool and Manchester, England, as well as Boston and New York. (Courtesy of Georgia Archives, Vanishing Georgia, ctm 345.)

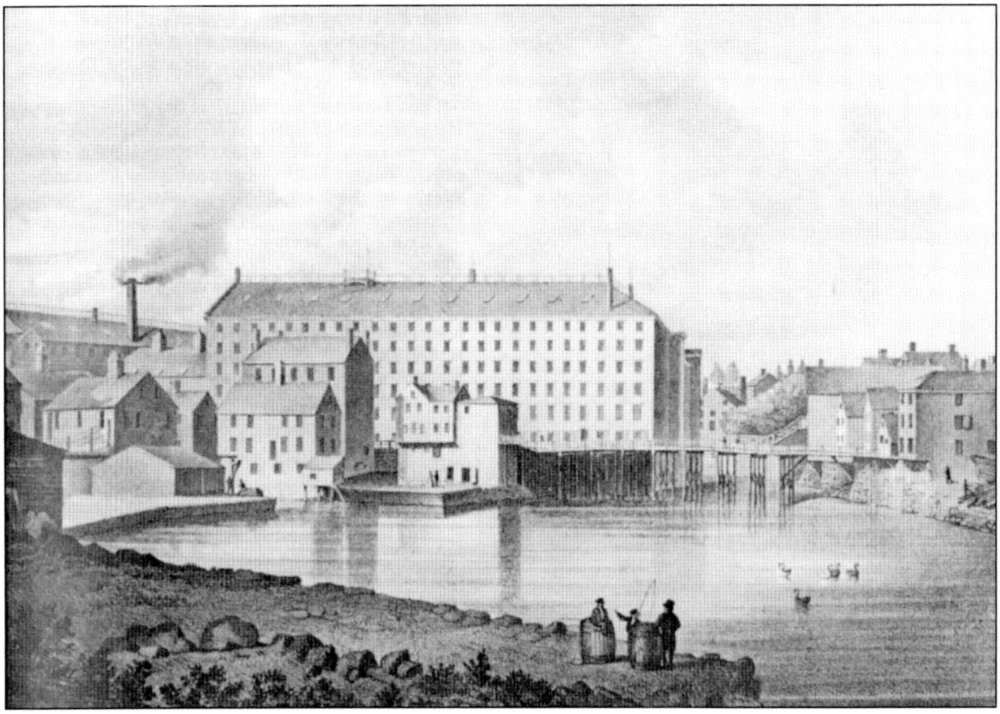

Before the Civil War, companies like Arlington Mills spun and wove Georgia cotton for the domestic and foreign market. With growing demand for cotton cloth and increased cotton production in Georgia and other Southern states, such mills expanded their operations throughout the North and into the South by the early 1900s. (Courtesy of the City of Lawrence, Massachusetts.)

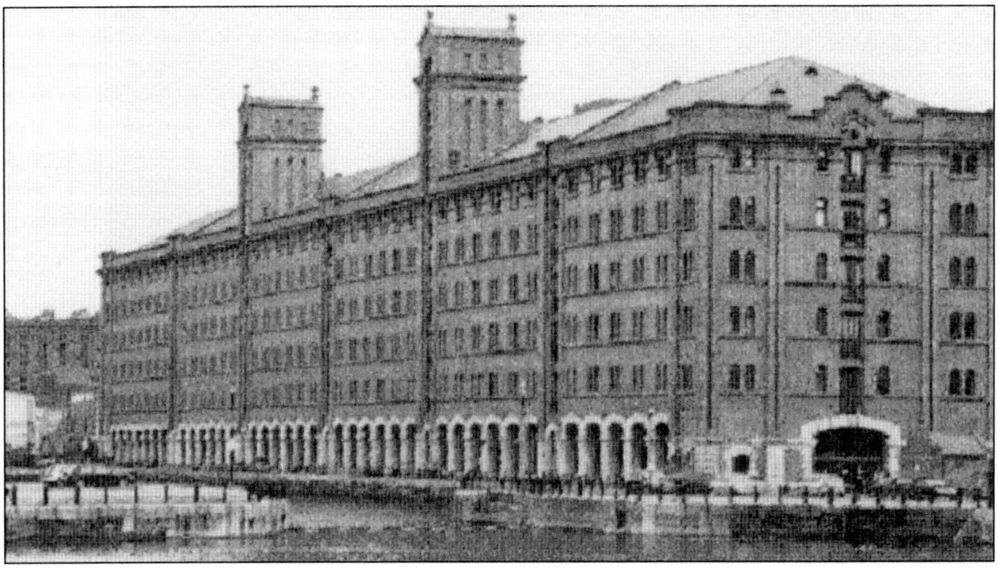

From Liverpool and other ports, Georgia cotton was transported to the key textile producing areas of Manchester and Lancashire, England. The livelihood of English and American mill workers and their families depended on the cotton trade. (Courtesy of the City of Manchester.)

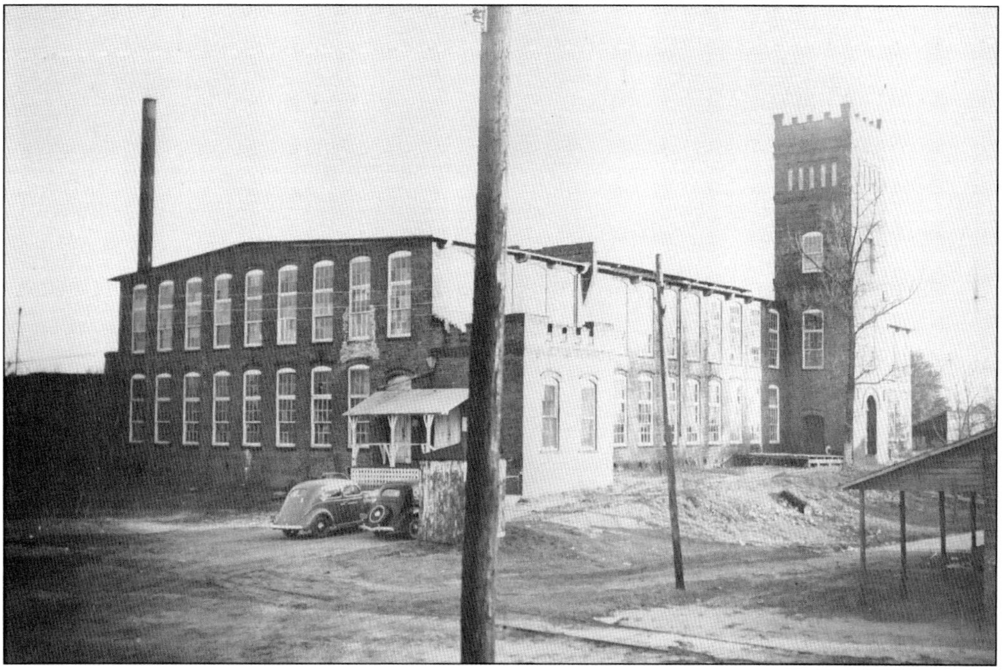

A cotton mill was established in Hawkinsville on a bluff above the Ocmulgee River in the early 1900s. For many Middle Georgians, the mill became an opportunity to escape the poverty they had known as sharecroppers or small landowners. The mills provided a steady wage and often houses near the mill that could either be leased or purchased. (Courtesy of Georgia Archives, Vanishing Georgia, pul 035.)

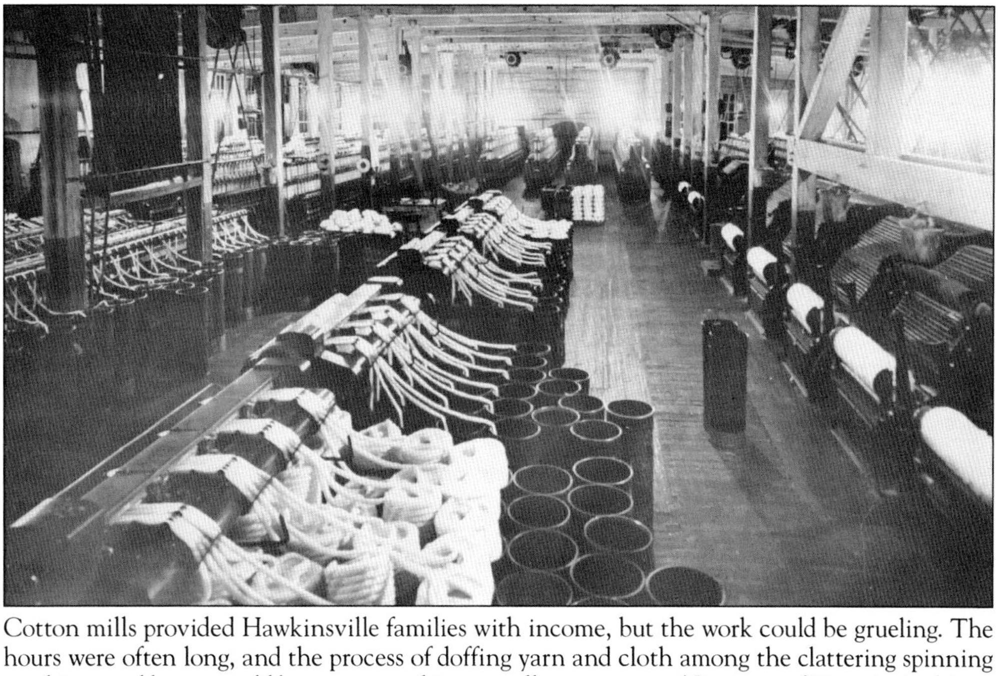

Cotton mills provided Hawkinsville families with income, but the work could be grueling. The hours were often long, and the process of doffing yarn and cloth among the clattering spinning machines and looms could be nerve-wracking as well as strenuous. (Courtesy of Georgia Archives, Vanishing Georgia, pul 049.)

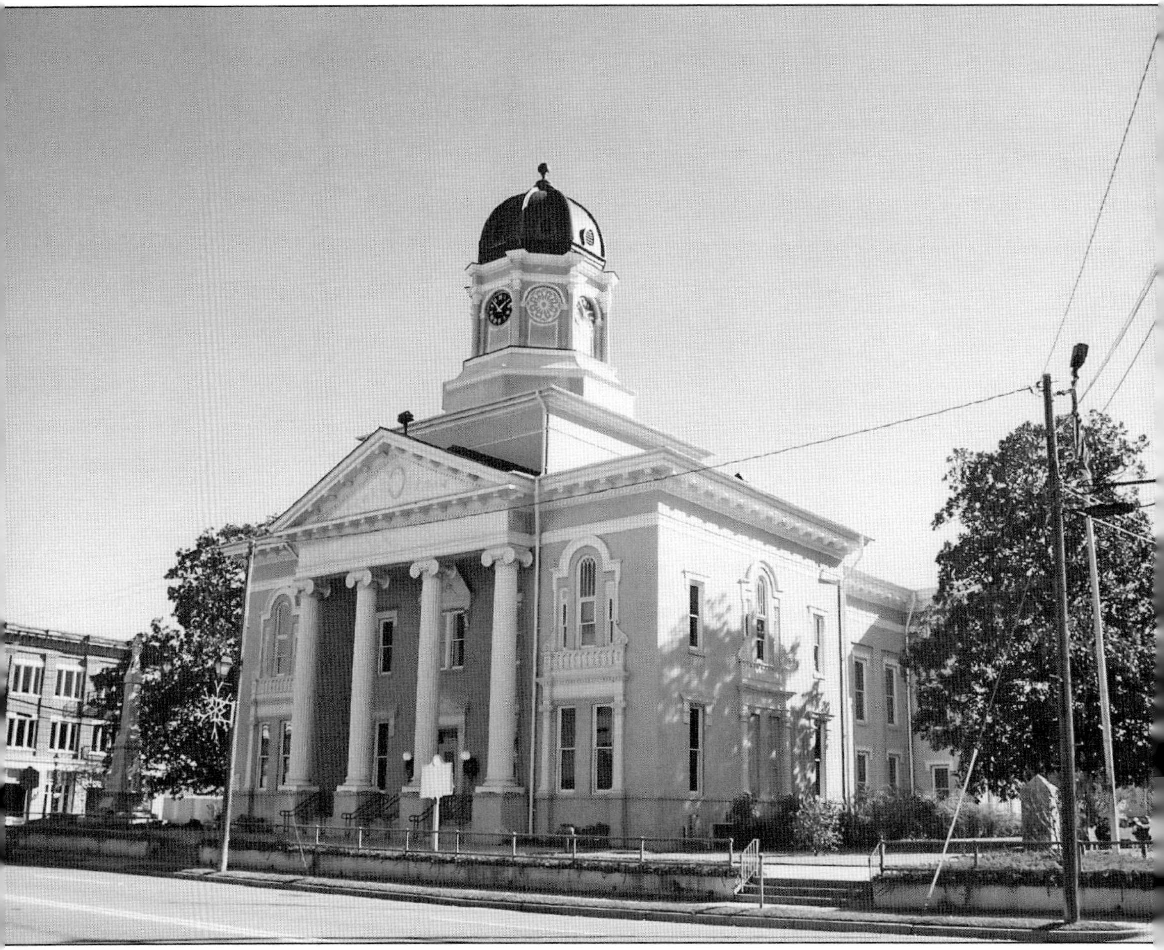

Constructed on Commerce Street in 1874 and later expanded to include a Colonial facade and two additional stories, the Pulaski County Courthouse stands as a symbol of Hawkinsville's transformation into a New South town. (Courtesy of Phillip A. Gibbs.)

Three

Queen of the Wiregrass

Hawkinsville was the queen of Wiregrass country. Before the Civil War, the town was already on the rise. Favorable cotton prices during the 1850s had made Hawkinsville a bustling commercial market. Cotton bales were shipped downriver on steamboats loaded at Hawkinsville's docks. Farmers came not only to sell their crops, but to also buy goods and obtain services. A thriving, professional, middle class of doctors, lawyers, merchants, artisans, and teachers catered to their needs.

During the Civil War, Hawkinsville continued to serve as a repository for cotton as well as a refugee center for whites and blacks alike. After the war, it became a model New South town. The refugee population provided temporary workers to build rail lines into the town. And high prices for the stored cotton kept Hawkinsville prosperous. By the 1880s, there were over 30 grocery, general merchandise, and dry goods stores. There were also numerous warehouses. Hawkinsville was more than just a warehouse town, however. It ginned and compressed cotton, and it also produced cottonseed oil. While other towns in the region withered and died, Hawkinsville flourished.

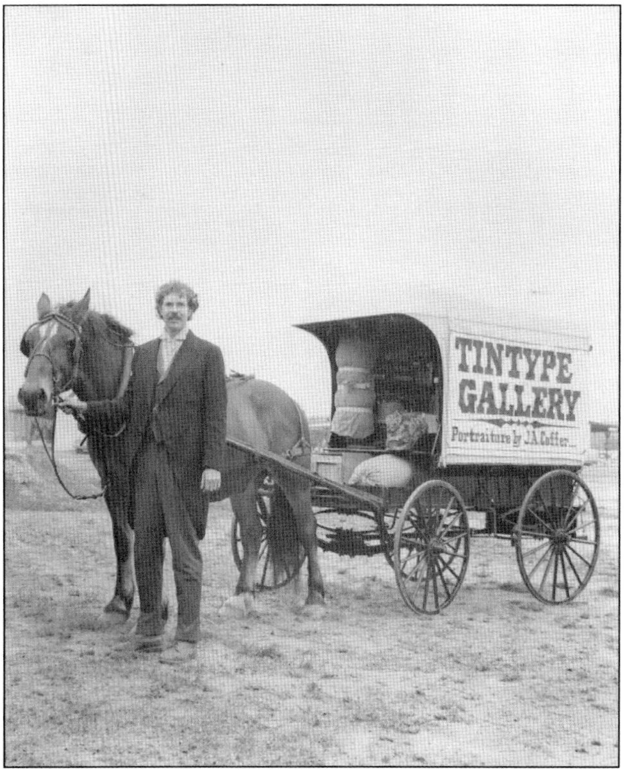

J. B. Cofield traveled throughout Middle Georgia making photographs of the region's people in the late 1890s and early 1900s. He maintained a studio in Hawkinsville for more than 50 years. The gentleman pictured here is dressed as a photographer in a 1970s photograph. (Courtesy of Georgia Archives, Vanishing Georgia, pul 032.)

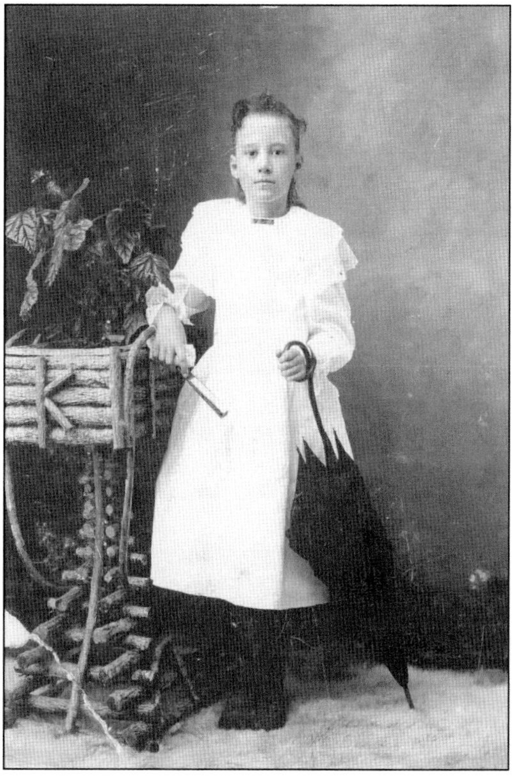

The young girl pictured here is just one of the many photographs Cofield made of the citizens of Hawkinsville during the late 1890s and early 1900s. (Courtesy of Pat Keller.)

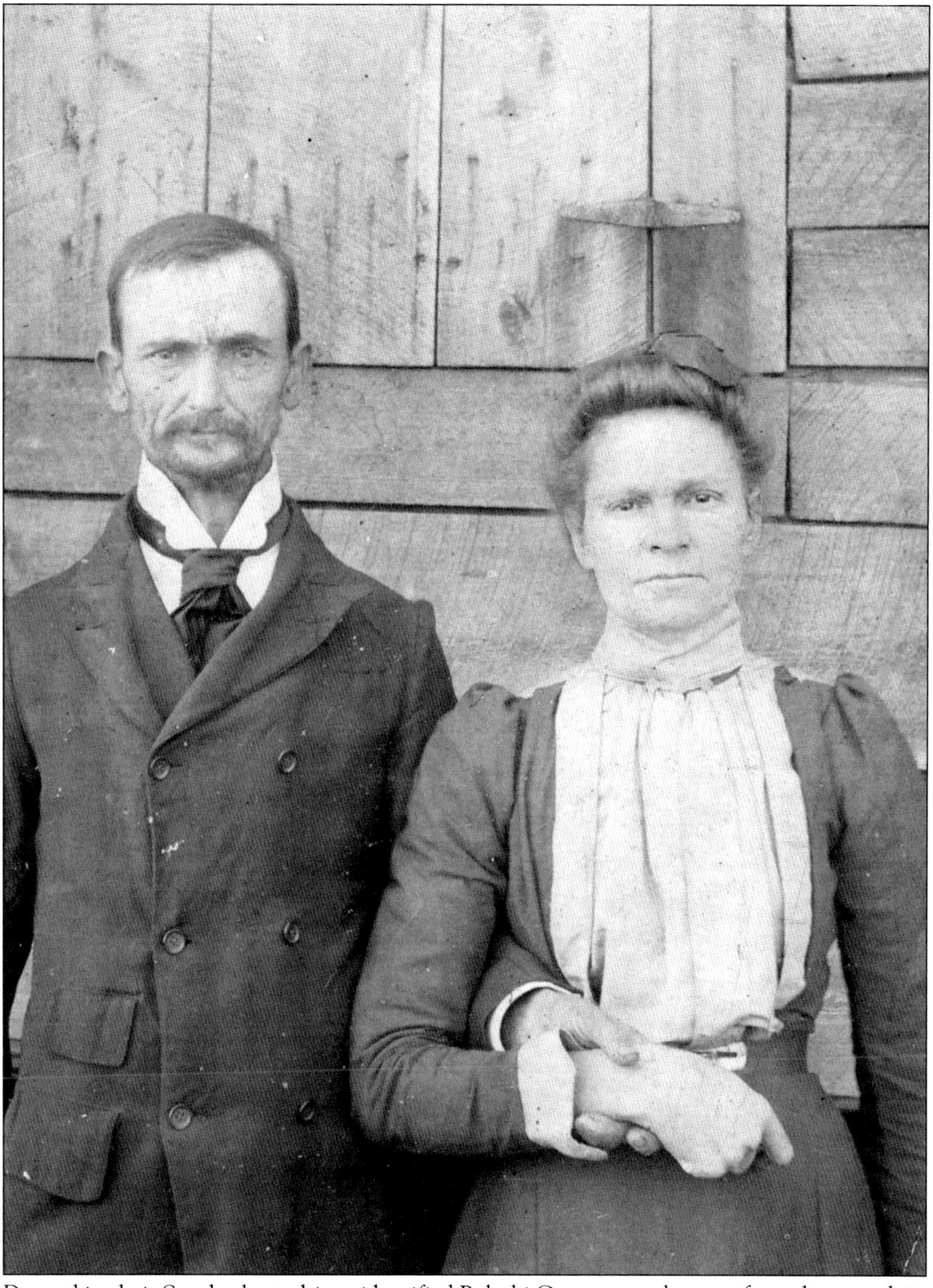

Dressed in their Sunday best, this unidentified Pulaski County couple poses for a photograph in front of their clapboard house. (Courtesy of Josh Wilcox.)

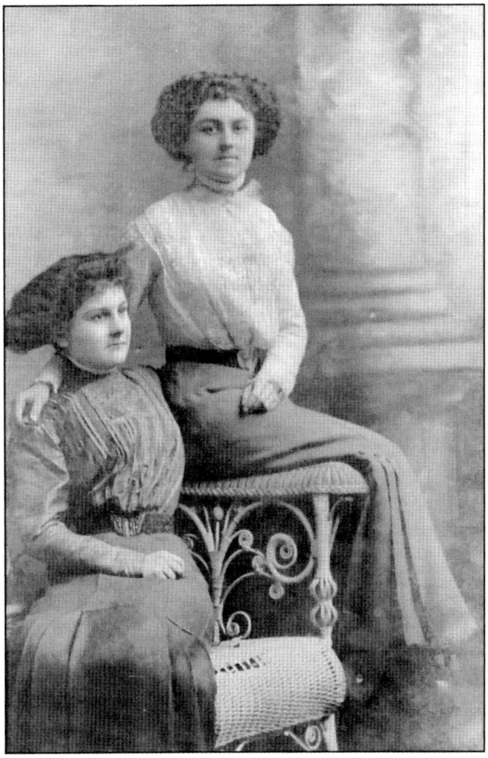

Dressed in 1890s fashion, these two ladies pose for a photograph in a Hawkinsville studio. (Courtesy of Pat Keller.)

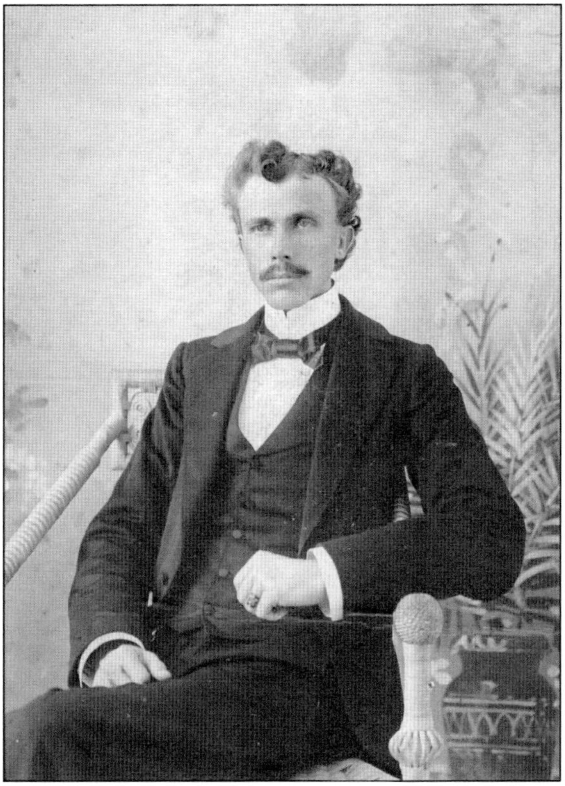

Young men of the planter-merchant elite in 19th-century Hawkinsville were rarely seen on the streets of the city, at church, or any social occasion unless they were impeccably dressed. (Courtesy of Pat Keller.)

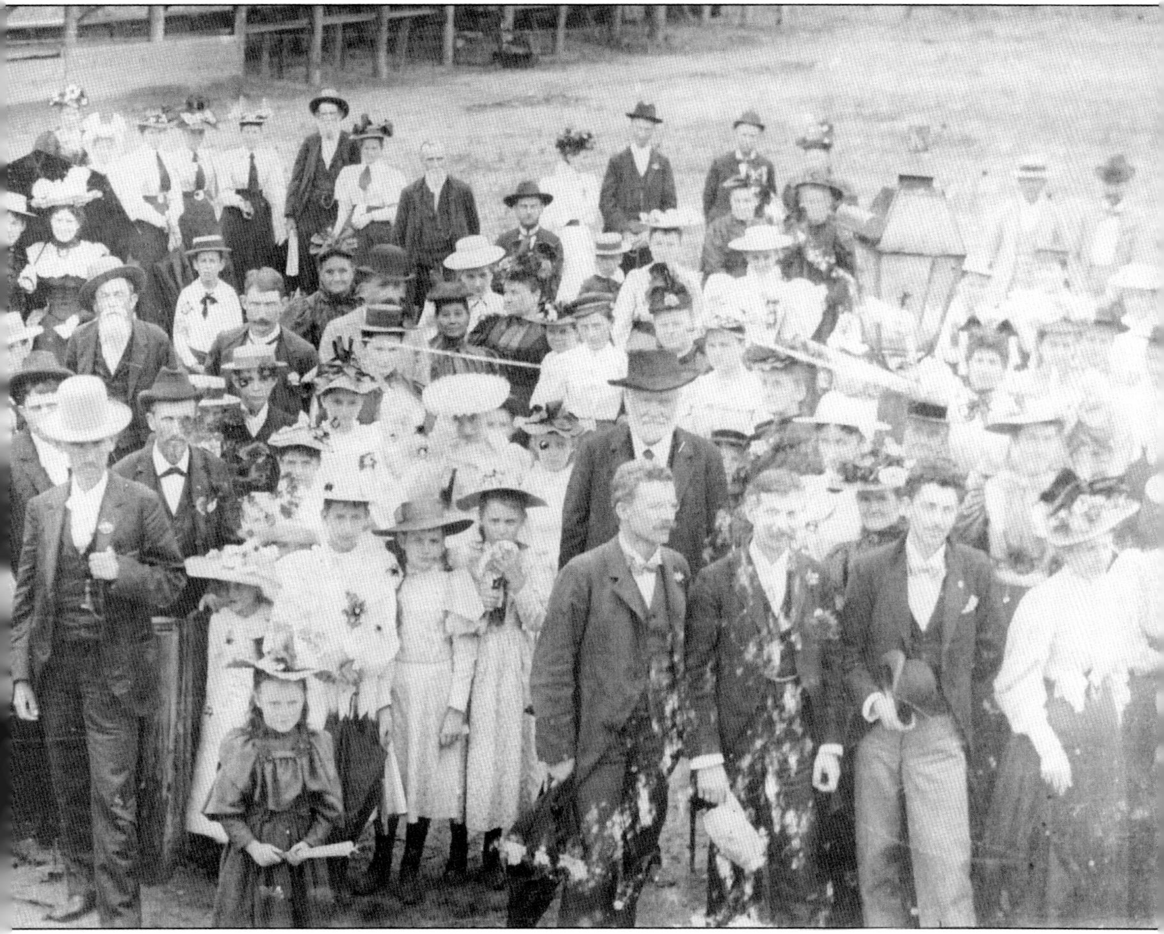

The numerous clothing and mercantile firms in Hawkinsville enabled the city's men, women, and children to dress in the latest fashions of the period. Although the social occasion is uncertain in this 1890s photograph, the citizens seemed to have spared little or no sartorial expense. (Courtesy of Hawkinsville *Dispatch and News*.)

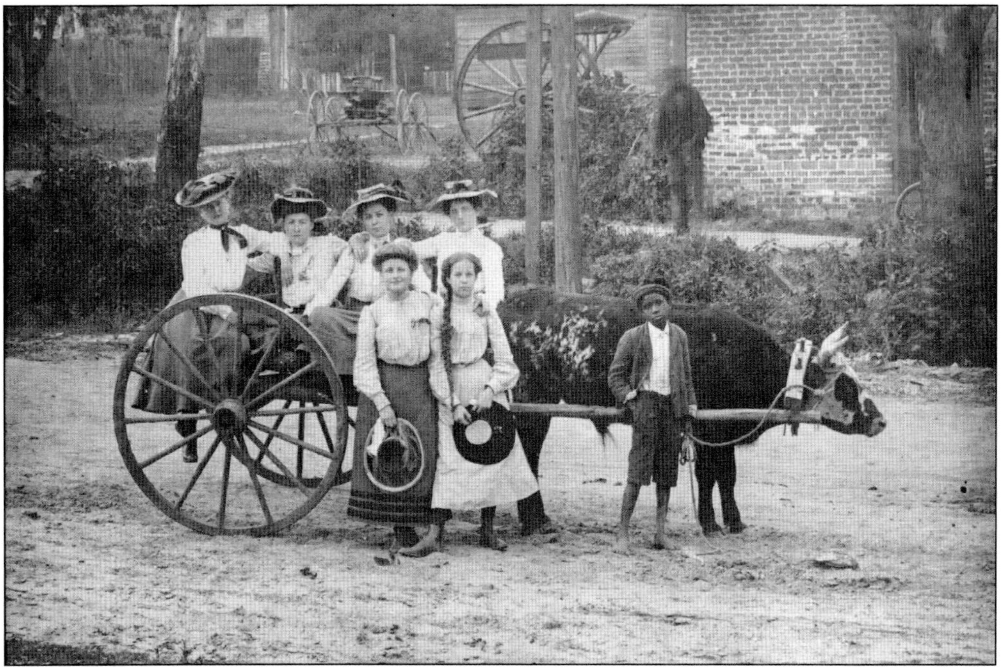

These fashionably dressed young women were perhaps out for a Sunday stroll in Hawkinsville when they decided to have their pictures taken on the young boy's oxcart. (Courtesy of Georgia Archives, Vanishing Georgia, pul 097.)

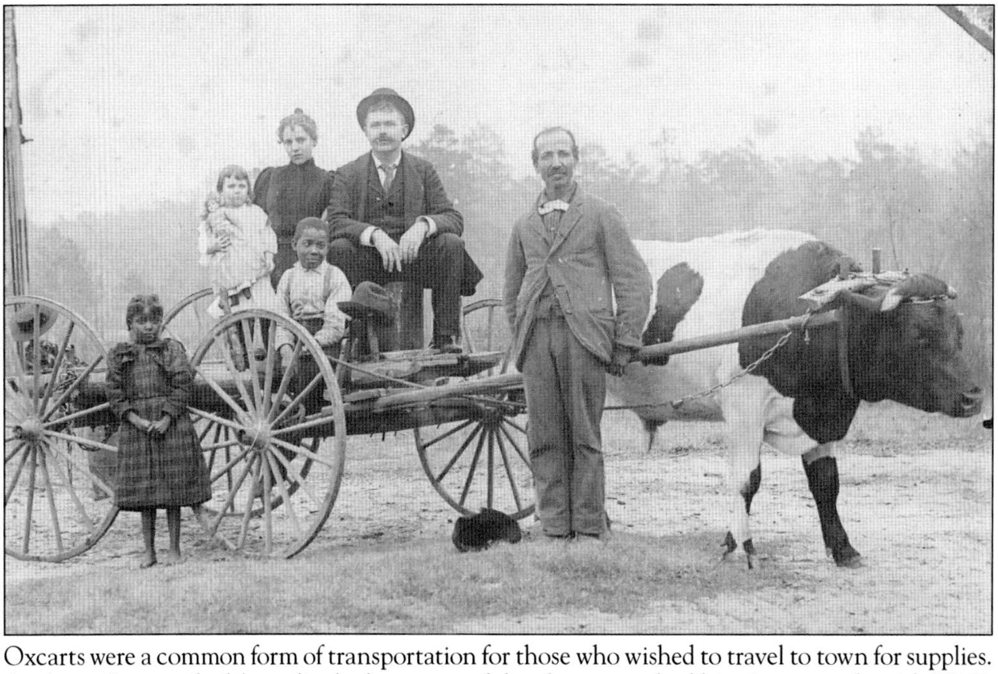

Oxcarts were a common form of transportation for those who wished to travel to town for supplies. Anthony Summerford (standing), the owner of the above cart, had his picture made with W. C. Kalor (the music teacher at the public school where Summerford was a janitor) and his family. The two black children are Pearl and Willie Mitchell. (Courtesy of Georgia Archives, Vanishing Georgia, pul 080.)

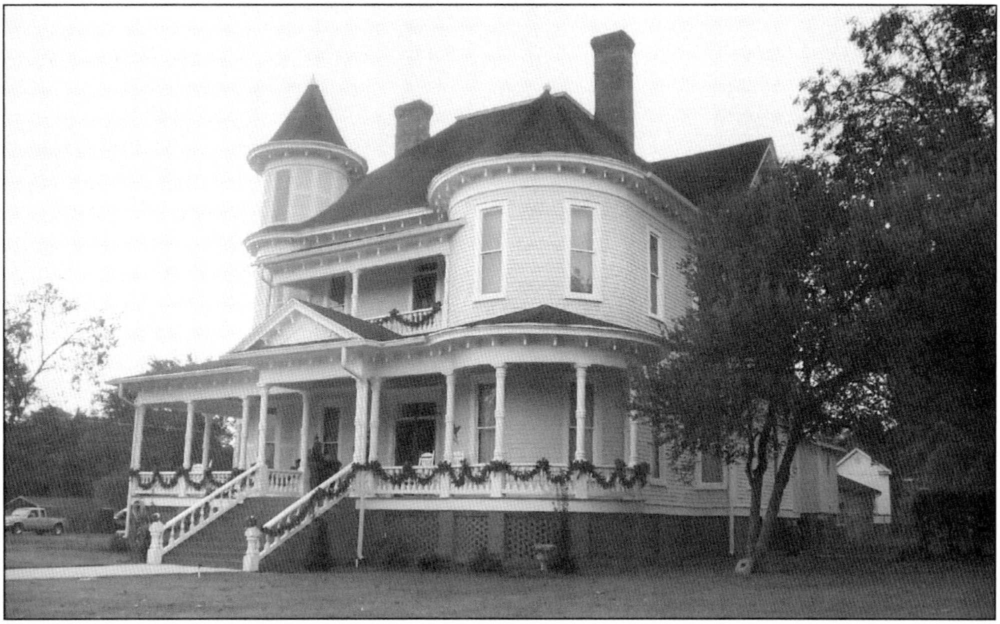

As Hawkinsville's population grew and prospered during the late 19th century, fashionable homes began to appear along the streets of the city. This magnificent house, modeled after an English castle, may well be the largest home in Hawkinsville. J. L. Huggins, the same contractor who built the Opera House, constructed this Victorian masterpiece as his personal home prior to 1900. It took five years for Huggins to locate the choicest lumber to be used in its construction and another five years to construct the home. Having completed the home, Huggins was only able to enjoy his work of art for six to eight years prior to his death. (Courtesy of Phillip A. Gibbs.)

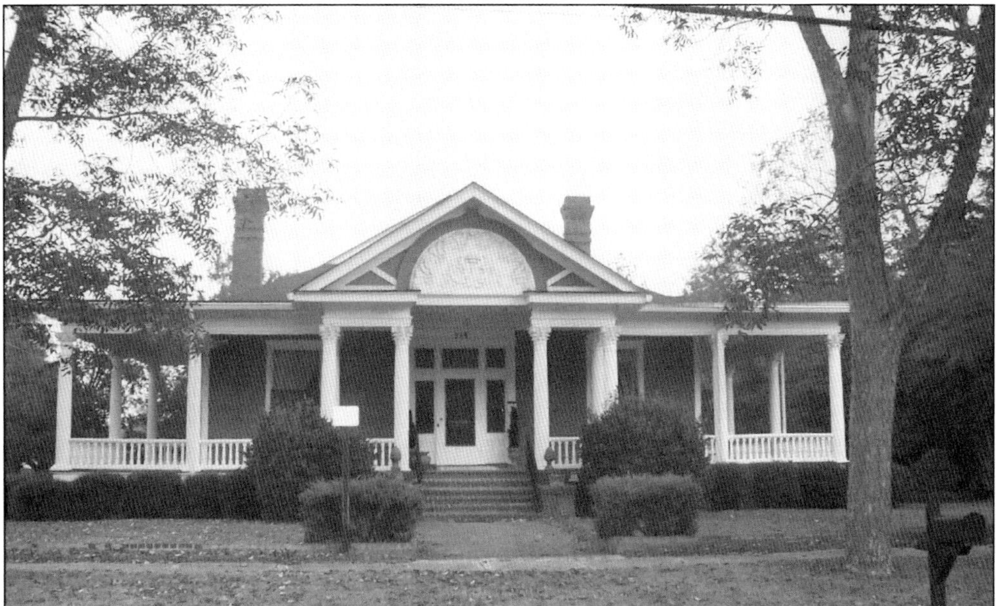

The Jelks-Dent House was built around 1910 by Gus and Lillia Jelks. Gus Jelks was the previous president of Planter's Bank. They lived in the home until their deaths. The Colonial brick and frame structure has been restored to its original state. (Courtesy of Phillip A. Gibbs.)

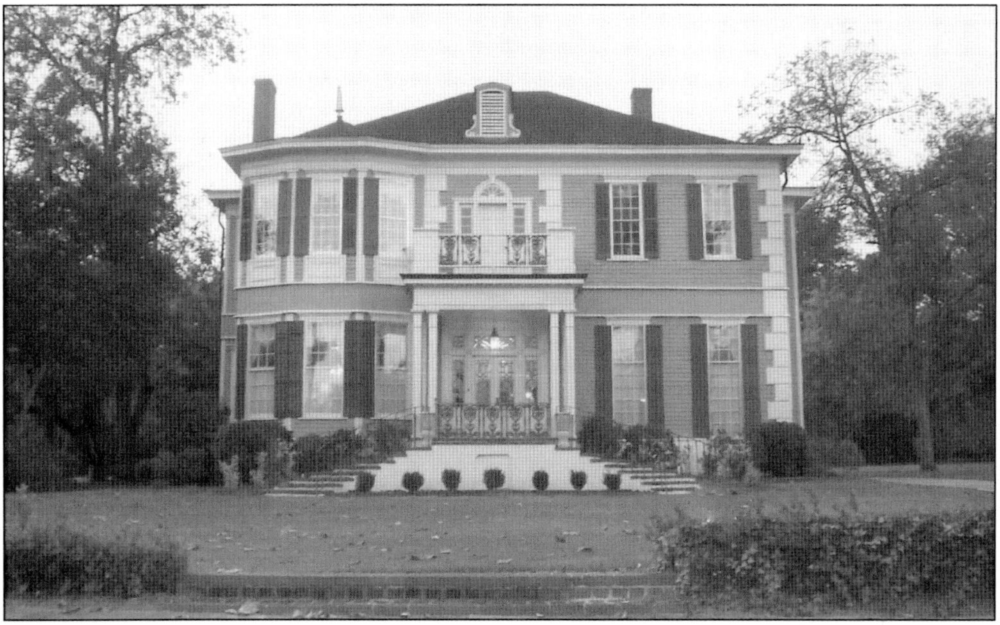

This elegant house was built around 1902 and was the home of J. J. Whitfield. Later the Cabero family purchased the home from Ed Chancey. The Caberos modernized the home while preserving the timeless treasure it is. The house contains a magnificent grand staircase, a parlor, a dining room, a sitting room, servants' quarters, large hallways, four bedrooms and two baths upstairs, and one bedroom and one bath downstairs. This home was superbly designed for cross ventilation throughout, and with a double porch both upstairs and downstairs, it was a home to enjoy during the changing seasons. (Courtesy of Phillip A. Gibbs.)

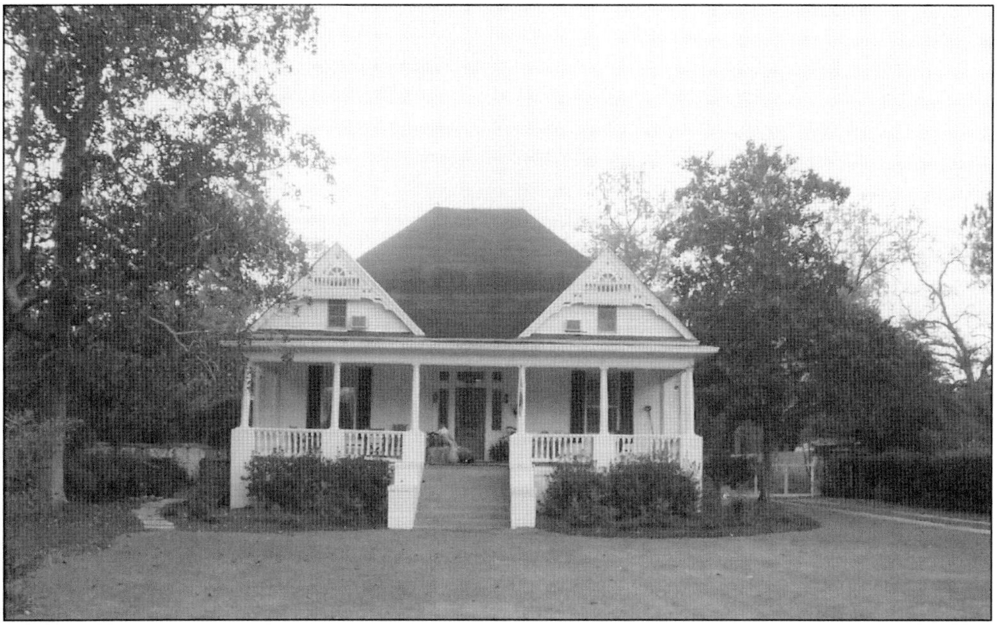

Built in the 1870s, this house was the home of Samuel Sommer's German grandparents. An affluent businessman, Samuel Sommer's family immigrated to the United States in the 1850s and then later to Hawkinsville in the 1880s. (Courtesy of Phillip A. Gibbs.)

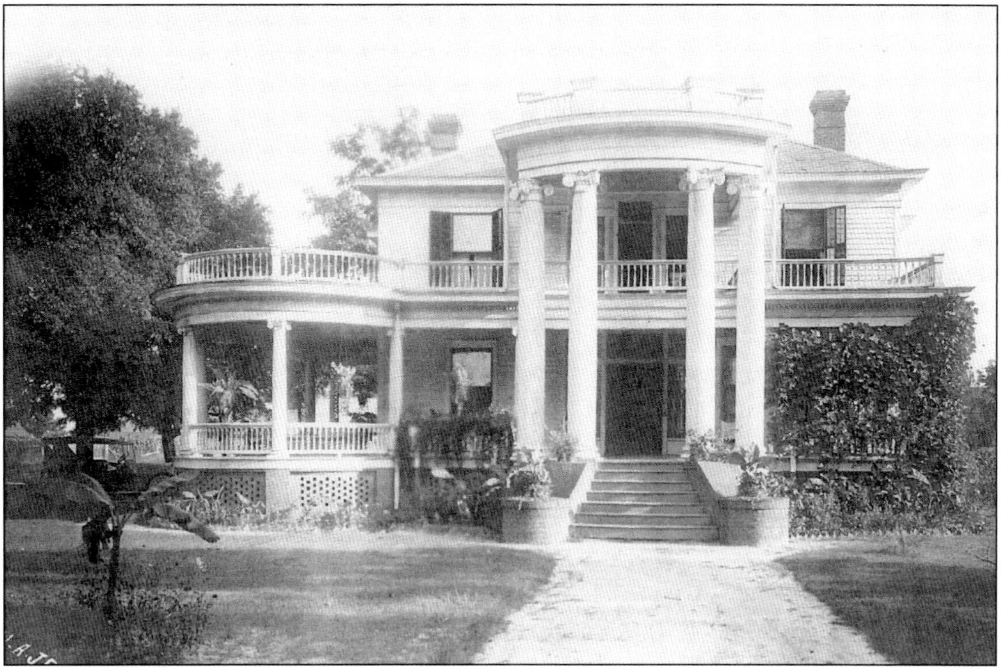

Samuel Sommer's family built this neoclassical home in the 1890s. W. A. Jennings, the founder of the Hawkinsville Phone Company, purchased the house in the early 1900s. (Courtesy of Lucille Bennett.)

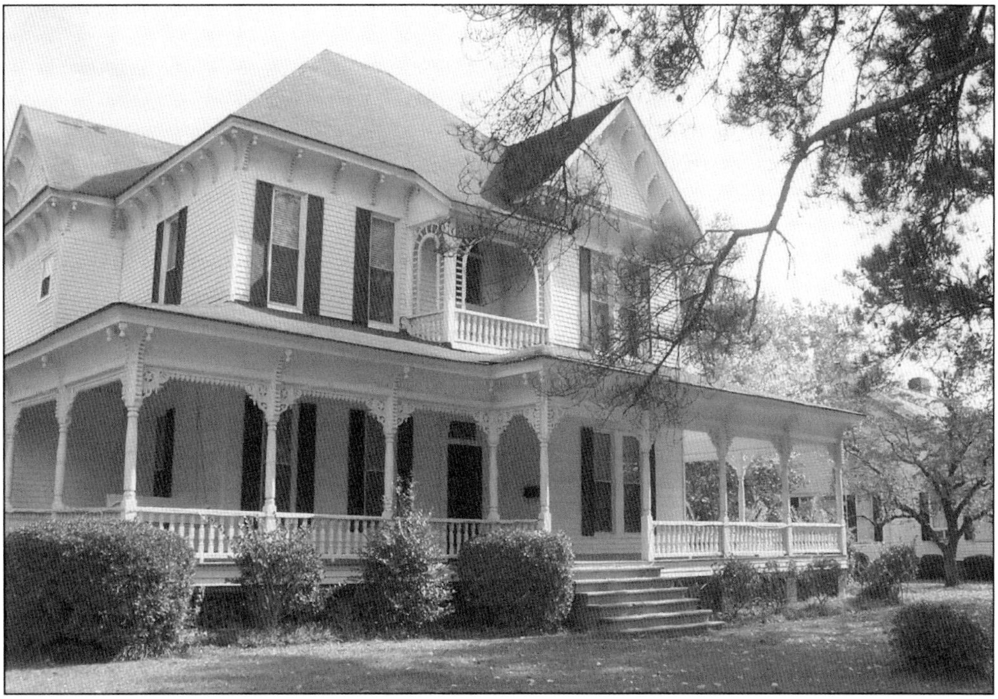

Samuel Way, a merchant, mayor, and state assemblyman, built this Victorian home in the 1890s. Way was the son of Dr. E. F. Way, who settled in Hawkinsville in the 1830s. (Courtesy of Phillip A. Gibbs.)

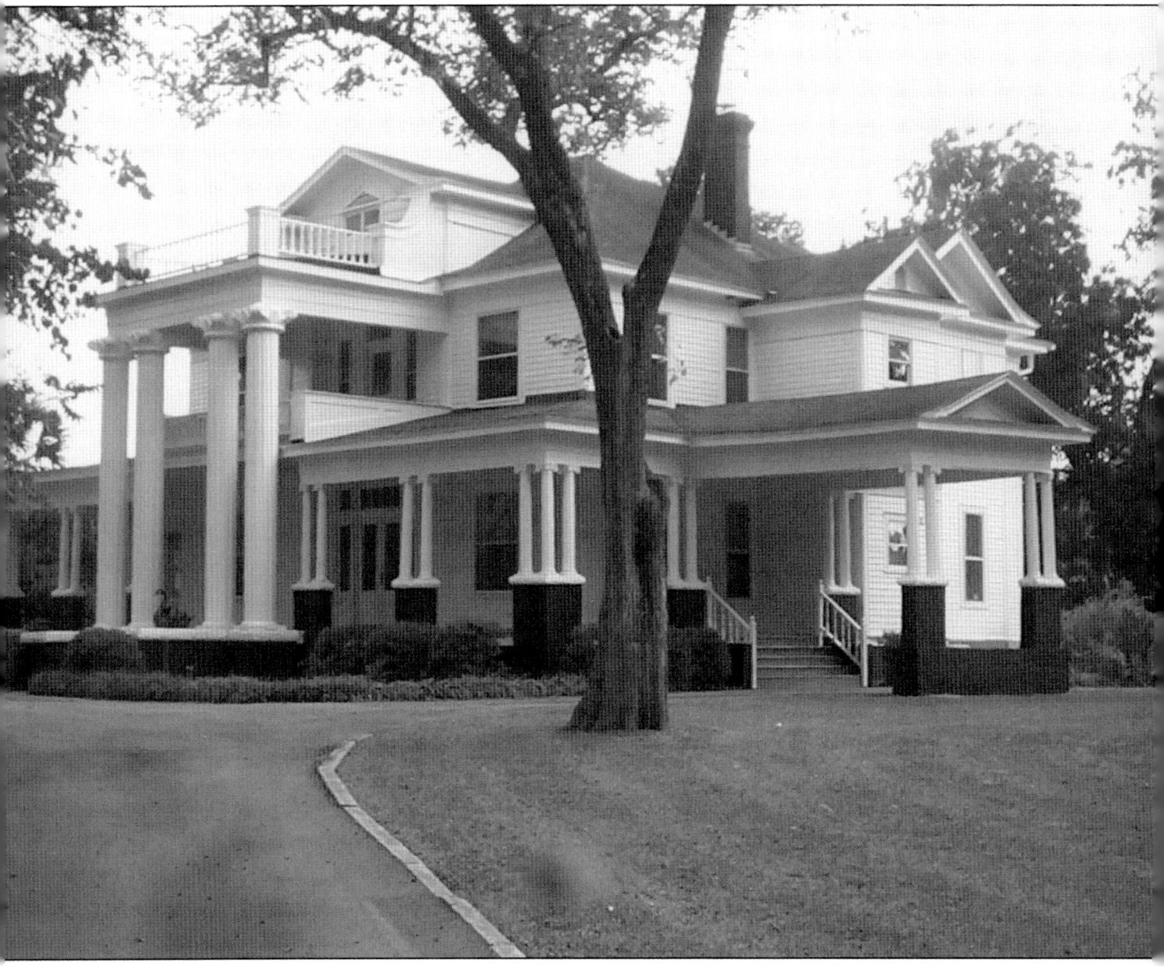

Byron Glover, a cotton broker, completed this Southern Colonial–style home with classic revival features about 1907. He later sold the property to the family of planter-politician James Pope Brown when he went to Savannah to make his fortune in the cotton export business. (Courtesy of Phillip A. Gibbs.)

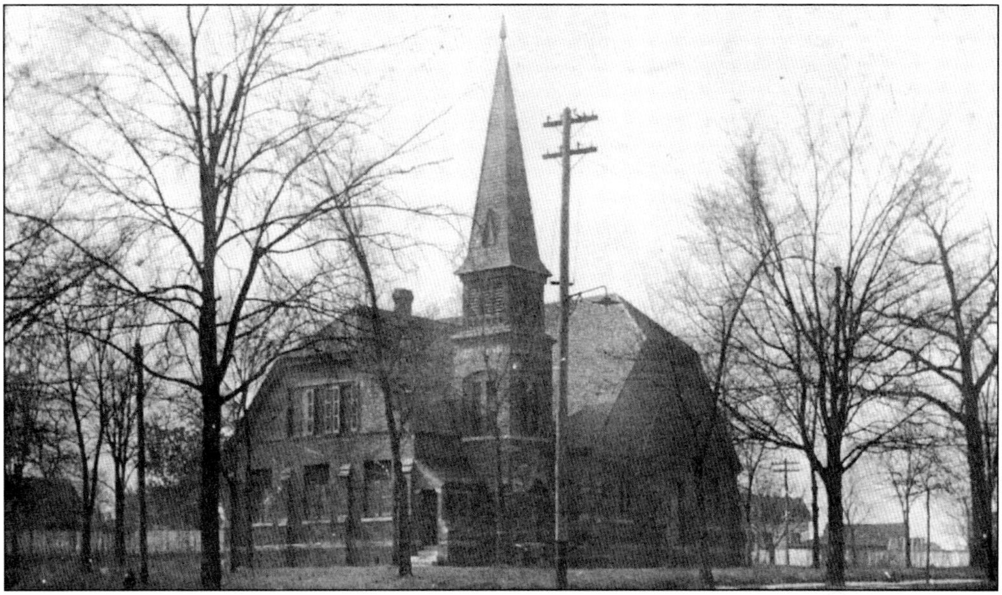

The First Baptist Church in Hawkinsville was first organized in 1830 in Old Hartford on the east side of the Ocmulgee River. The church, then called Hartford Baptist, held services for two years in the Hartford courthouse. In 1839, the church moved from Hartford to a schoolhouse near Bembry's Mill. The church relocated to Hawkinsville in 1842 and was renamed Hawkinsville Baptist. In 1916, the name was changed to First Baptist Church of Hawkinsville. John Rawls, an early city father, donated the lot where the present church now stands, and in 1844, a frame building was erected. In 1885, this wood frame building was replaced with a red-brick church. (Courtesy of First Baptist Church.)

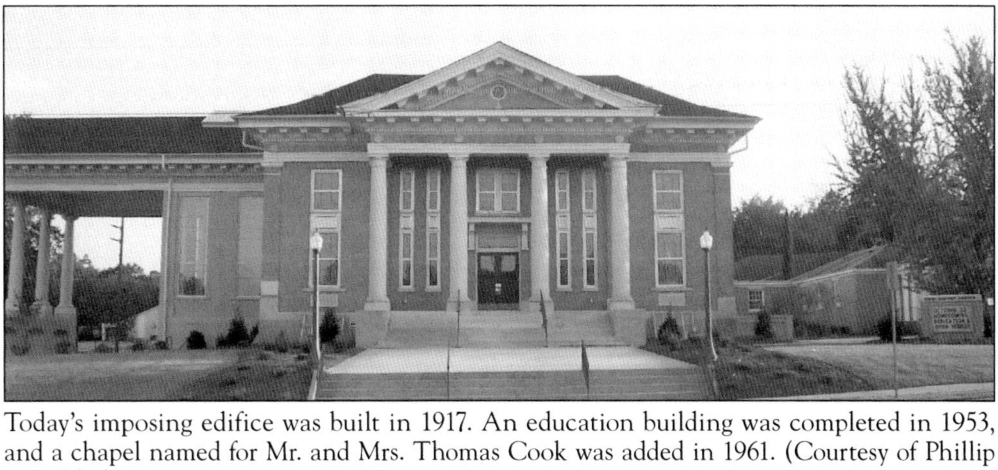

Today's imposing edifice was built in 1917. An education building was completed in 1953, and a chapel named for Mr. and Mrs. Thomas Cook was added in 1961. (Courtesy of Phillip A. Gibbs.)

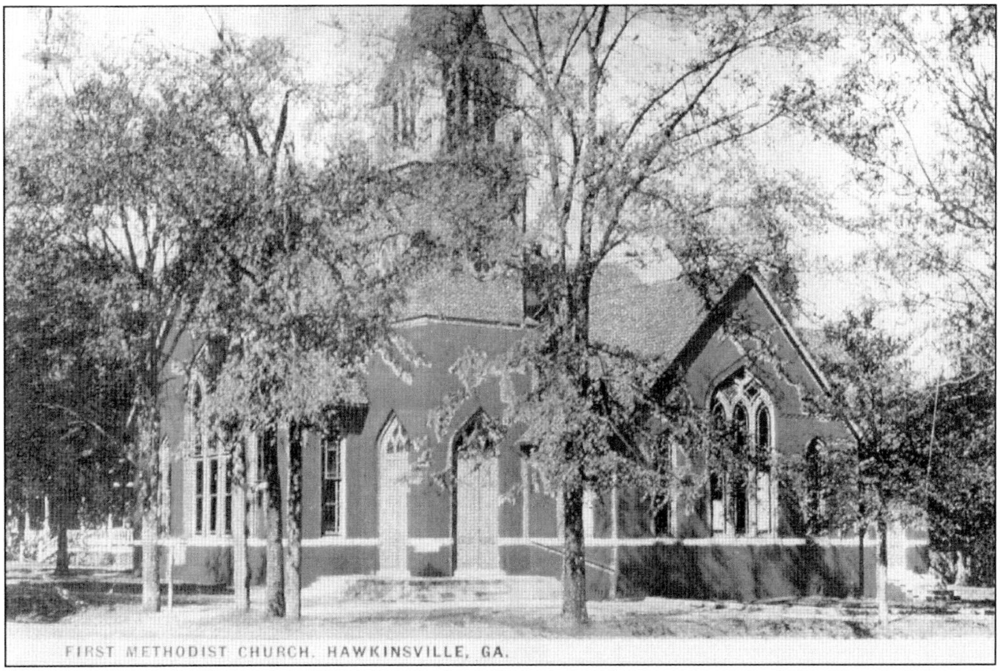

The First United Methodist Church was founded in 1825 as a mission of the South Carolina Conference of the Methodist Episcopal Church. The congregation's first church building was erected on North Dooly Street sometime prior to 1832. This low-lying area, however, was frequently covered with standing water. As a consequence, the congregation voted in 1857 to relocate to the present site. In 1895, the congregation erected this brick structure. (Courtesy of First Methodist Church.)

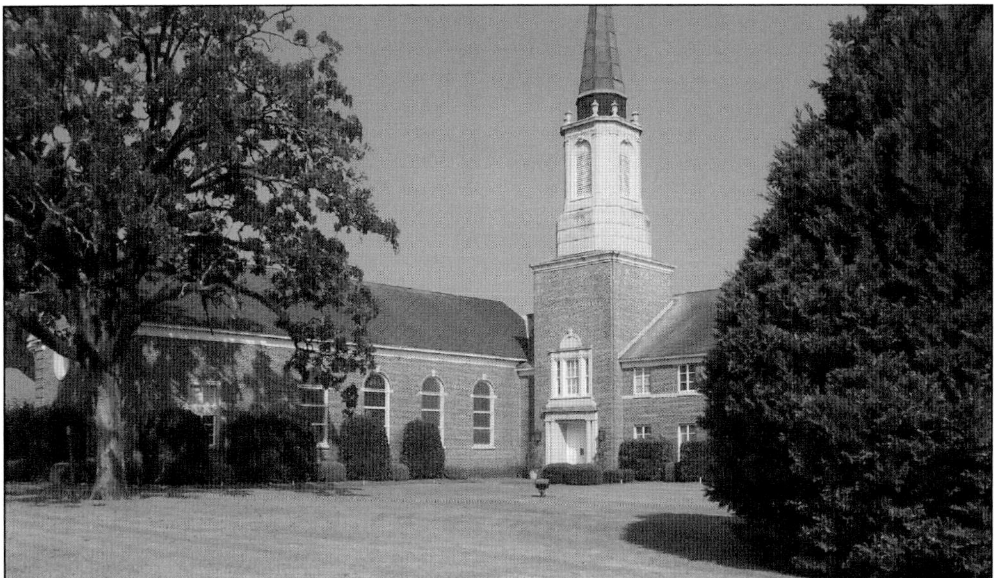

By 1942, the congregation had grown, and there was a need for a new building. To make way for the new facility, the old church and parsonage were dismantled. The current sanctuary, with its beautiful stained-glass windows and chapel, was constructed in 1949. (Courtesy of Phillip A. Gibbs.)

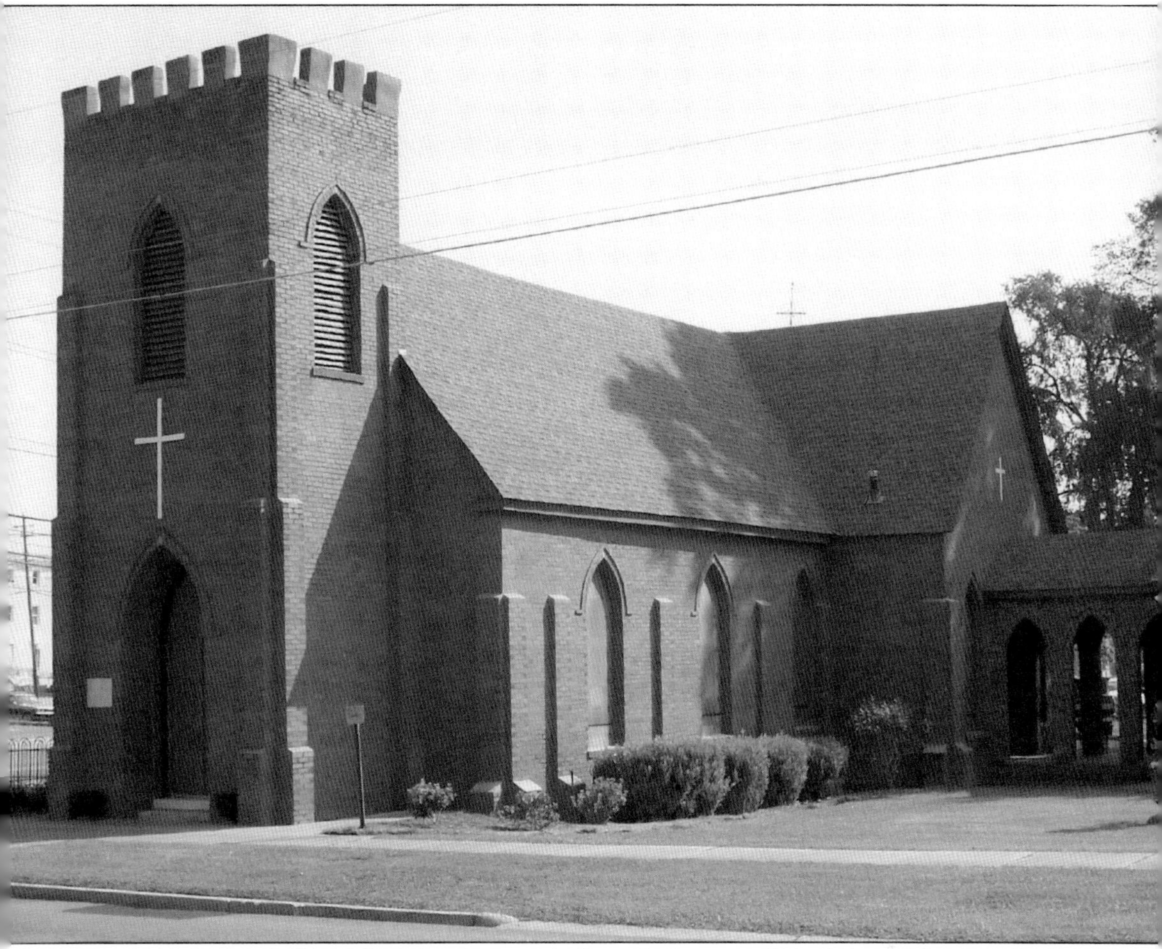

St. Luke's Episcopal Church has played a major role in the history of Hawkinsville for more than 125 years. St. Luke's was built in 1871 of wood-frame construction. Brick veneer was added later to the wood-frame building in 1916, along with other improvements to the interior design. The architecture of the church relies heavily on symbolism. The structure, for example, is cruciform in design. The entry and the nave form the base of the cross, the sanctuary forms the head, and the vestry on the north and the sacristy on the south form the transepts, or arms, of the cross. Today the original structure still stands within the exterior brick and is most evident in the rough-hewn timbers in the high-vaulted ceiling of the nave. Although St. Luke's is not completely in its original state, it is the oldest building in Pulaski County that has seen continuous use. (Courtesy of Phillip A. Gibbs.)

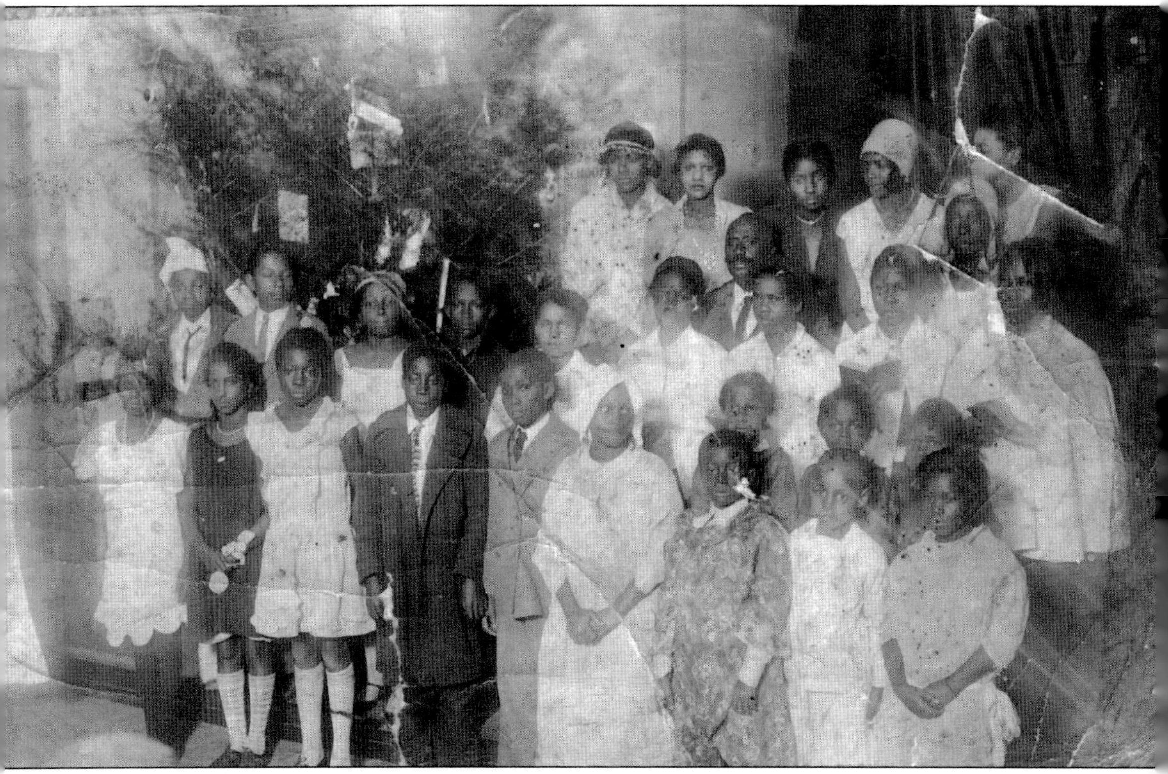

Young people in the community often performed in Christmas musicals at their churches. In this early-1900s picture, boys and girls pose for the camera either before or after a performance. (Courtesy of Mary Colson.)

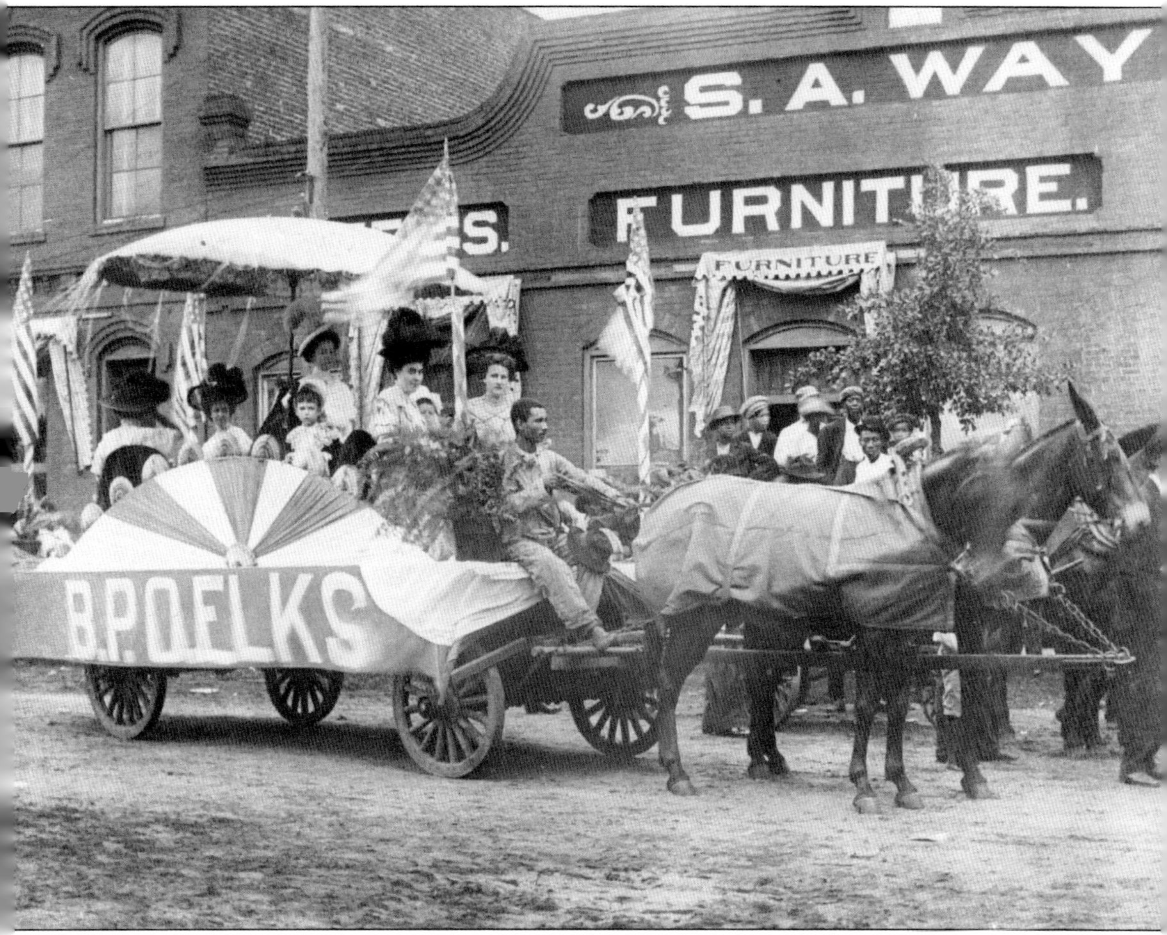

Hawkinsville citizens joined numerous civic and social organizations during the late 1890s and early 1900s. The Benevolent Protective Order of Elks, shown in this late 19th-century picture, was just one of many such organizations. (Courtesy of Sam Way.)

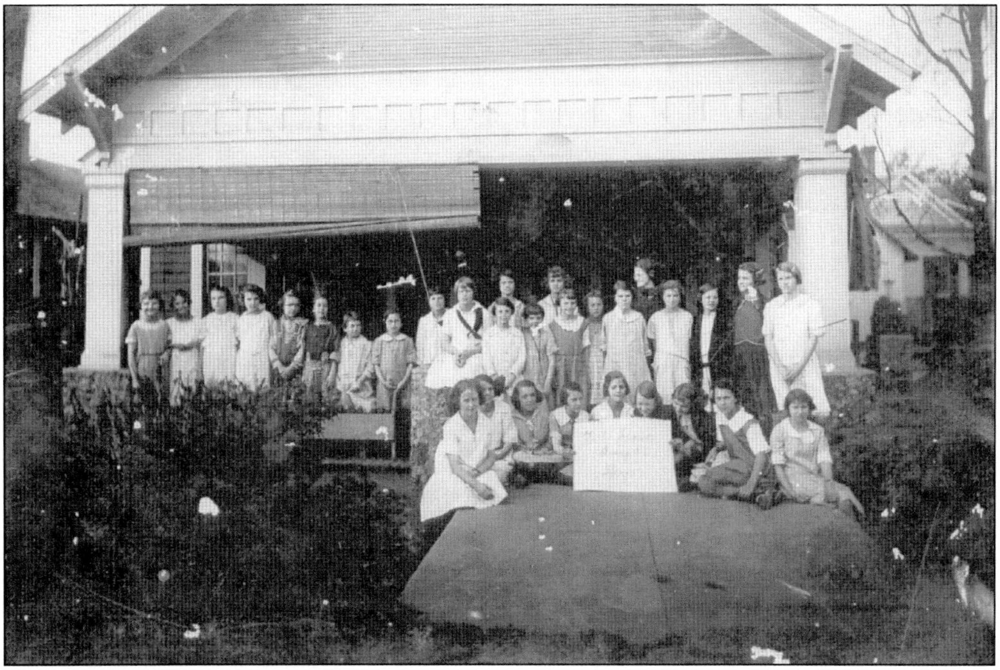

Founded by Savannah native Juliette Gordon Low, the Girl Scouts were a popular organization in Hawkinsville. Here members of a local troop pose for a picture at an unidentified home. (Courtesy of Barbara and Hugh Lawson.)

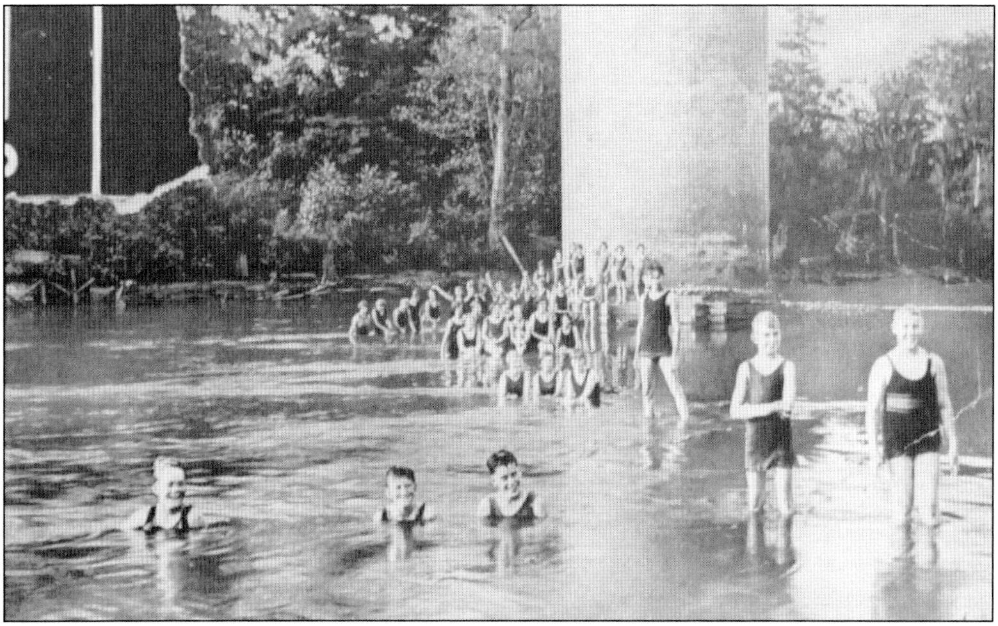

Many young boys in Hawkinsville joined the Boy Scouts in the 1920s. Here members of a local troop frolic in the Ocmulgee River after the flood of 1925. (Courtesy of Georgia Archives, Vanishing Georgia, pul 086.)

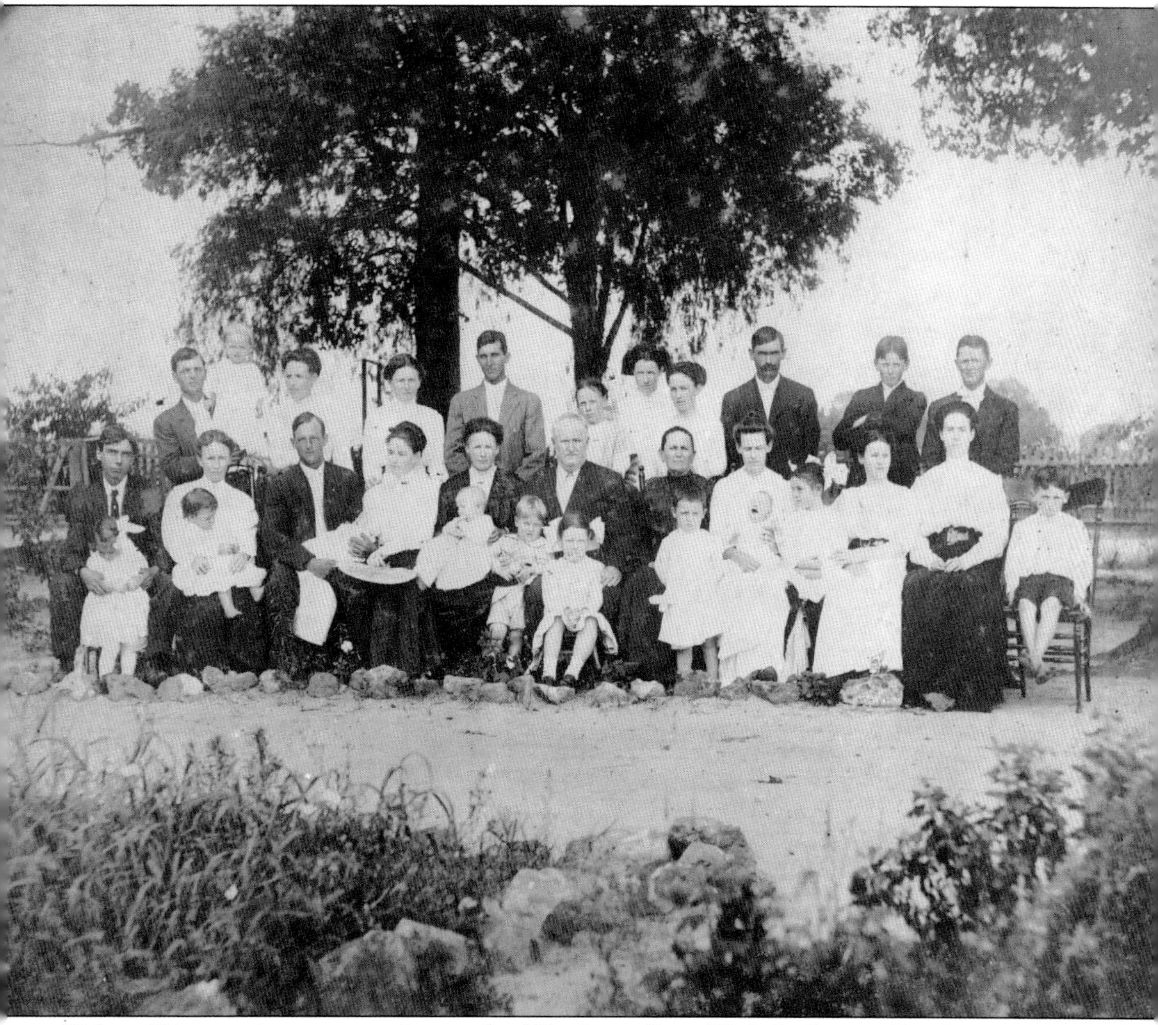

Kith and kin were important to the people of Hawkinsville and Pulaski County. Family reunions like that of the Buchan family pictured here afforded relatives an opportunity to reconnect and enjoy a large repast. (Courtesy of Georgia Archives, Vanishing Georgia, pul 091.)

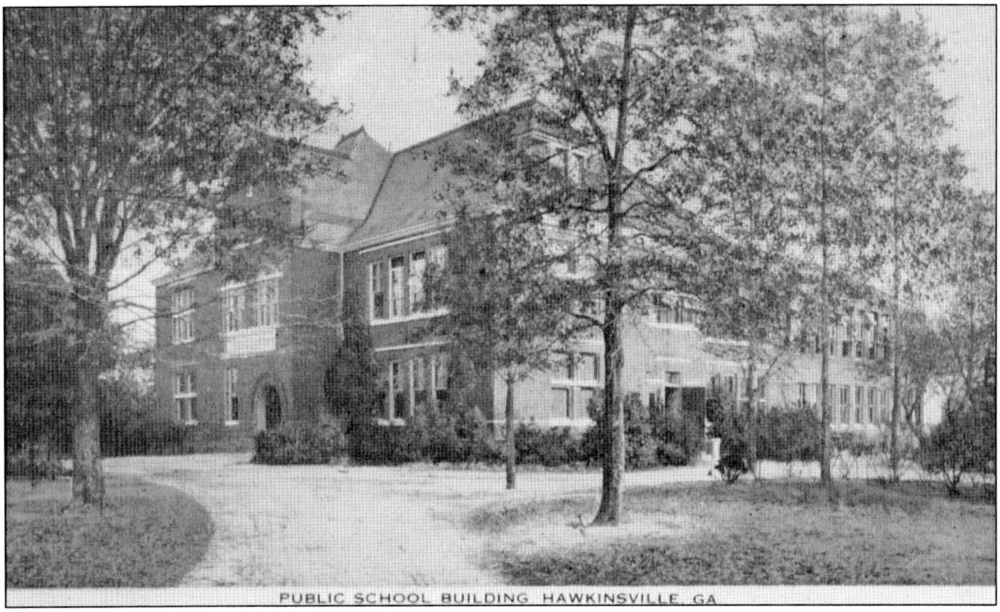

Until the 1890s, students in Hawkinsville were educated in private academies. But the town's growing population convinced citizens and the town council to build a public school. (Courtesy of Georgia Archives, Vanishing Georgia, pul 004.)

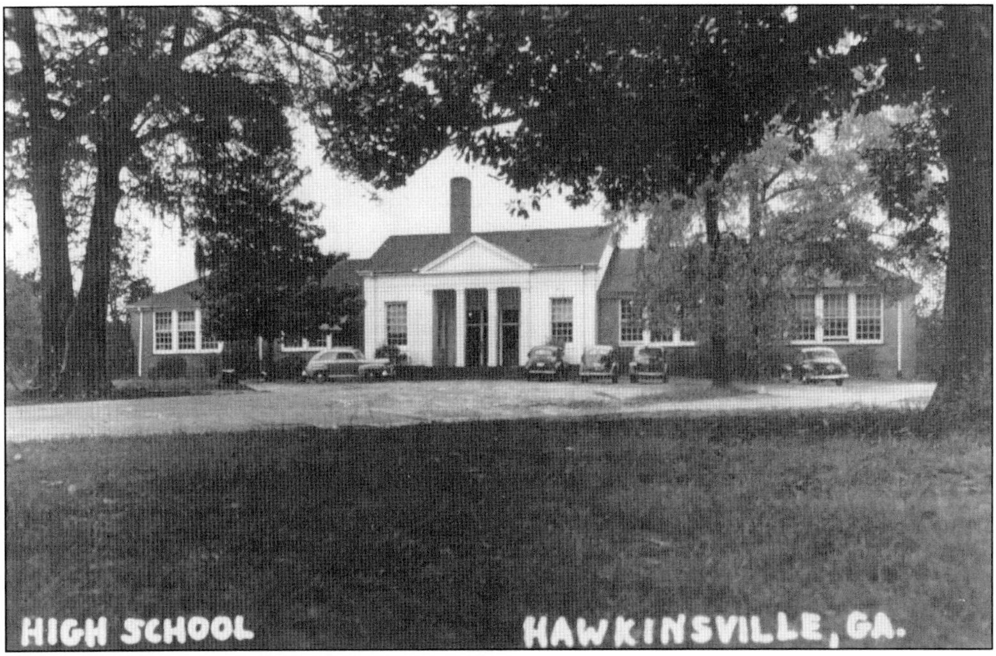

Although the existing public school served the community well for many years, a decision was made in 1936 to tear down the structure and build a new school. The new facility included a gymnasium and an auditorium. (Courtesy of Georgia Archives, Vanishing Georgia, pul 039.)

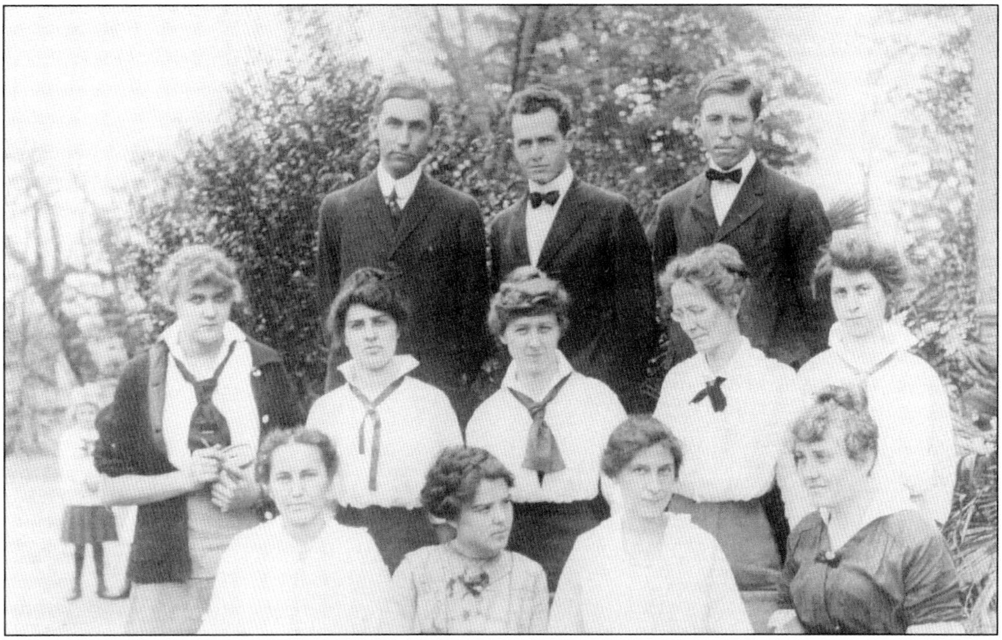

The members of the faculty at the public school were often trained at teacher's colleges. Most were responsible for instructing students in rhetoric, Latin, declamation, and even home economics. (Courtesy of Hawkinsville *Dispatch and News*.)

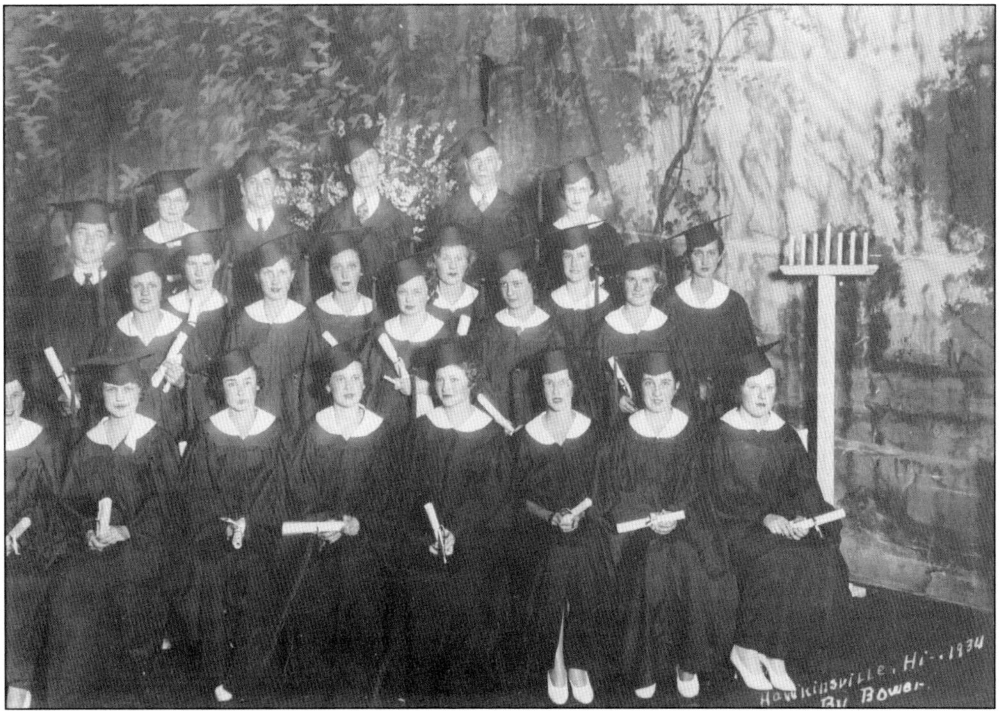

Women made up a large number of the graduates at Hawkinsville Public School. Young men often left school to take over their parents' farms or to pursue a trade. (Courtesy of Georgia Archives, Vanishing Georgia, pul 094.)

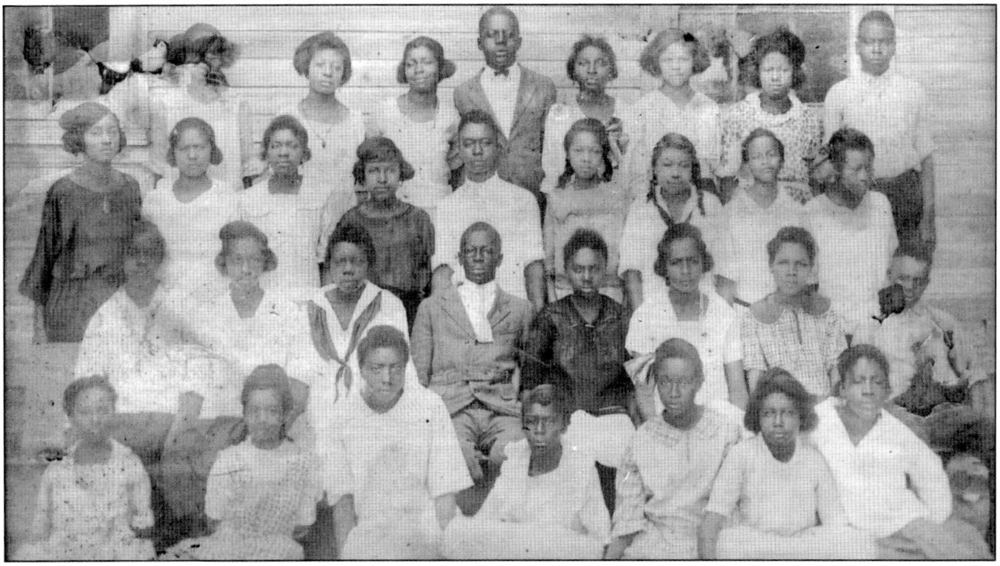

Determined to maintain a strict line of segregation, the white citizens of Hawkinsville refused to allow black students to attend the public school. Nevertheless, white and black citizens joined together in the late 1890s to establish an industrial school for the training of black students. (Courtesy of Mary Colson.)

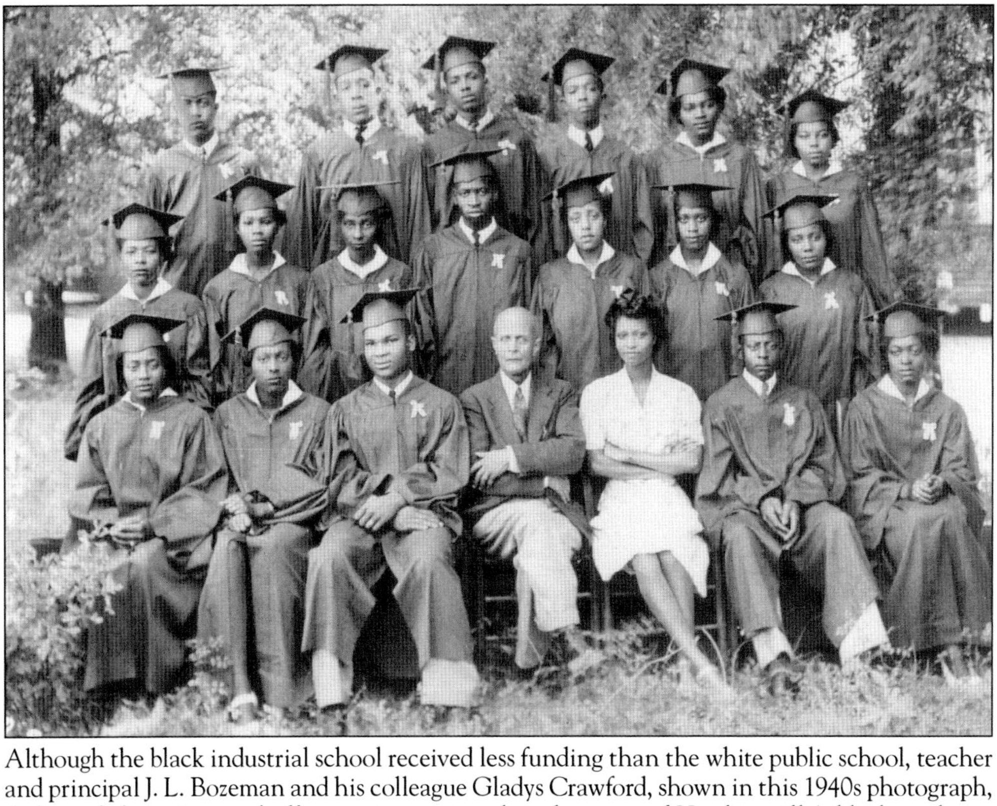

Although the black industrial school received less funding than the white public school, teacher and principal J. L. Bozeman and his colleague Gladys Crawford, shown in this 1940s photograph, dedicated their time and efforts to improving the education of Hawkinsville's black students. (Courtesy of Mary Colson.)

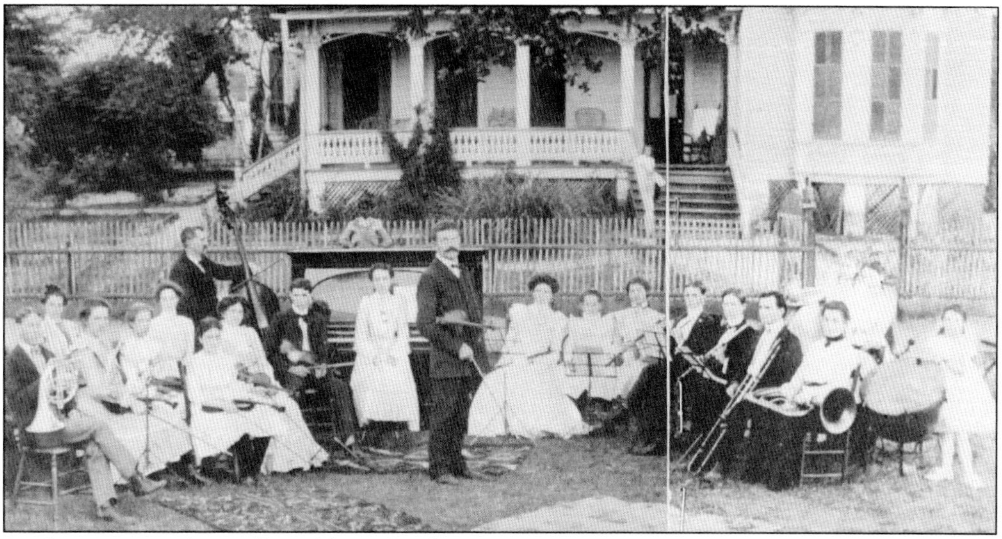

Students in Hawkinsville Public School were encouraged to appreciate art and music. Here students from the school prepare for an outdoor concert with their teacher, W. C. Kalor (standing). (Courtesy of Georgia Archives, Vanishing Georgia, pul 103.)

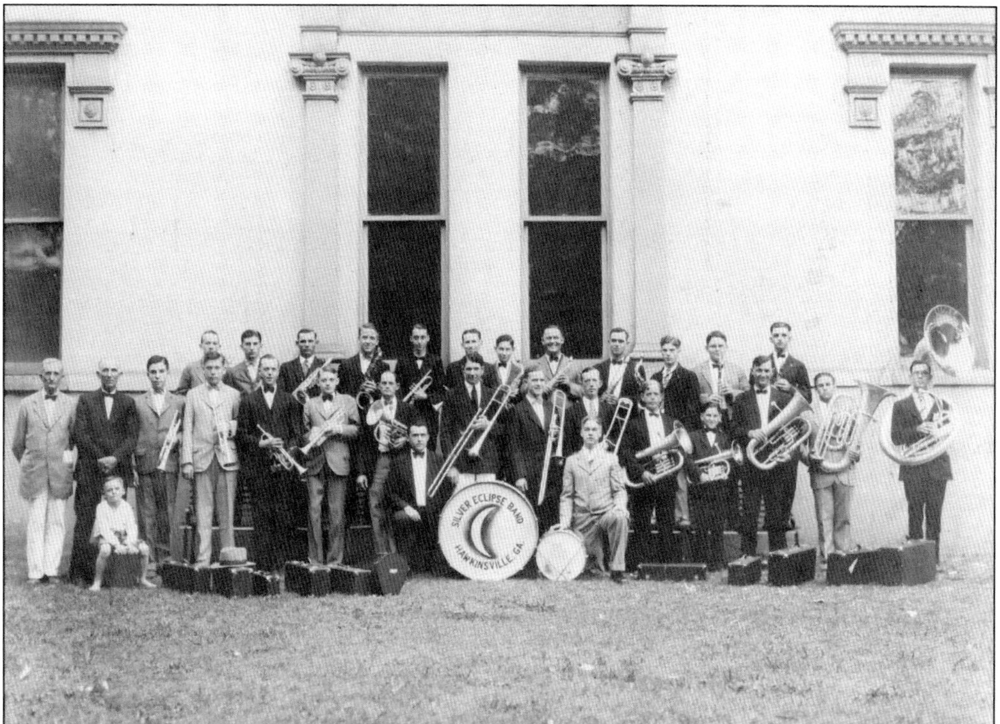

After graduating from public school, some young men and women continued to perform in local ensembles and orchestras like the Silver Eclipse Band. (Courtesy of Georgia Archives, Vanishing Georgia, pul 073.)

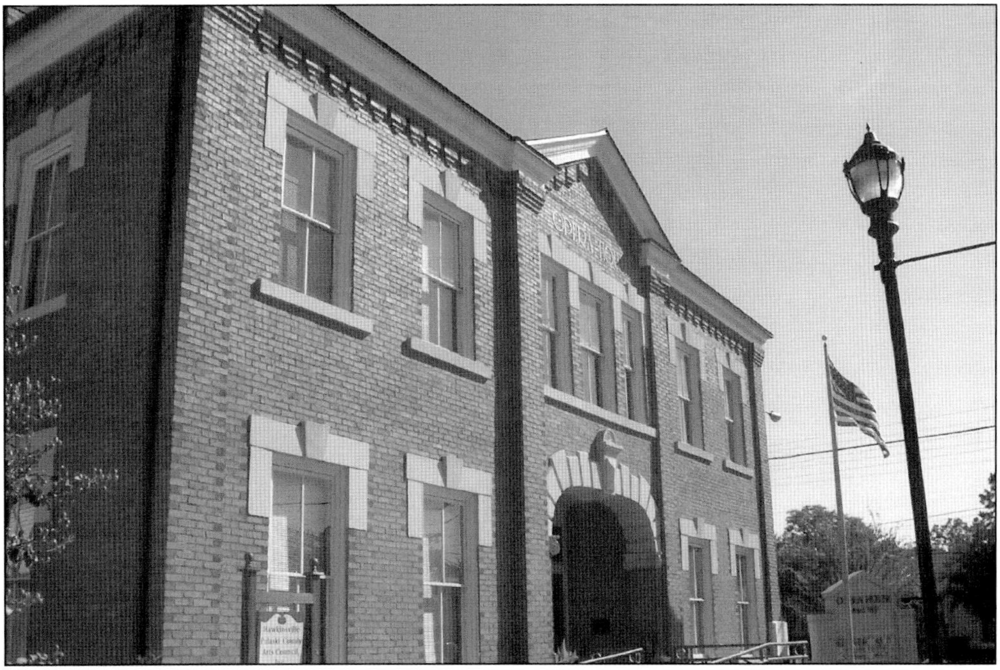

Built in 1907 and listed on the National Register of Historic Places in 1973, the old Opera House has hosted much of the community's entertainment over the years. At one time, the Opera House served as a city hall and an auditorium. After a new city hall was built in the 1950s, the old Opera House lost much of its status as the civic cultural hub of community life, and in 1977, the dilapidated building was threatened with demolition. A group of preservation-minded citizens formed the Pulaski Historical Commission, Inc., to lease and restore this vintage landmark. Once the restoration was completed, the historical commission reopened the building for concerts, plays, and other entertainment. (Courtesy of Phillip A. Gibbs.)

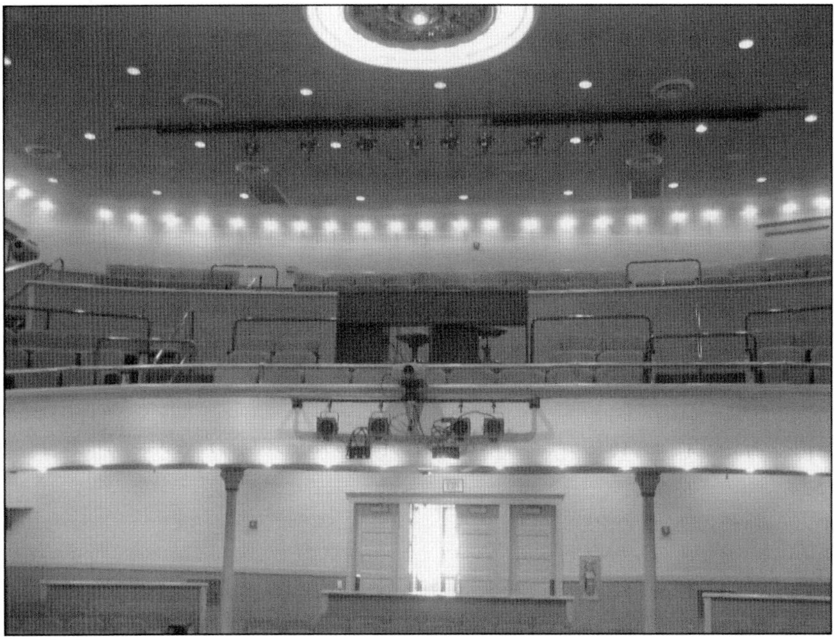

The Opera House's beautiful interior and excellent acoustics have made it ideal for plays, musicals, concerts, and operas. (Courtesy of Mike Newman.)

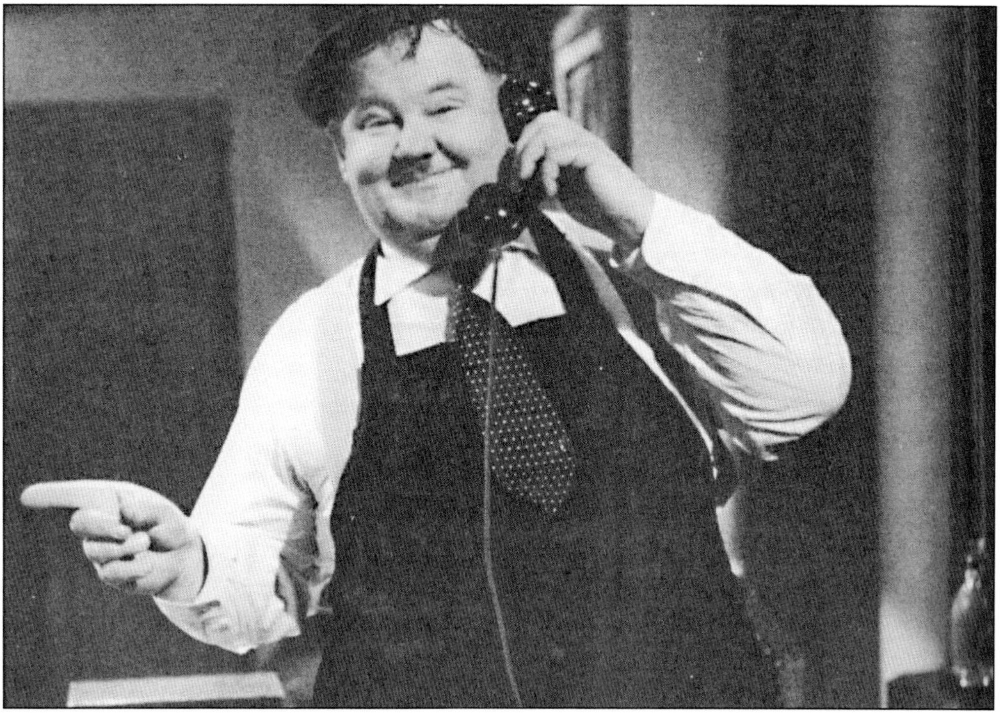

As a young boy, future comedian Oliver Hardy sang on the Opera House stage during one of his many visits to his aunt's home in Hawkinsville. (Courtesy of Library of Congress.)

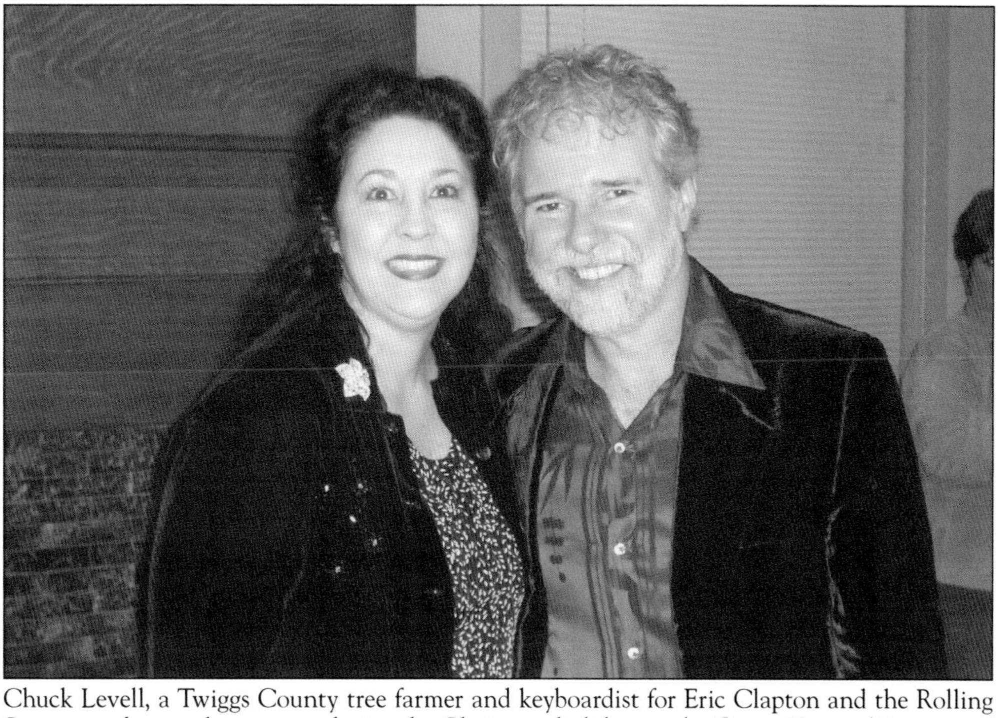

Chuck Levell, a Twiggs County tree farmer and keyboardist for Eric Clapton and the Rolling Stones, performs solo concerts during the Christmas holidays at the Opera House. (Courtesy of Julie Stewart.)

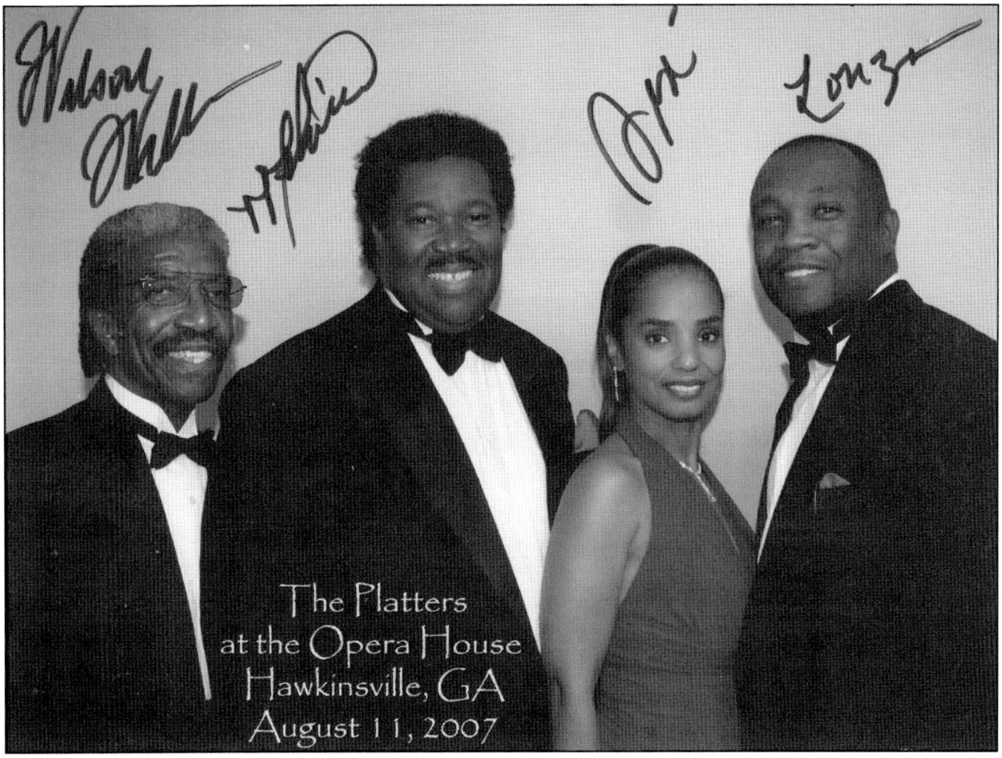

Best known for their song "The Great Pretender," the Platters and other 1950s and 1960s groups have appeared on the Opera House stage. (Courtesy of Julie Stewart.)

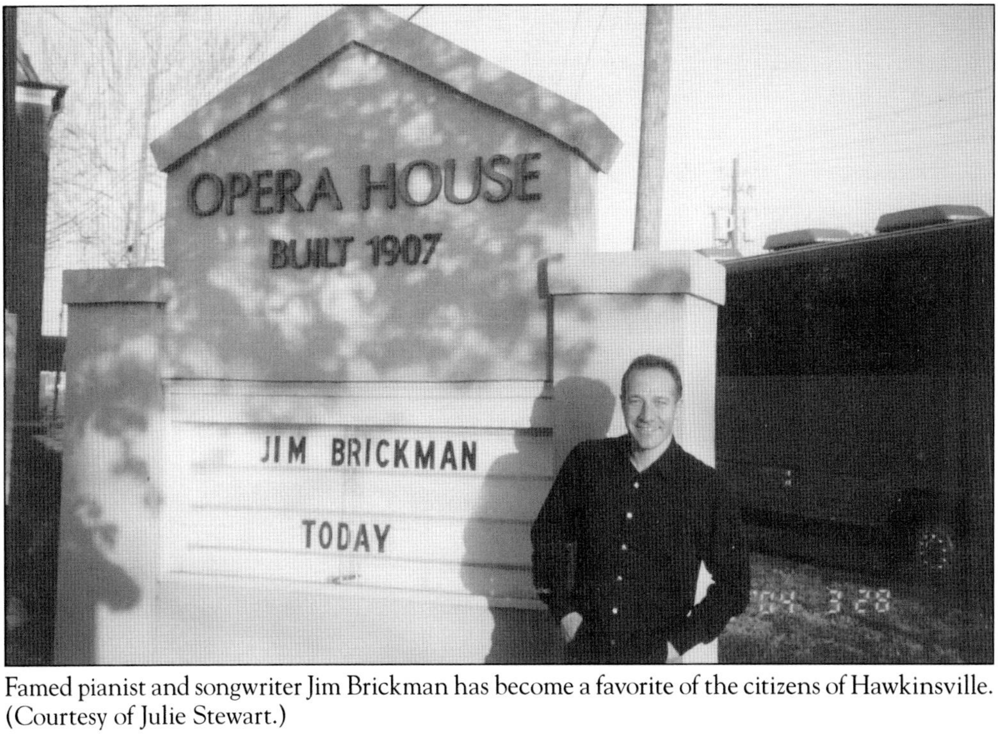

Famed pianist and songwriter Jim Brickman has become a favorite of the citizens of Hawkinsville. (Courtesy of Julie Stewart.)

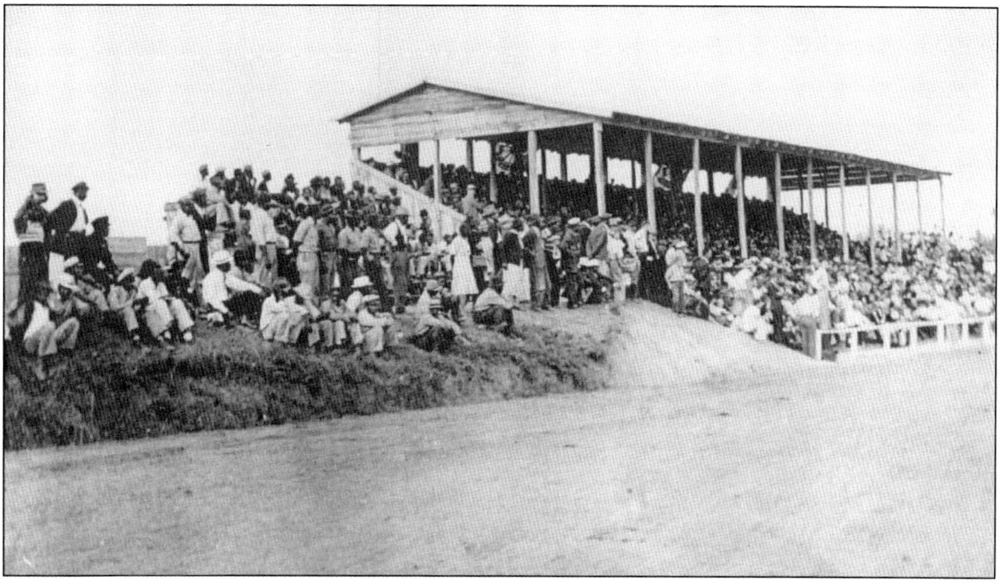

In the 1890s, Northern horsemen introduced harness racing to Hawkinsville. Since that time, the city has been known as the "Harness Horse Capital of Georgia." The city's past and present connection to the sport is celebrated each year at the spring Harness Festival. (Courtesy of Lucille Bennett.)

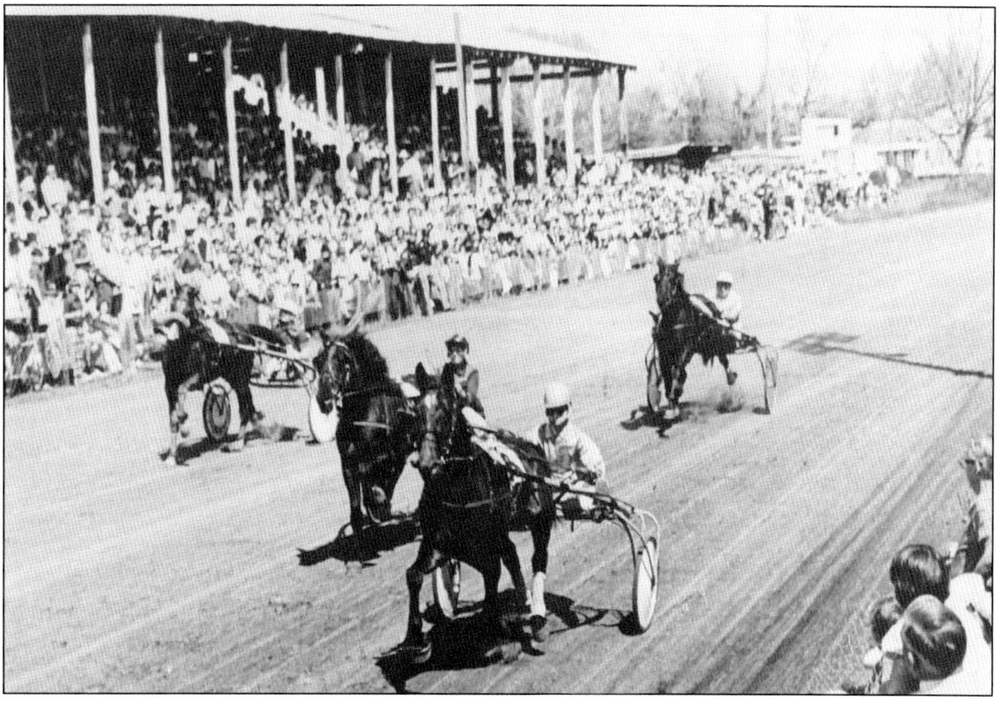

For many years, Hawkinsville citizens and tourists enjoyed the spring races at the harness track. Although harness races are no longer held at the city-owned track and grounds, people from all over the United States and Canada come to Hawkinsville to train their horses at one of the premier training facilities in the southeastern United States. (Courtesy of Georgia Archives, Vanishing Georgia, pul 019.)

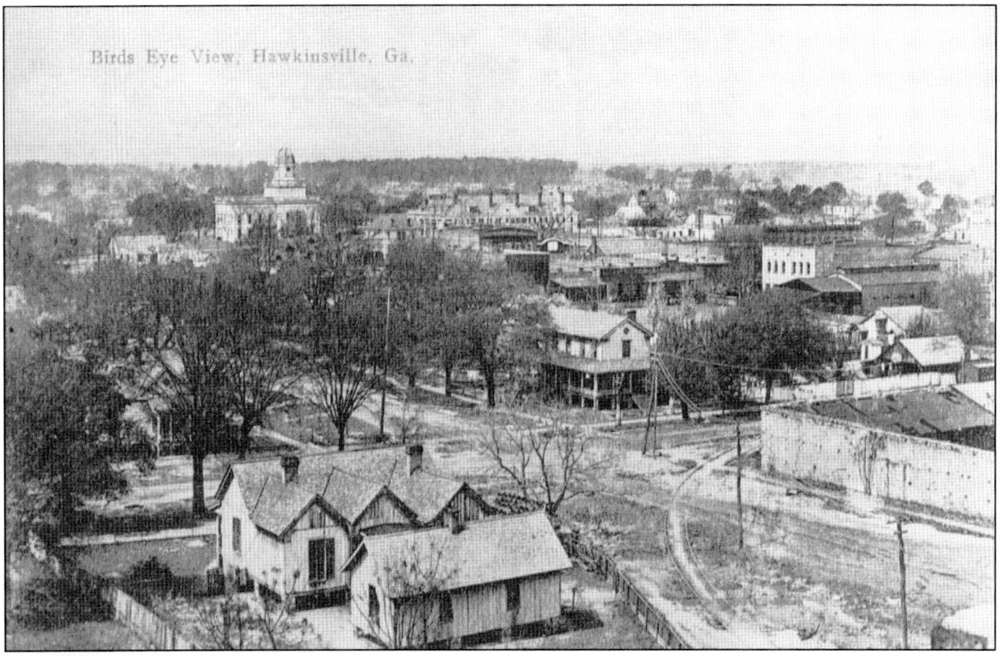

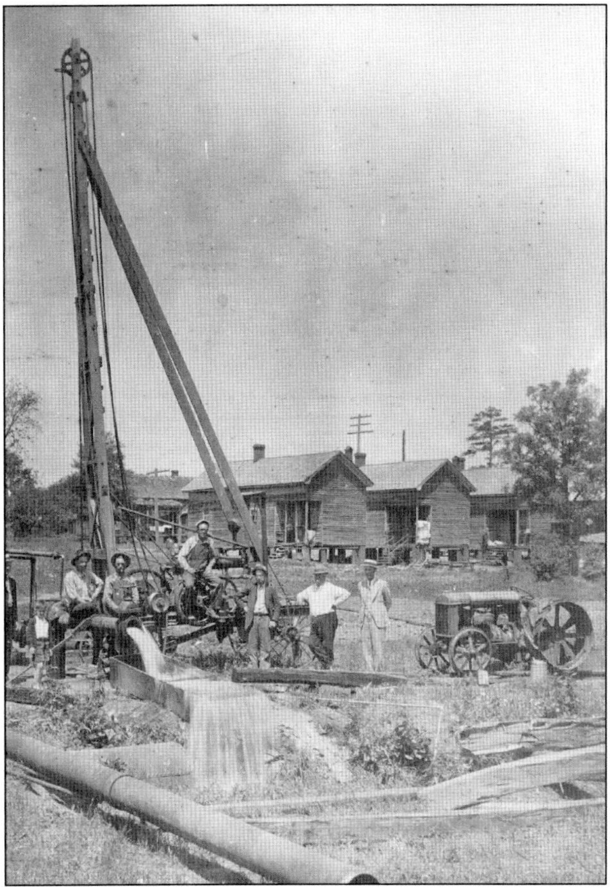

Sitting on the river's edge and at the juncture of several trade routes, Hawkinsville thrived. Numerous shops, businesses, and warehouses were located here. Prosperous, and in some cases rich, the citizens enjoyed numerous amenities generally reserved for larger cities. For these reasons, Hawkinsville was considered to be the "Queen of the Wiregrass." (Courtesy of Georgia Archives, Vanishing Georgia, pul 105-85.)

Fresh water supplies are vital to any city, and Hawkinsville was no exception. This artesian well, dug around 1900, was located at the corner of Houston and Commerce Streets. It served mainly the downtown businesses. (Courtesy of Georgia Archives, Vanishing Georgia, pul 002.)

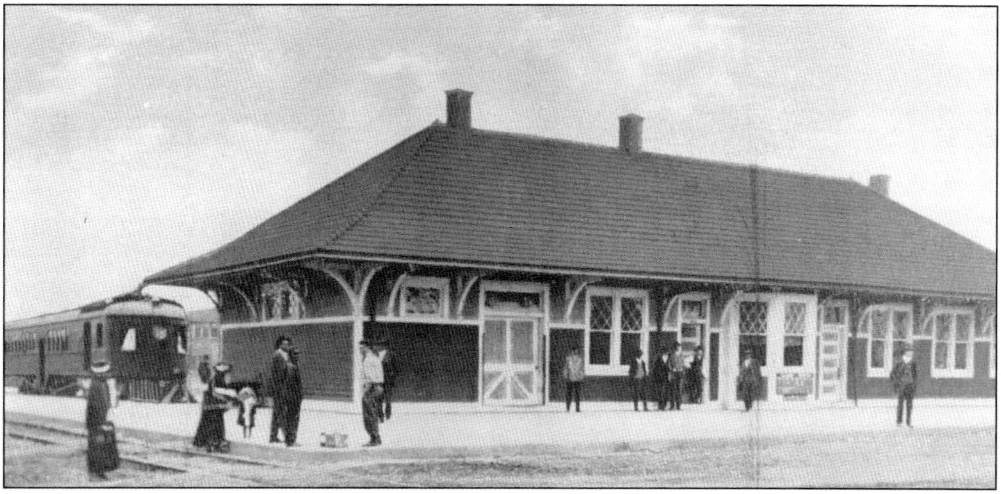

Shortly after the Civil War, the Macon and Brunswick Railroad opened a spur from Cochran to Hawkinsville. Not only did this give the railroad river access, but it opened up Hawkinsville to new commerce and travel. Other rail lines soon followed. During the 1890s, a line was added to Worth, and in 1902, the Oconee and Western built a short line from Hawkinsville to Tennille. (Courtesy of Pulaski Historical Society.)

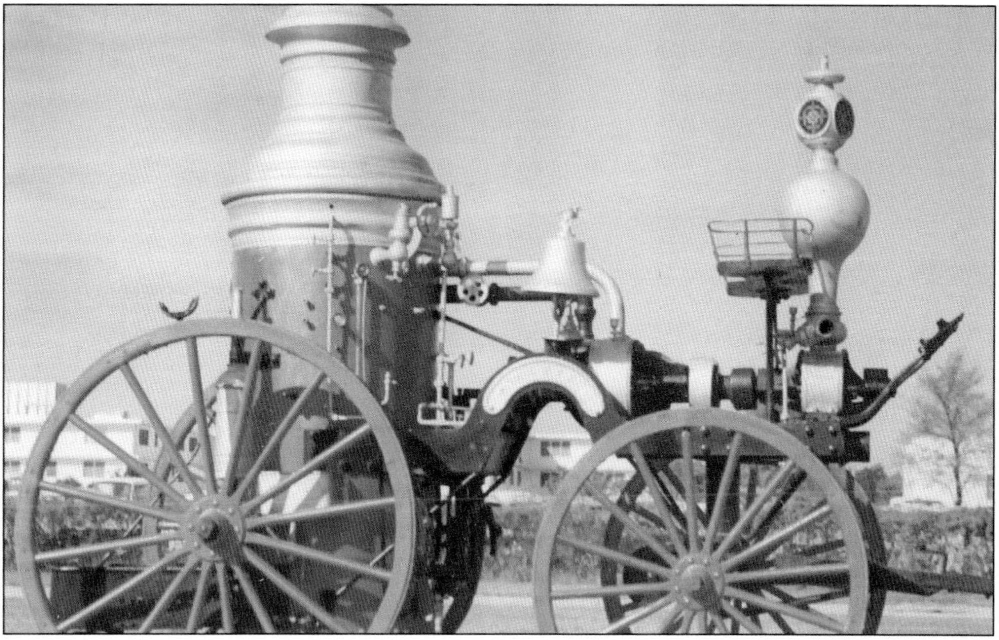

Located on the Broad Street side of the Opera House is "Katy," one of the world's oldest steam pumps, which was made by the Le France Company of Elmira, New York. The City of Hawkinsville purchased her in November 1883 for $3,267. She was promptly dubbed Katy in honor of the fire chief's daughter. To provide water to the steamer, an artesian well or underground reservoir was built under the town's main intersection. Katy saw service in the downtown section until 1906. That year, a major fire burned several businesses, but thanks to Katy, the rest of the town was spared. She was then retired to a quiet spot off Broad Street where she sat forgotten until the late 1960s when the local newspaper spearheaded restoration efforts. Today Katy sits in all her glory, a tribute to 19th-century know-how and community spirit. (Courtesy of Karen Bailey.)

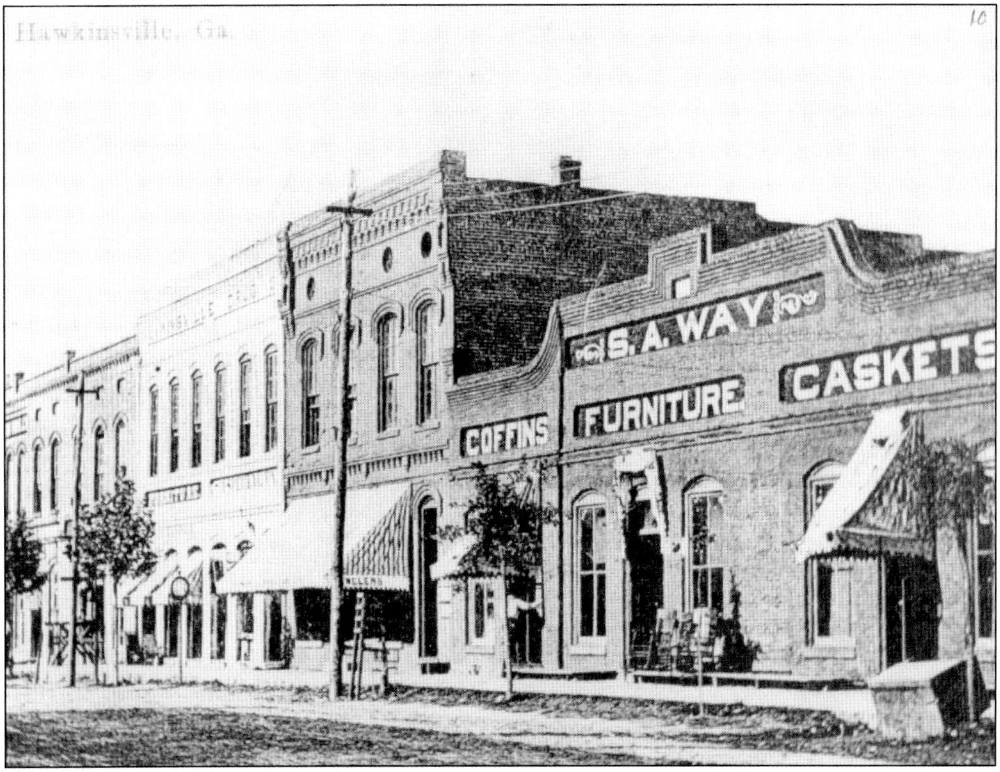

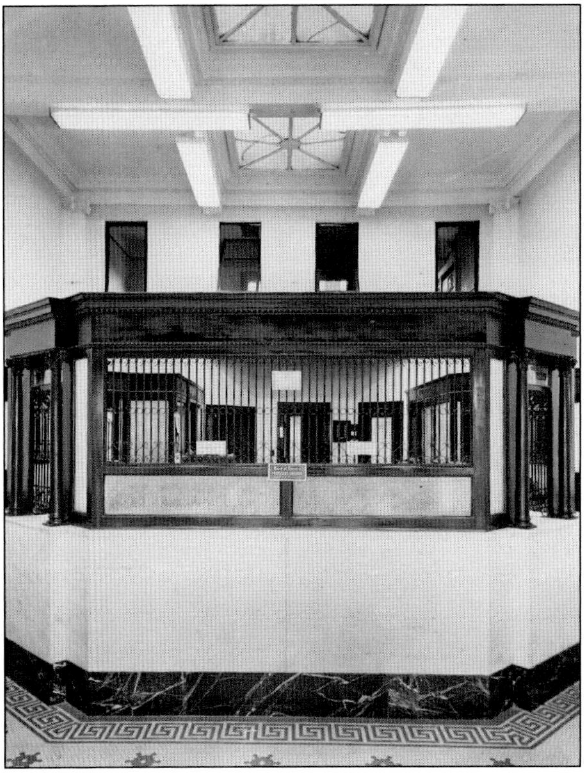

Downtown businesses catered to the needs of their clients. Sam A. Way's store provided the necessities for both life and death, selling furniture, dry goods, and coffins in the early 1900s. This family-run store would become Hawkinsville's first car dealership in the early 20th century. Way prospered and became an active member of the community. He also served as mayor. (Courtesy of Pulaski Historical Society.)

Hawkinsville Bank and Trust was established in 1872 by several leading citizens of the town. Located downtown on Commerce Street, it served the interests of businesses and citizens alike. (Courtesy of Pulaski Historical Society.)

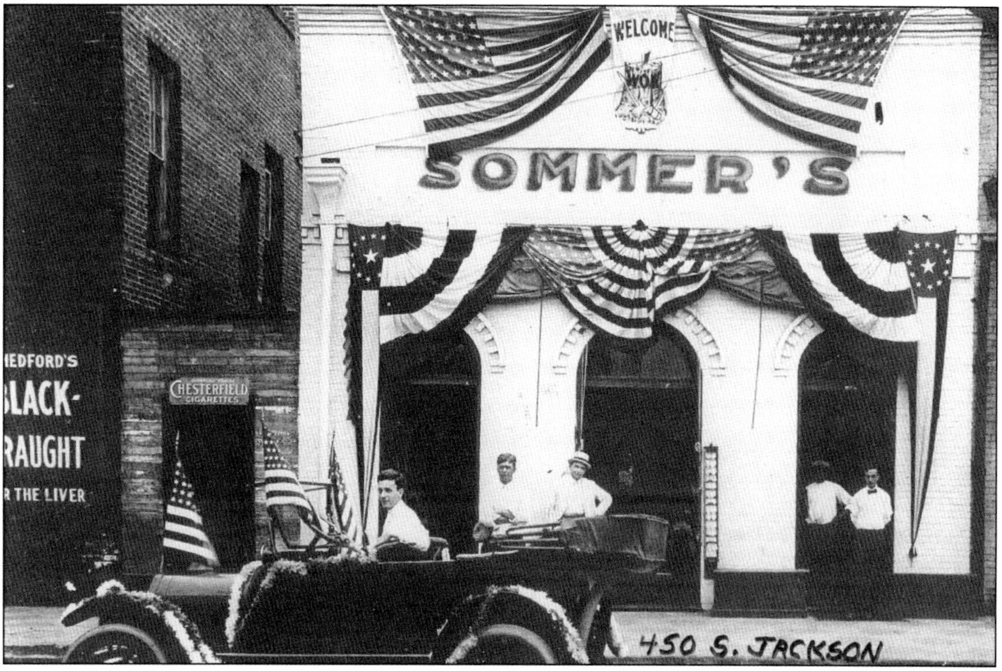

During the 1880s, the Sommer family settled in Hawkinsville and began a number of businesses. Samuel Sommer later opened Samuel Sommer's Dry Goods, a general merchandise store that featured clothing, particularly hand-tailored suits. (Courtesy of Georgia Archives, Vanishing Georgia, pul 104-82.)

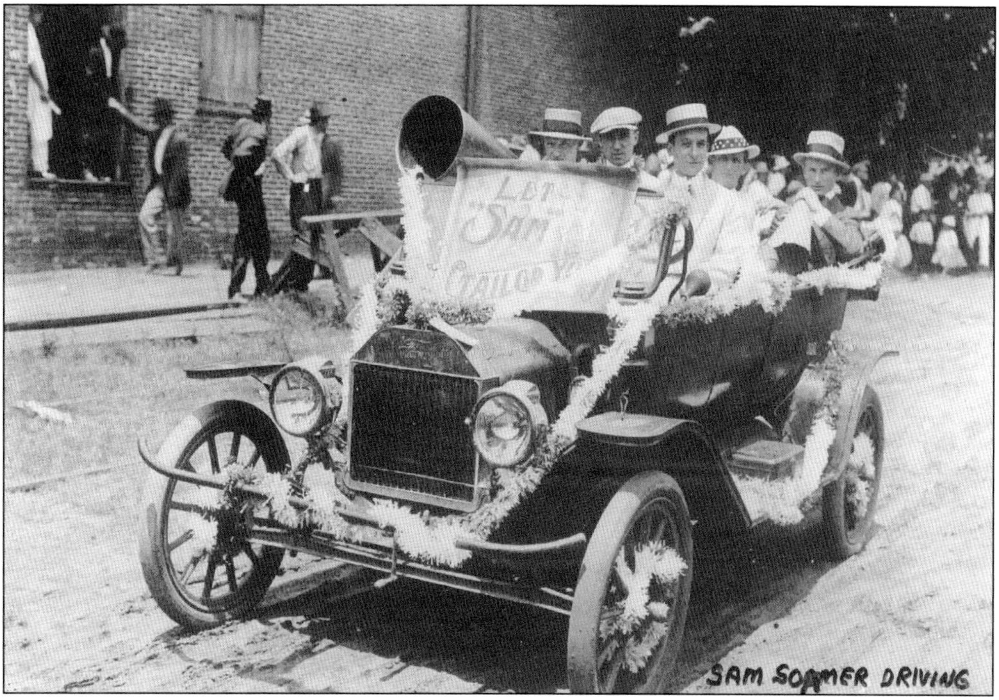

Ever the entrepreneur, Samuel Sommer advertised his clothing and tailoring business from the driver's seat of his Ford Model T during the early 1900s. (Courtesy of Pulaski Historical Society.)

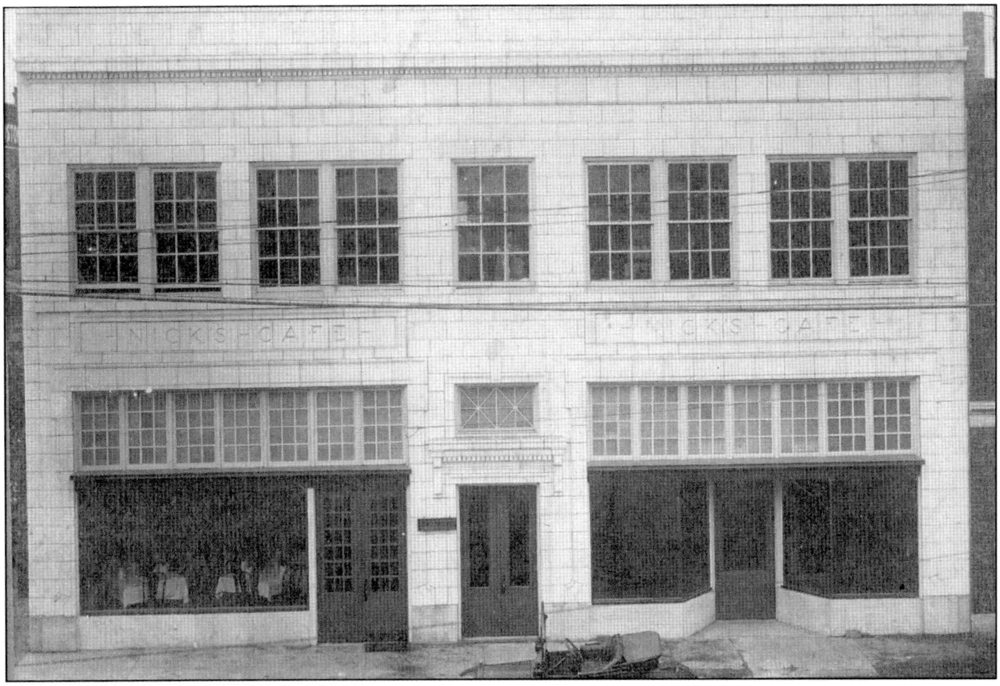

Nick Cabero and his brother Leonidias ("Lee") emigrated from Greece in the first decade of the 1900s. Hardworking and ambitious, the brothers opened several downtown shops, including Nick's Café. The building, erected in 1917, was later demolished and is now Cabero Park. (Courtesy of Nick Cabero.)

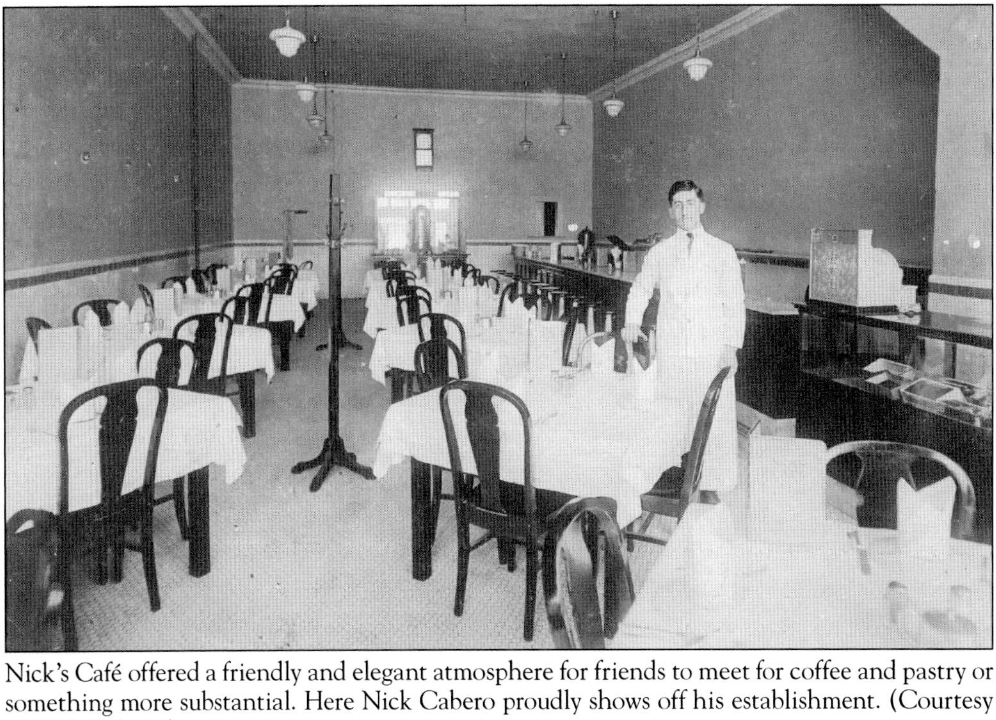

Nick's Café offered a friendly and elegant atmosphere for friends to meet for coffee and pastry or something more substantial. Here Nick Cabero proudly shows off his establishment. (Courtesy of Nick Cabero.)

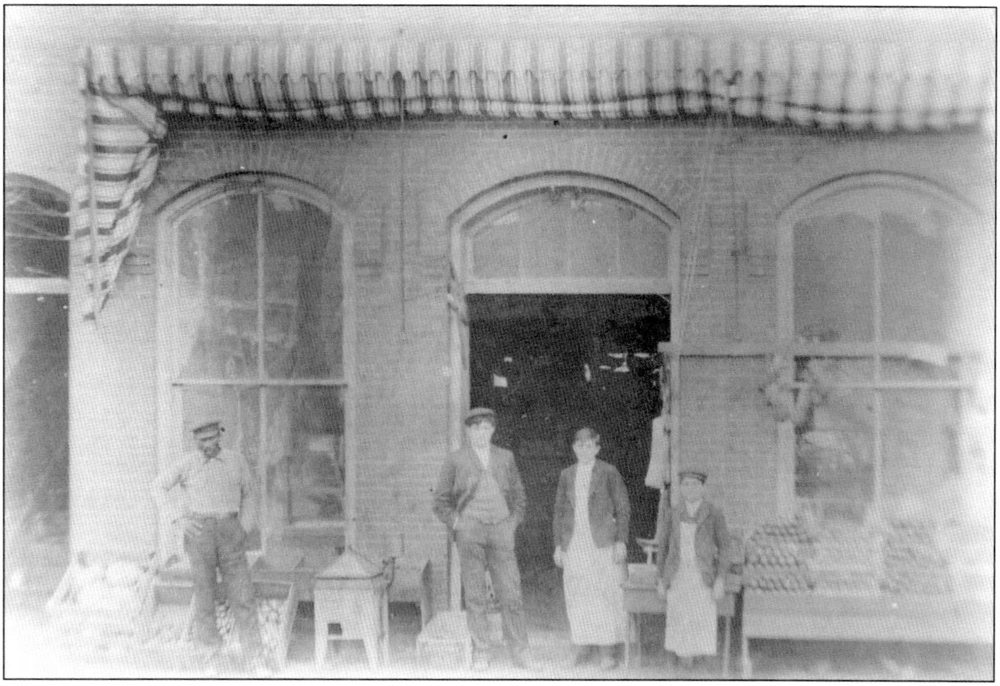

Among the businesses the Cabero brothers operated was the Hawkinsville Fruit and Candy Company. Fresh fruit can be seen in crates along the exterior as Lee Cabero stands with several of his employees. (Courtesy of Nick Cabero.)

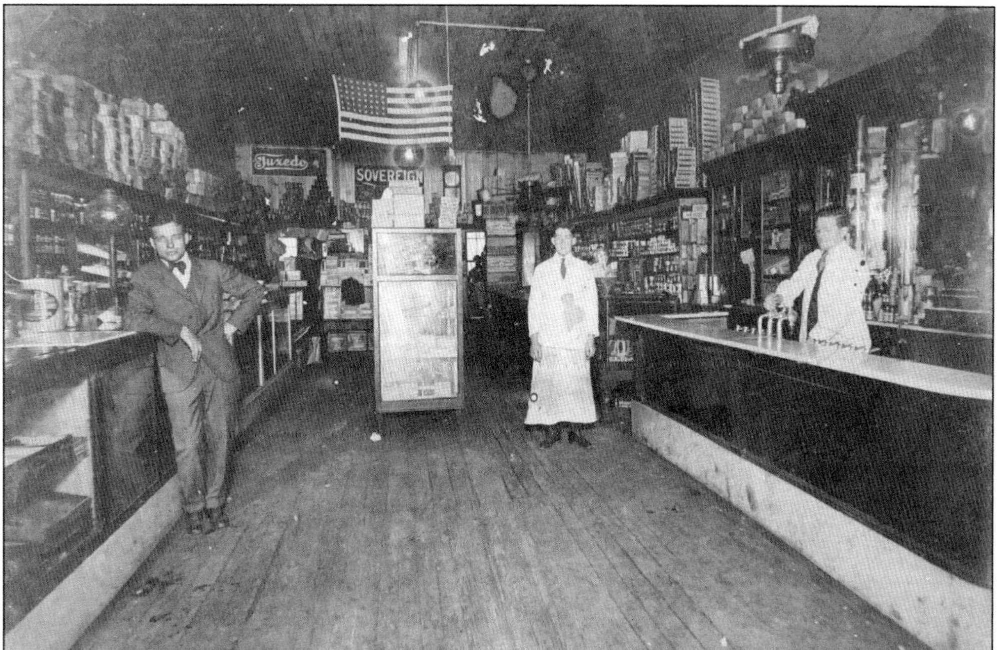

The interior of the Hawkinsville Fruit and Candy Company offered treasures and treats for all ages. The soda fountain dispensed Coca-Cola and other drinks. Licorice, gumdrops, and peppermint could be found in other counters. (Courtesy of Nick Cabero.)

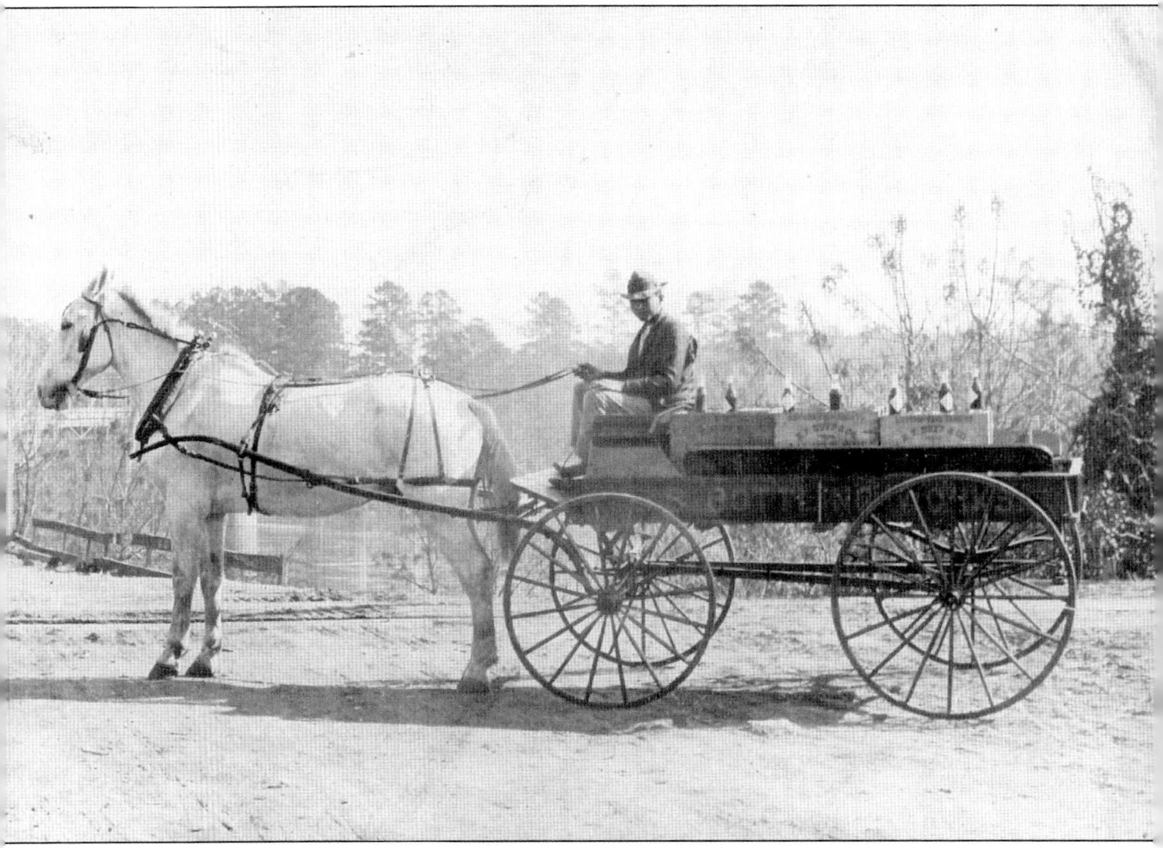

The Buff and Bennett Bottling Company, based in Hawkinsville, was an early manufacturer of Coca-Cola and Chero-Cola. This was the first delivery of America's favorite beverage to local stores. (Courtesy of Pulaski Historical Society.)

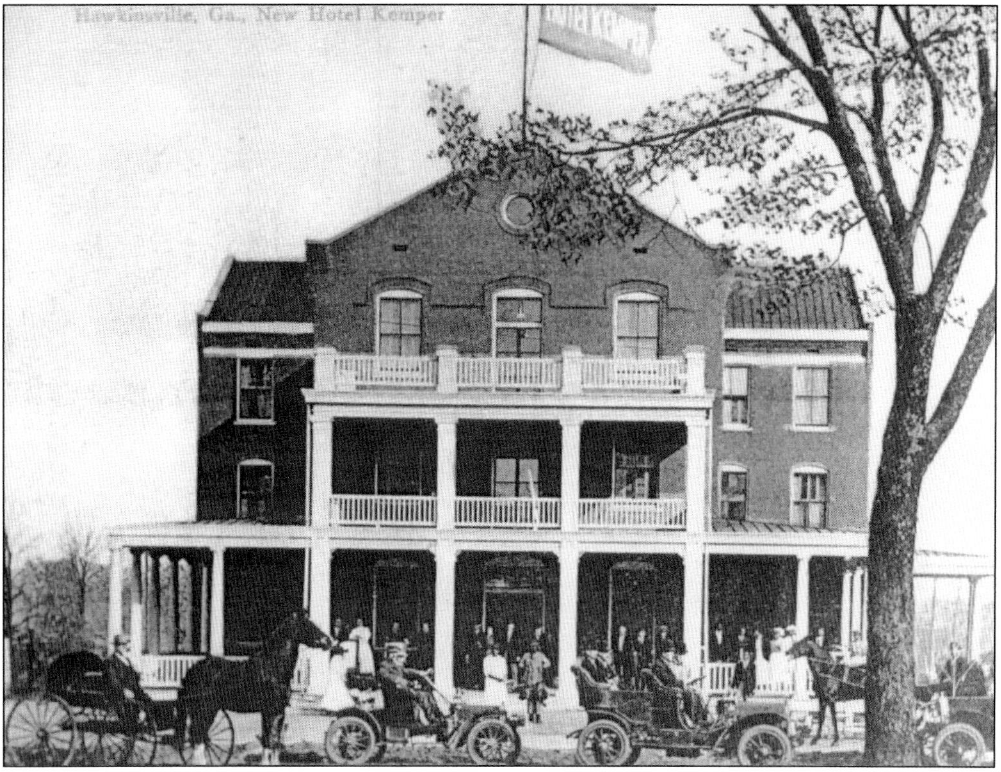

Weary travelers needed places to stay in Hawkinsville, and the Hotel Kemper, later the Brown Hotel, was one of several establishments that served them. Since it was located on Commerce Street at the end of the business district, guests did not need to travel far to eat or shop. (Courtesy of Pulaski Historical Society.)

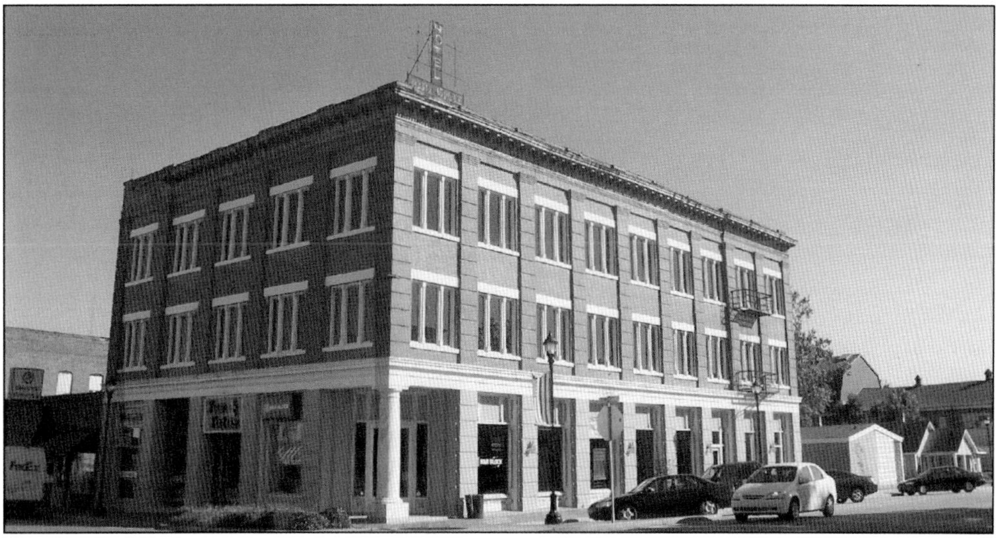

The New Pulaski Hotel was constructed out of existing office space at the corner of Commerce and Lumpkin Streets. It was later renamed the Hotel Hawkinsville. Situated kitty-corner to the Hotel Kemper, it also offered an elegant place to stay not far from the attractions of downtown. (Courtesy of Phillip A. Gibbs.)

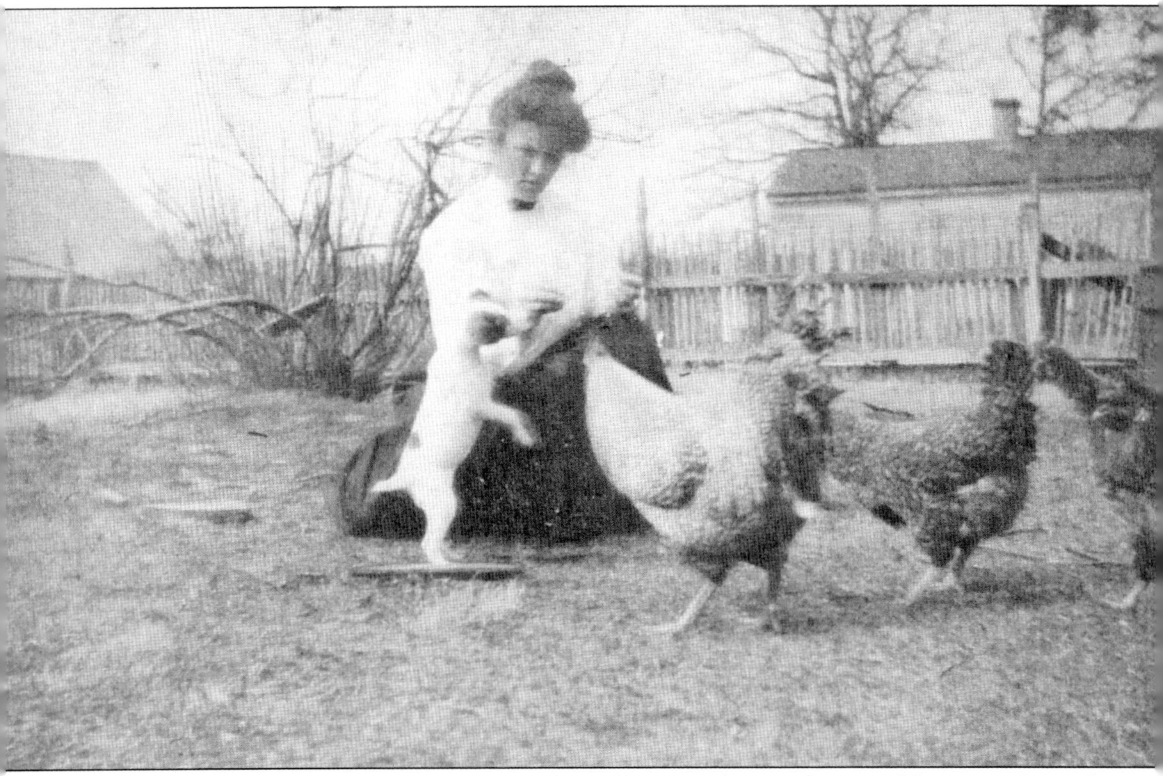

Despite its cosmopolitan flair, Hawkinsville still retained part of its rural heritage. One of Hawkinsville's leading citizens, Rena Brandon Lawson, kept chickens at her home on Lumpkin Street during the 1920s. (Courtesy of Hugh and Barbara Lawson.)

Four

New Century, New World

The new century brought many changes to Hawkinsville. Conveniences that made their debut in the previous century—electric lights, radios, and the telephone—became commonplace in the city's homes and businesses. As a transportation hub, it was only fitting that Hawkinsville soon became home to an automobile dealership. A new bridge was built over the Ocmulgee River to facilitate travel and was dedicated to those who had given their lives in the Great War.

New immigrants brought a cosmopolitan feel to Hawkinsville as well as swelling its population. With the good also came the bad. When the nation went to war, many of Hawkinsville's sons answered the call. Many never saw the Wiregrass again. Even before Prohibition was national, the temperance movement was forcing Hawkinsville dry. When the Depression hit, Hawkinsville suffered along with the rest of America. The city persevered, and at the dawn of the 21st century, it is flourishing again.

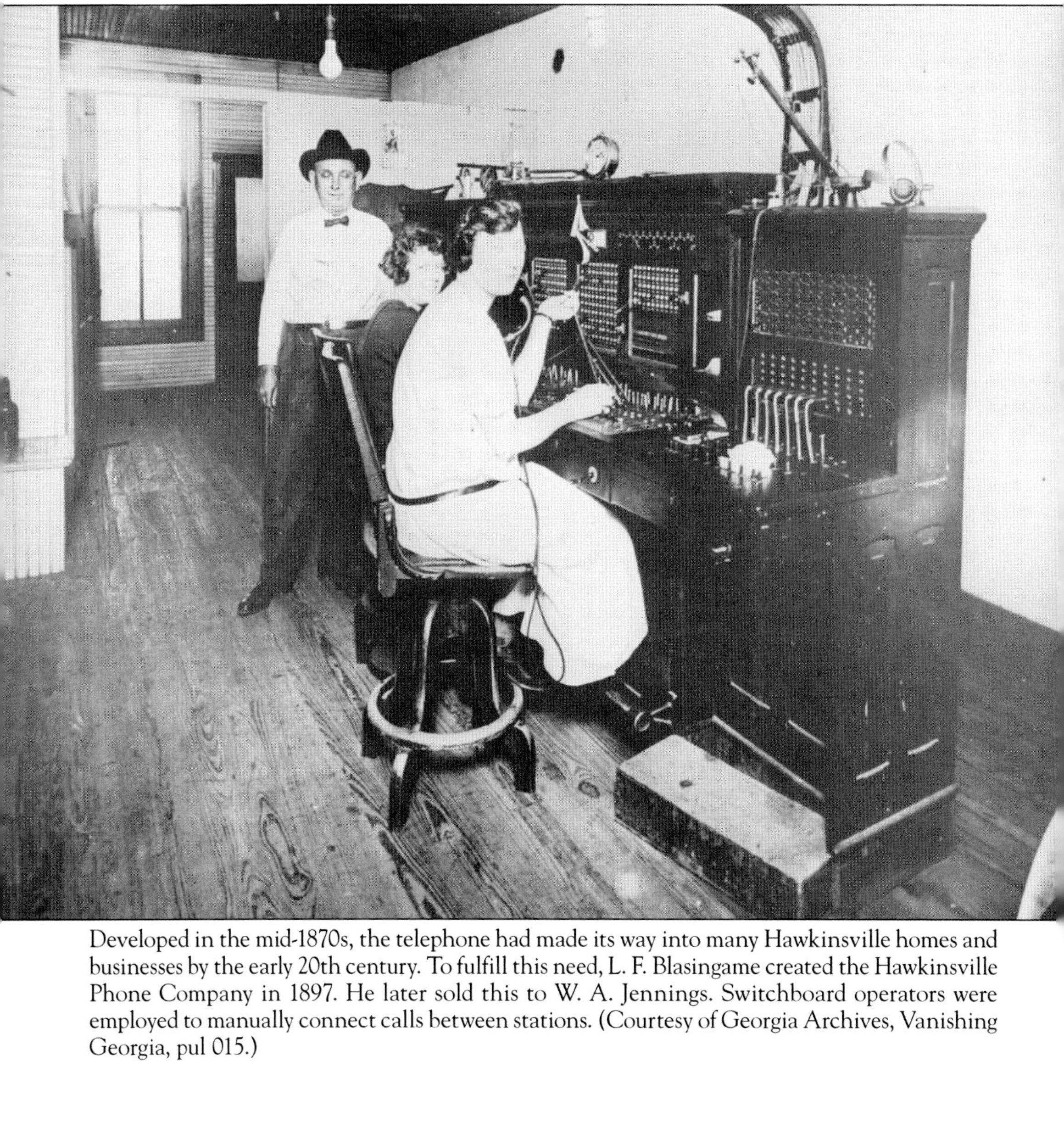

Developed in the mid-1870s, the telephone had made its way into many Hawkinsville homes and businesses by the early 20th century. To fulfill this need, L. F. Blasingame created the Hawkinsville Phone Company in 1897. He later sold this to W. A. Jennings. Switchboard operators were employed to manually connect calls between stations. (Courtesy of Georgia Archives, Vanishing Georgia, pul 015.)

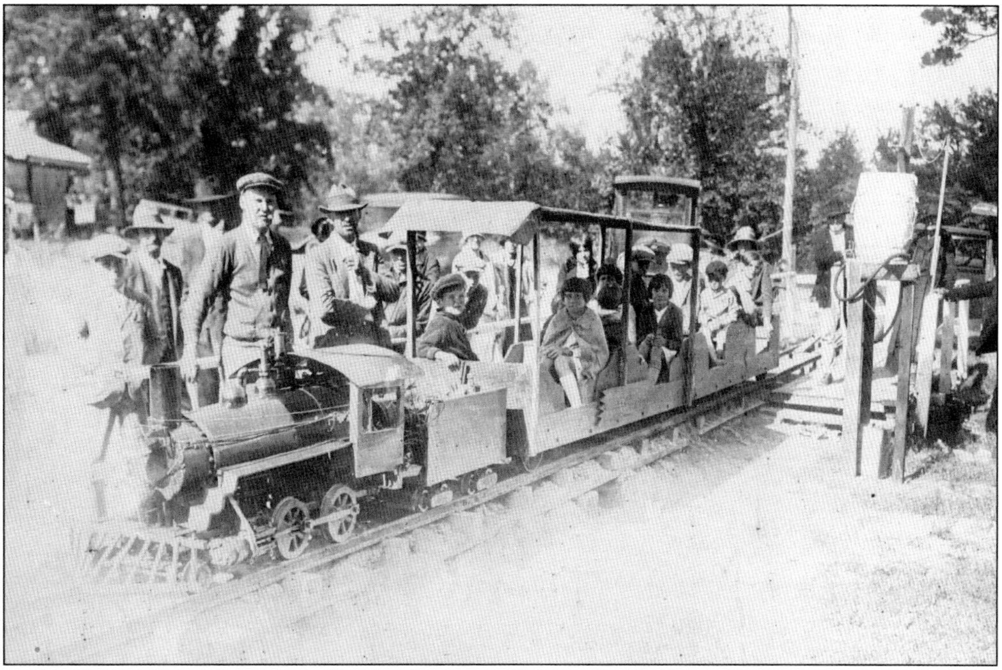

This miniature train delighted children at the fairgrounds in the mid-1920s. All of the train's cars were built to scale as a hobby by A. M. Mobley, owner of Mobley's Garage and Machine Works. (Courtesy of Georgia Archives, Vanishing Georgia, pul 008.)

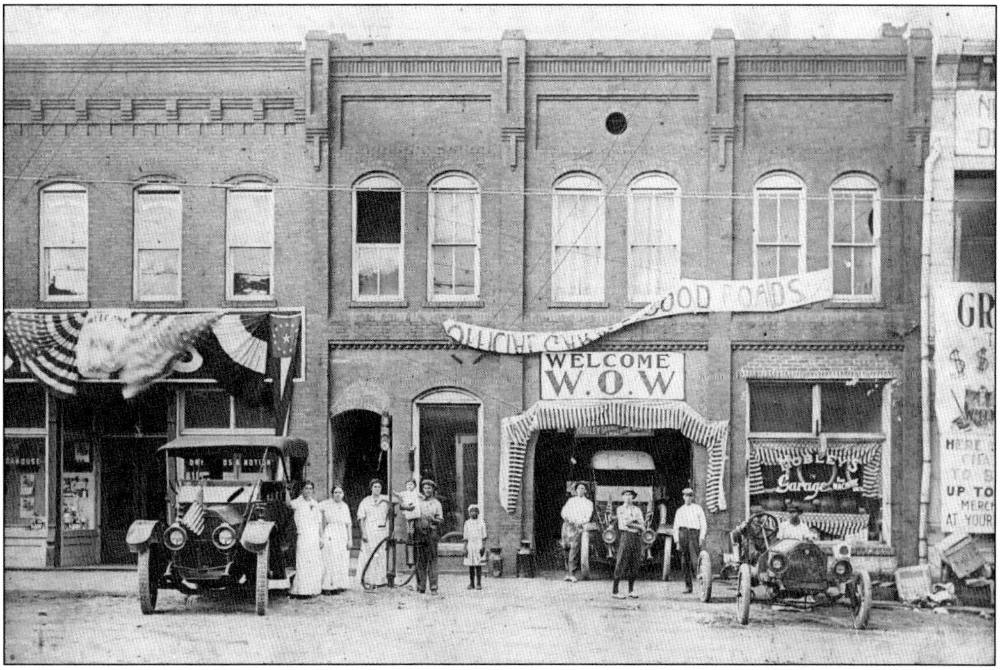

Mobley's Garage and Machine Works serviced the town's automobiles beginning about 1910. Owned by A. M. Mobley, the garage was located on Commerce Street and saw a brisk business. Mobley's is believed to be the first service station and gas pump in town. (Courtesy of Georgia Archives, Vanishing Georgia, pul 010.)

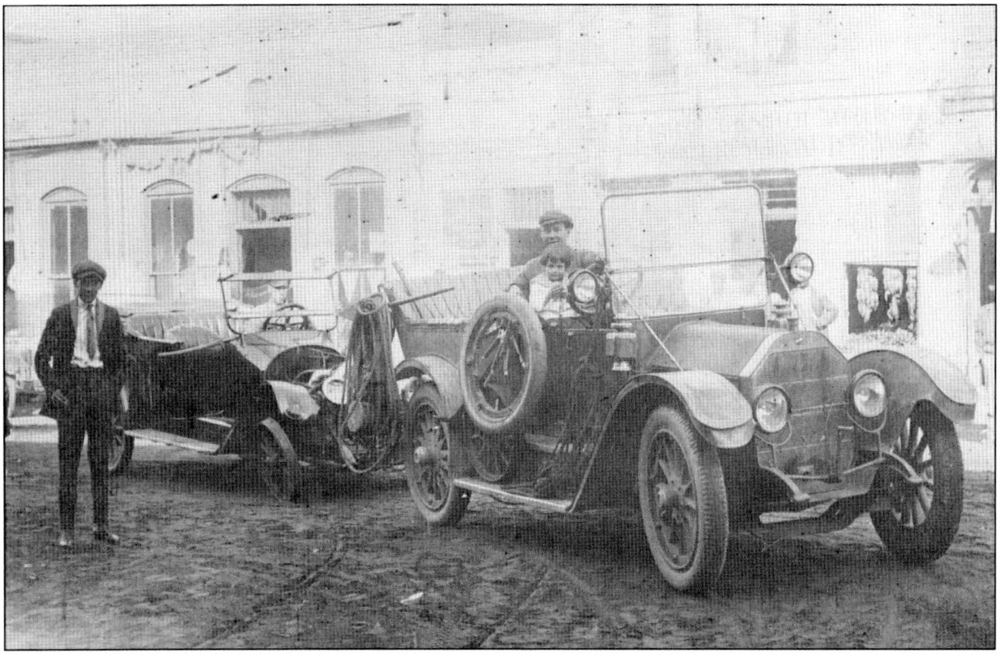

Without tow trucks, other automobiles were pressed into service to pull wrecked vehicles to repair stations. These two are headed to Mobley's Garage and Machine Works around 1917. (Courtesy of Georgia Archives, Vanishing Georgia, pul 013.)

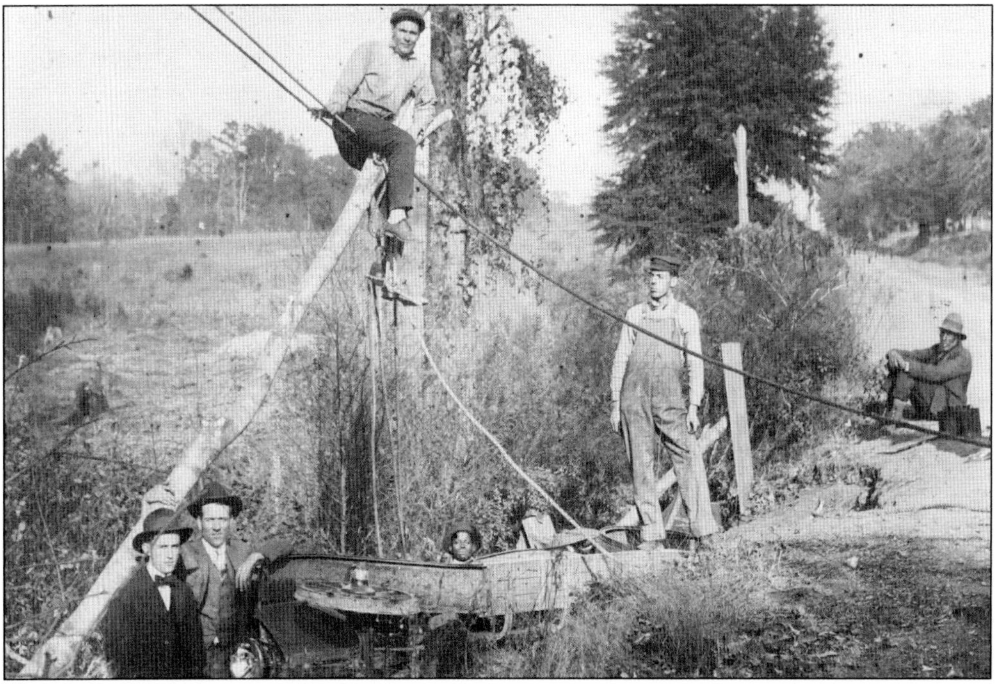

The roads near Hawkinsville were often treacherous, and the drivers were not always careful. Several men are seen here attempting to haul a wrecked automobile out of a ditch about a mile and a half east of town in 1917. The wrecked car would have been towed to A. M. Mobley's garage for repairs. (Courtesy of Georgia Archives, Vanishing Georgia, pul 012.)

Thomas Eugene Lovejoy grew up in Hawkinsville, went on to become the president of the Gulf Line Railroad, and served as the chief executive officer of the Montgomery Bank and Trust Company. He also served as a banking executive, and from 1913 until his death in 1939, he was the president of the Manhattan Life Insurance Company based in New York. (Courtesy of Pulaski Historical Society.)

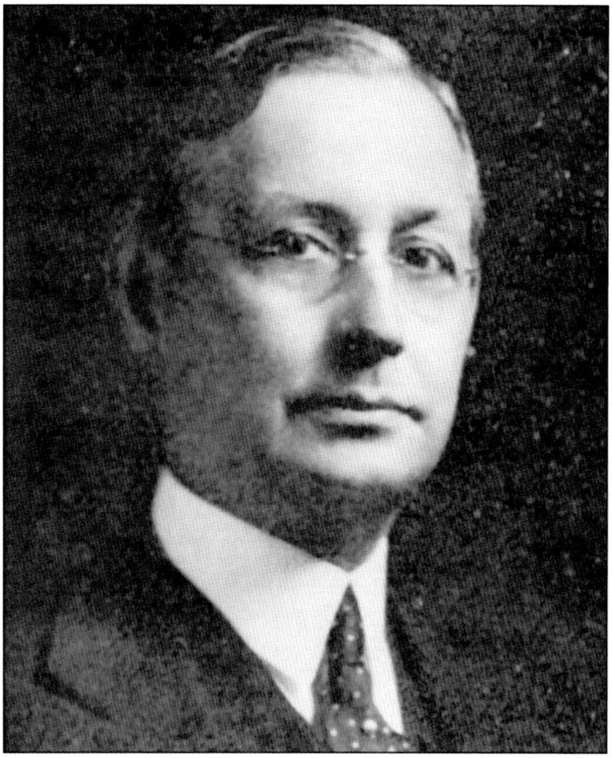

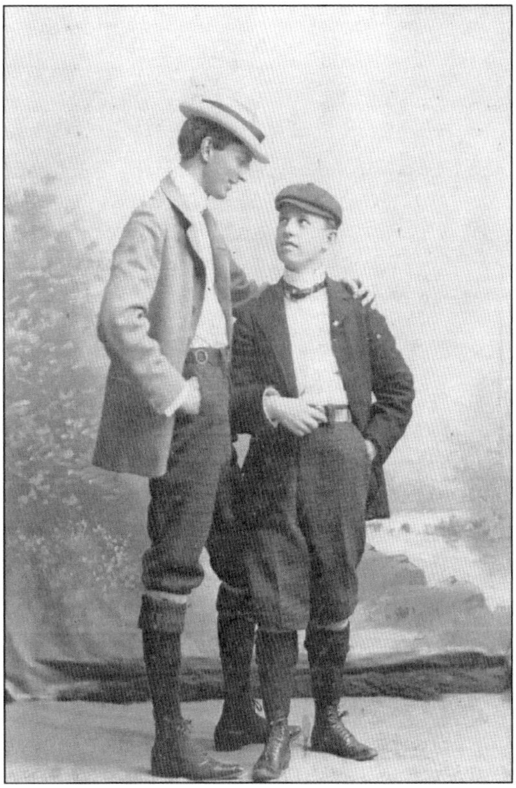

Harley Lawson (right) is pictured with a schoolmate in this Mercer University picture taken around 1900. Lawson briefly taught school while studying law. After being admitted to the bar, he set up a thriving practice in Hawkinsville. He was one of the premier lawyers in the town and a pillar of the community. (Courtesy of Pulaski Historical Society.)

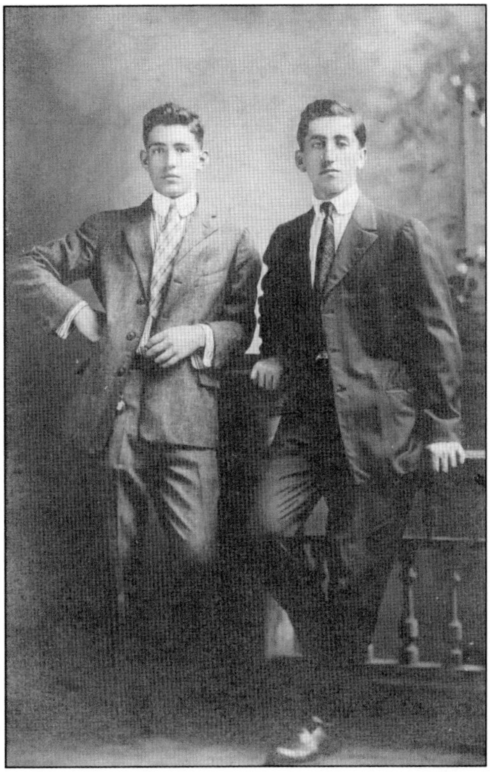

Andrew (left) and Freeman Cabero immigrated to America from Greece in 1904 and 1907, respectively, as children. They joined their older brother Spiro and uncle Louis Leopold, who owned the Hawkinsville Fruit and Candy Company. Both boys learned English and worked at their uncle's store until they bought it in 1907. Spiro returned to Greece in 1911, but another brother immigrated to Hawkinsville in 1912. (Courtesy of Nick Cabero.)

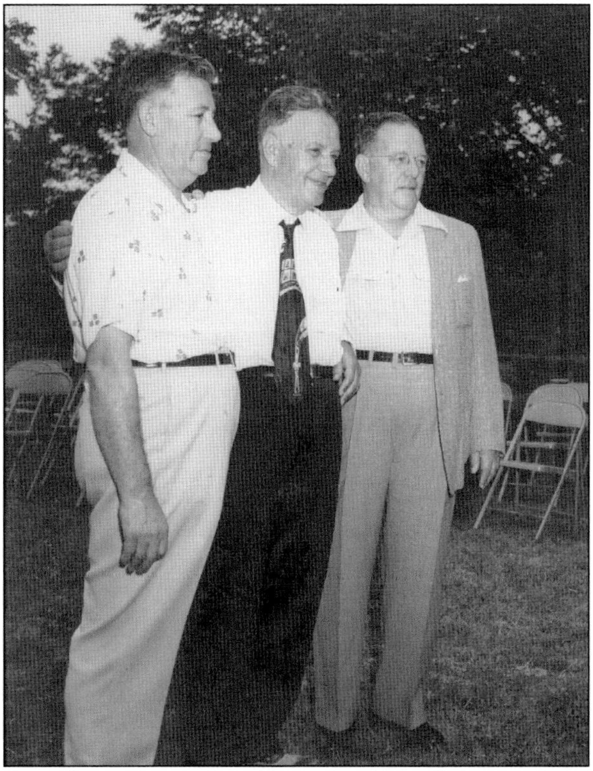

In 1954, Nick Cabero (center) celebrated the 50th anniversary of his arrival in America. Since stepping off the boat in Savannah at age 12, Nick, along with his brothers Andrew (left) and Lee (right), had owned numerous downtown businesses and had become an integral part of Hawkinsville. (Courtesy of Nick Cabero.)

Several of Hawkinsville's sons answered the drum during World War I. Clinton Duncan Pate was commissioned as a second lieutenant in the army in 1918. He was posted to France in August of that year. He was mustered out shortly after the war ended. (Courtesy of Pulaski Historical Society.)

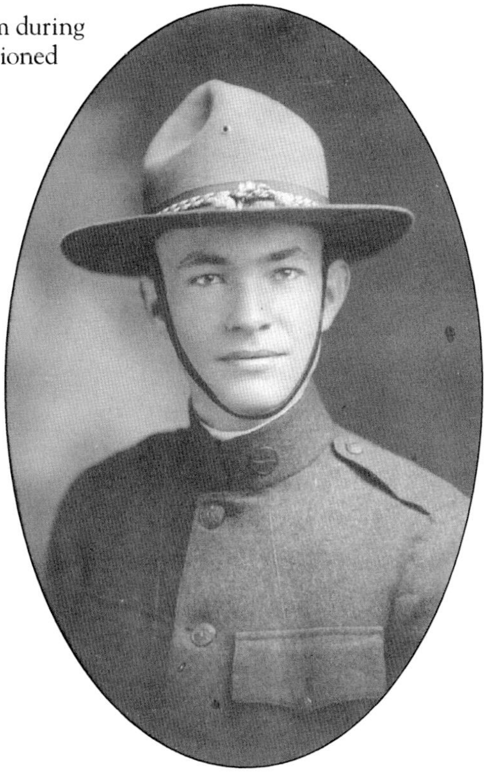

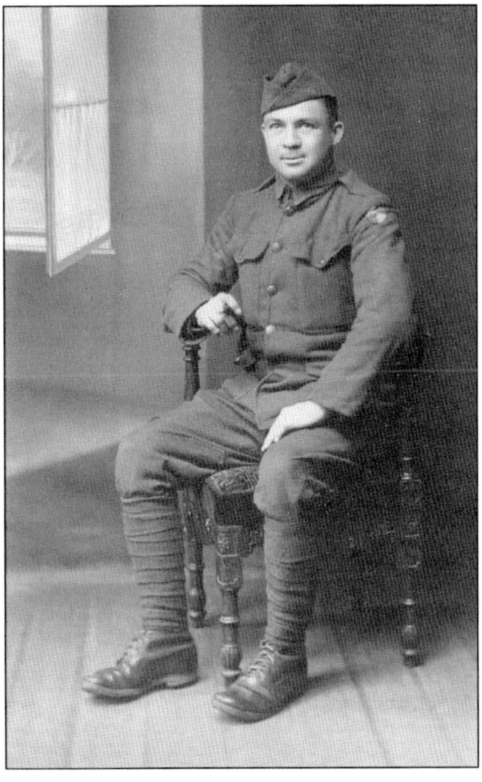

Pete Jelks served on the western front during the Great War. Writing his sister shortly after the armistice, he included this picture of himself. His letters home were brief, upbeat, and, of course, censored. (Courtesy of Pulaski Historical Society.)

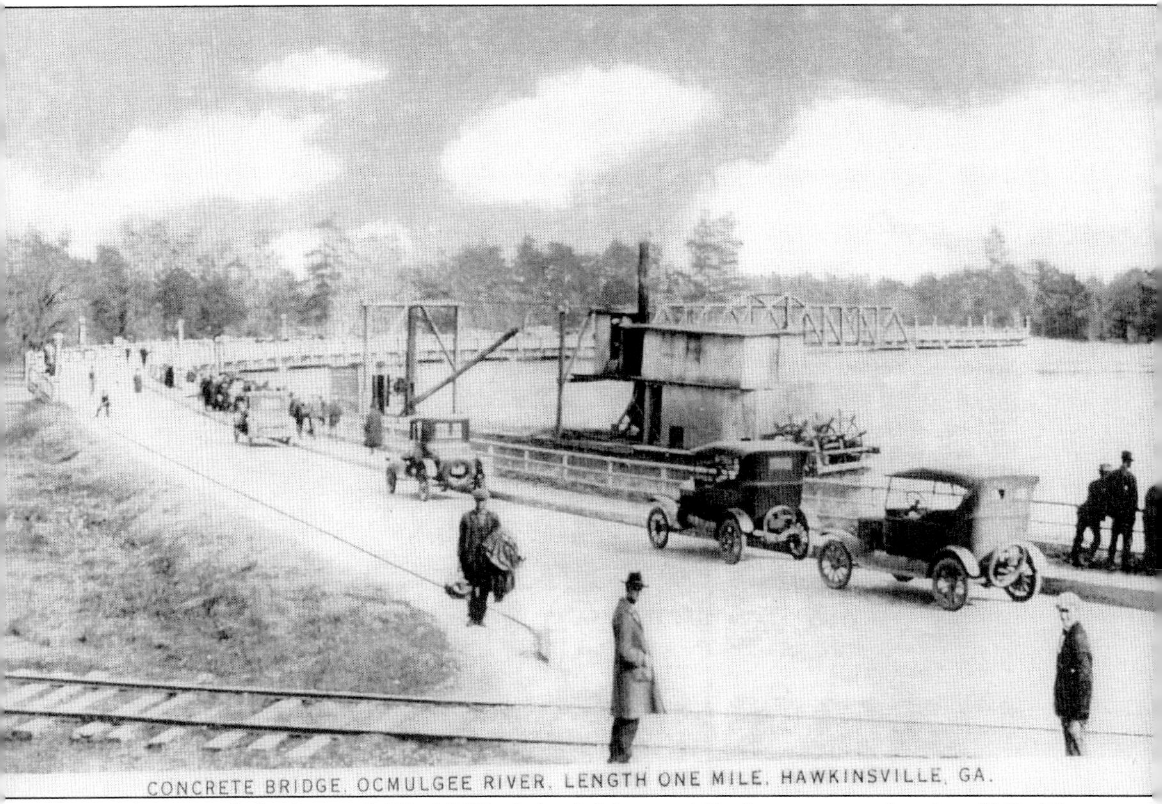

To honor Pulaski County's World War I dead, Memorial Bridge was completed in 1920. This bridge was replaced in the 1950s. (Courtesy of Pulaski Historical Society.)

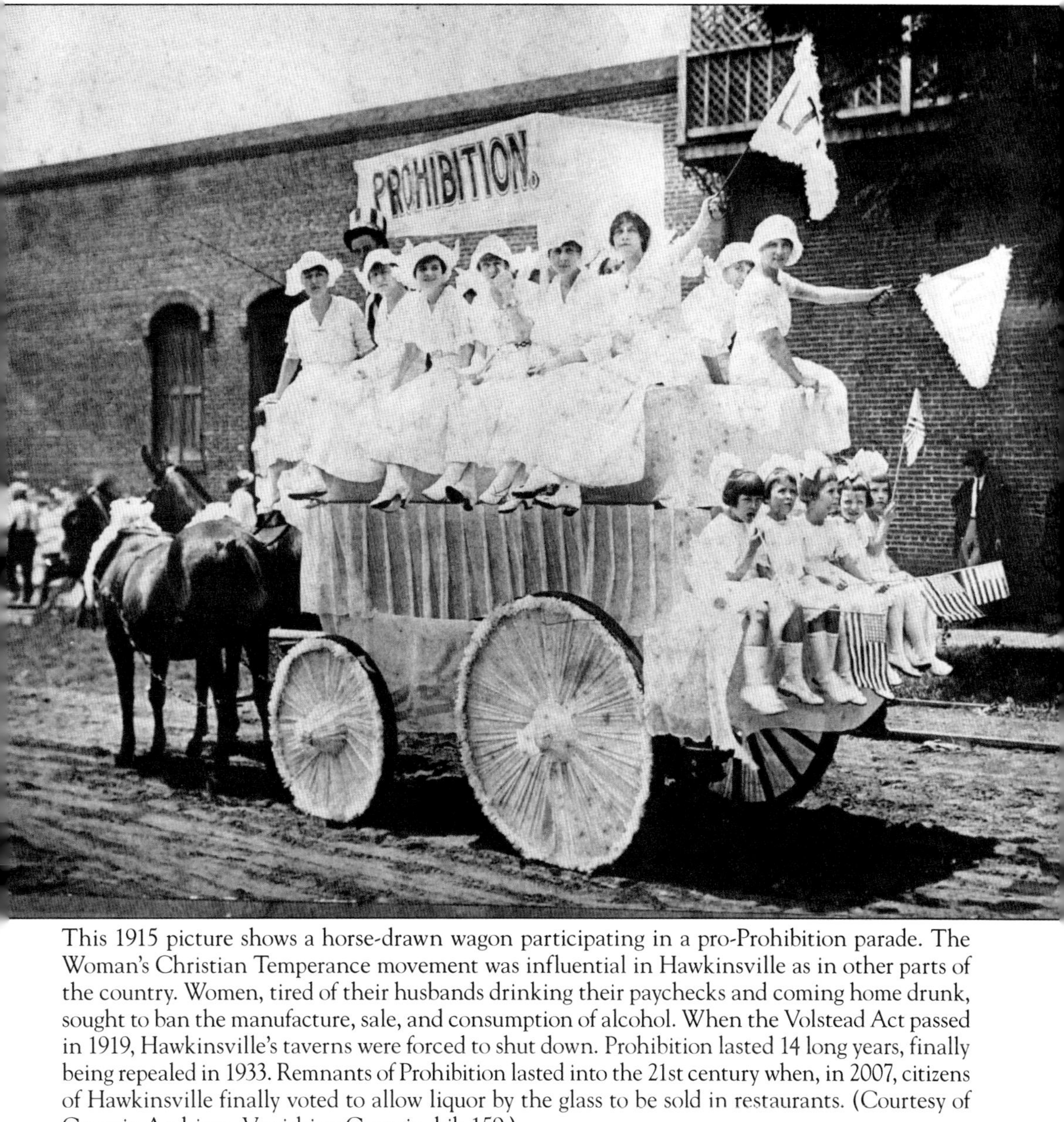

This 1915 picture shows a horse-drawn wagon participating in a pro-Prohibition parade. The Woman's Christian Temperance movement was influential in Hawkinsville as in other parts of the country. Women, tired of their husbands drinking their paychecks and coming home drunk, sought to ban the manufacture, sale, and consumption of alcohol. When the Volstead Act passed in 1919, Hawkinsville's taverns were forced to shut down. Prohibition lasted 14 long years, finally being repealed in 1933. Remnants of Prohibition lasted into the 21st century when, in 2007, citizens of Hawkinsville finally voted to allow liquor by the glass to be sold in restaurants. (Courtesy of Georgia Archives, Vanishing Georgia, bib 159.)

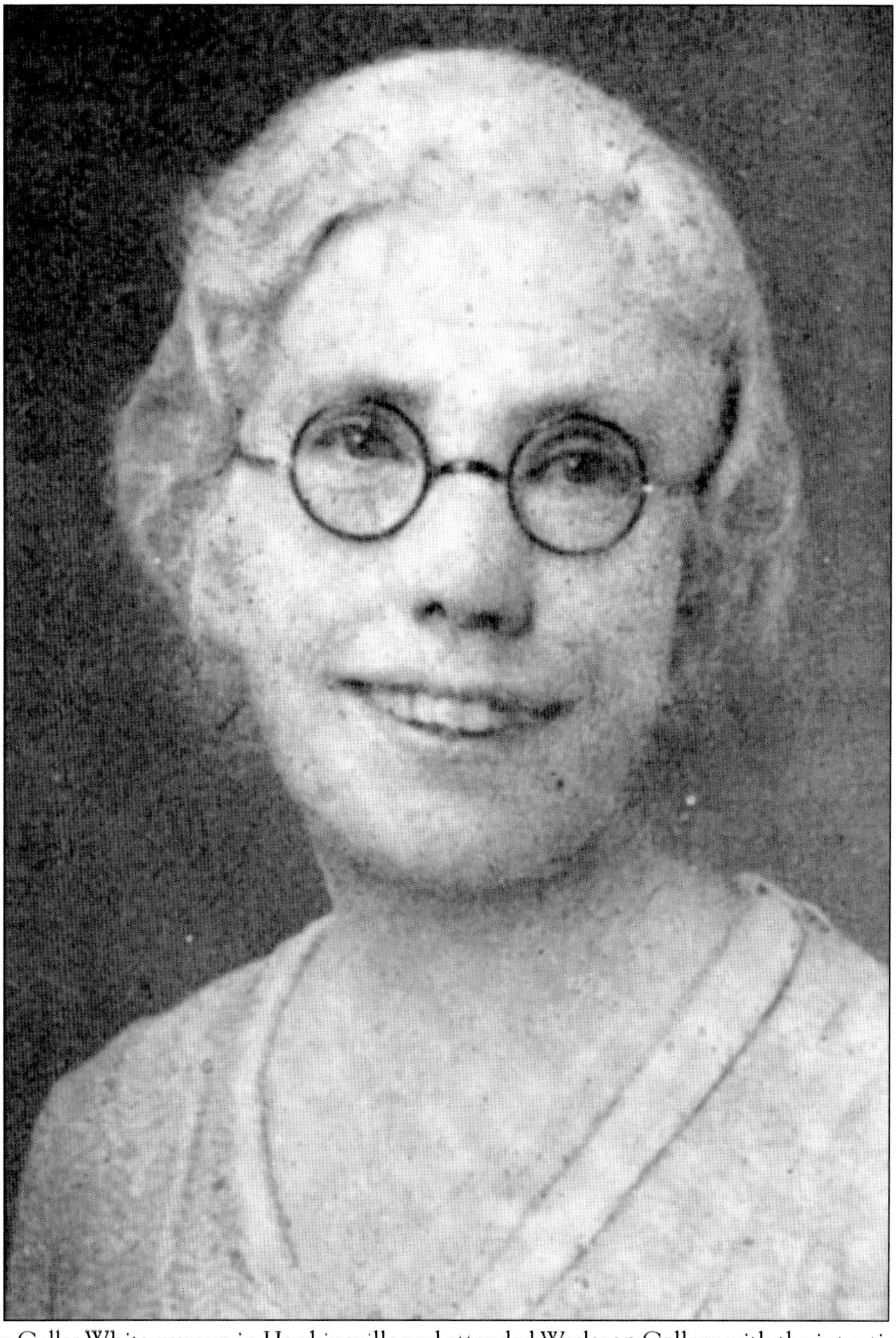

Mary Culler White grew up in Hawkinsville and attended Wesleyan College with the intention of becoming an artist. She abandoned this idea and entered the Scarrit Bible and Training School to become a missionary. After graduation, she was sent to China, where she worked tirelessly. After the Japanese invasion of China in 1937, she fled to the safety of the mountains with her Chinese staff. Until the Japanese attack on Pearl Harbor, White looked after some 5,000 refugees. After Japan went to war with America, White was first restricted and then interned by Japanese authorities while in China. She was repatriated in 1943. (Courtesy of Pulaski Historical Society.)

When the boll weevil decimated cotton in the 1930s, farmers were forced to find alternate crops to grow. One of the most popular was the peanut. It grows well in the sandy soil around Hawkinsville and allowed many farmers to hold on until the blight was over. (Courtesy of Georgia Archives, Vanishing Georgia, pul 023.)

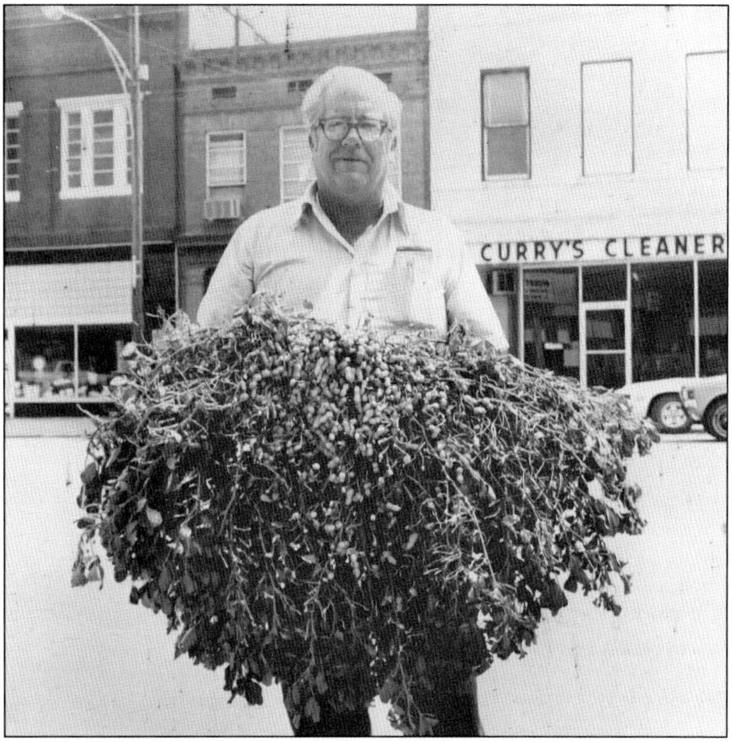

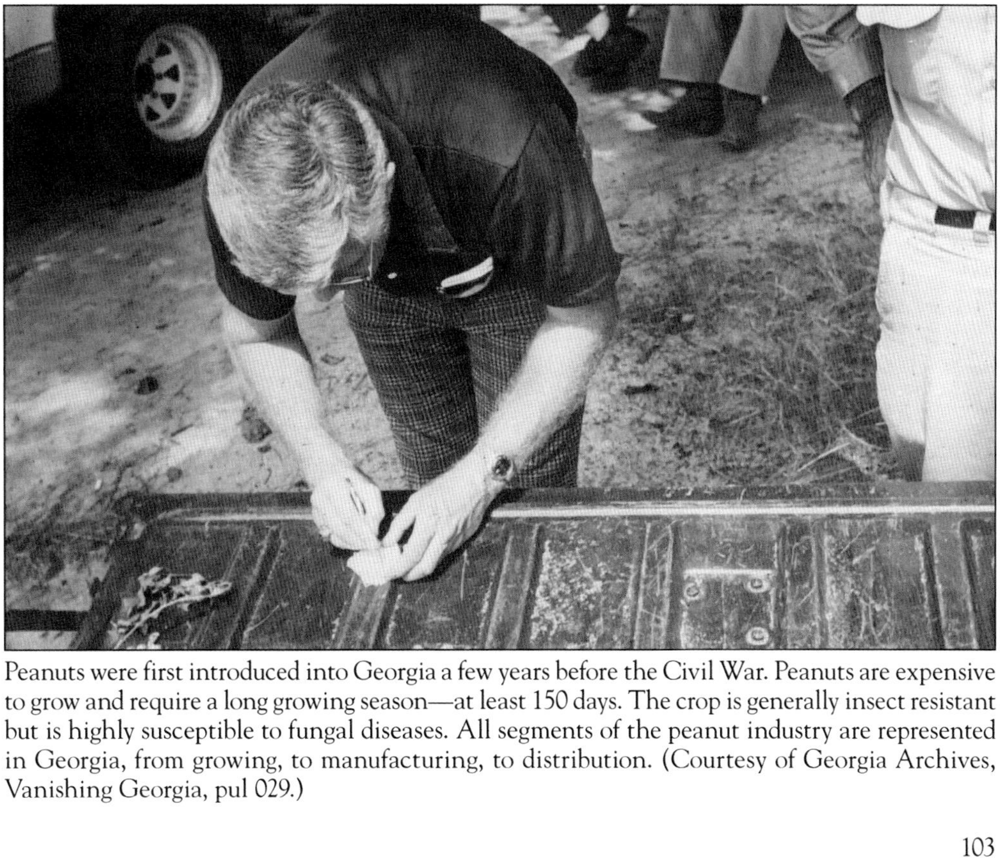

Peanuts were first introduced into Georgia a few years before the Civil War. Peanuts are expensive to grow and require a long growing season—at least 150 days. The crop is generally insect resistant but is highly susceptible to fungal diseases. All segments of the peanut industry are represented in Georgia, from growing, to manufacturing, to distribution. (Courtesy of Georgia Archives, Vanishing Georgia, pul 029.)

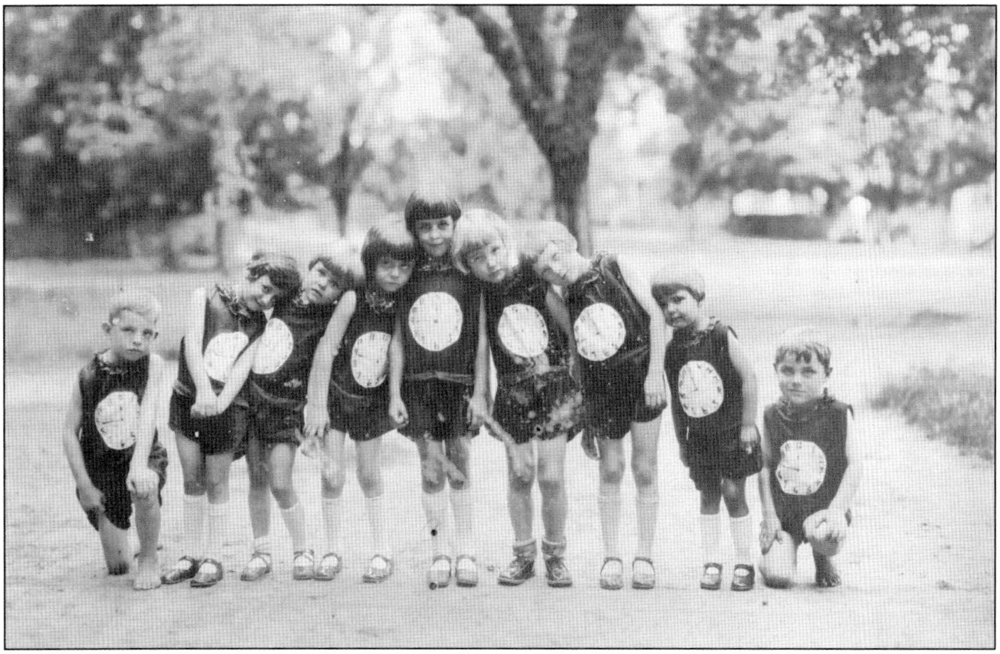

Hawkinsville, much as the rest of America, was hit hard by the Great Depression. With the election of Franklin D. Roosevelt and the implementation of the New Deal, the city slowly began to climb out of the economic devastation. The Works Progress Administration put millions of people back to work building important civil projects. Here children are shown taking part in a 1930s WPA recreation project. (Courtesy of Georgia Archives, Vanishing Georgia, pul 083.)

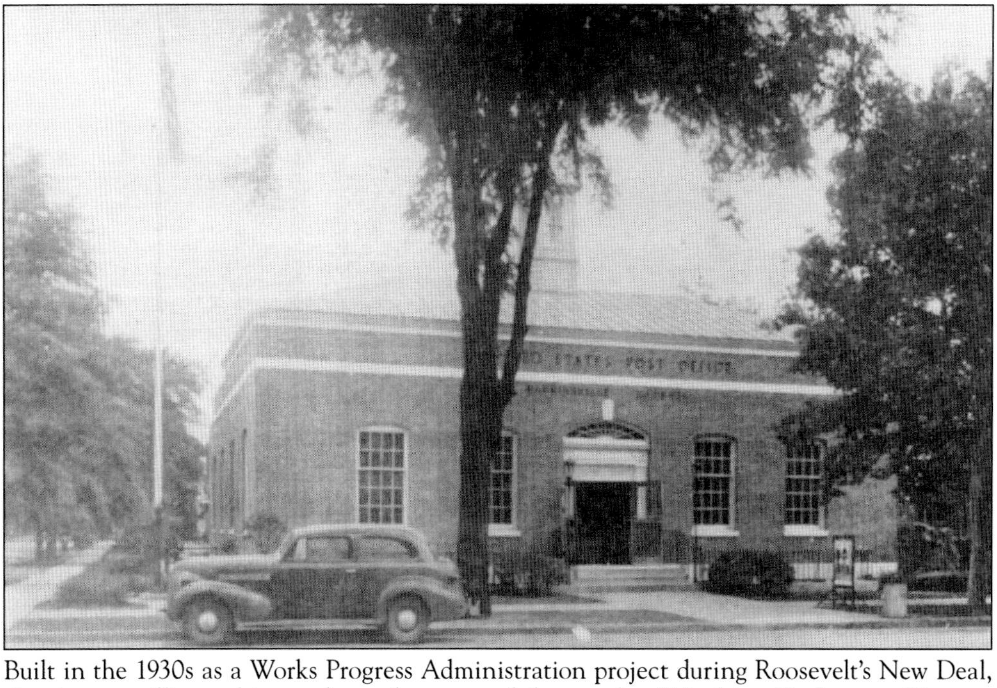

Built in the 1930s as a Works Progress Administration project during Roosevelt's New Deal, the city post office and its employees have served the people of Hawkinsville for over 70 years. (Courtesy of Pulaski Historical Society.)

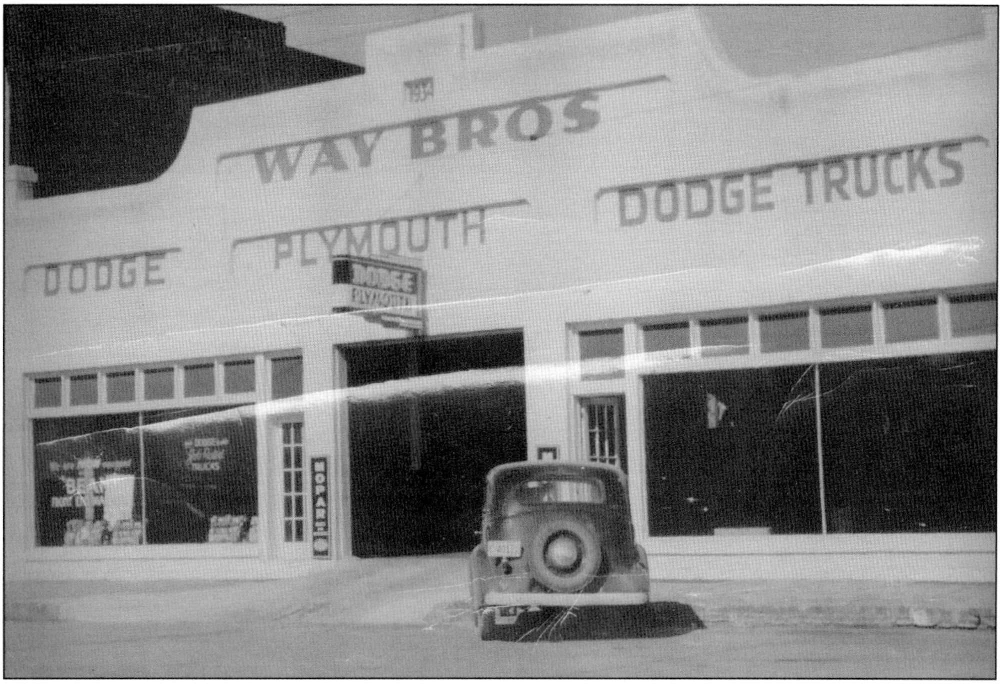

In the same building as his father's furniture store, Samuel Albert Way Jr. opened Way Brothers car dealership with his brother Robert Glover Way in 1933. Although long since moved from this site, Way Brothers is one of the city's oldest businesses. (Courtesy of the Way family.)

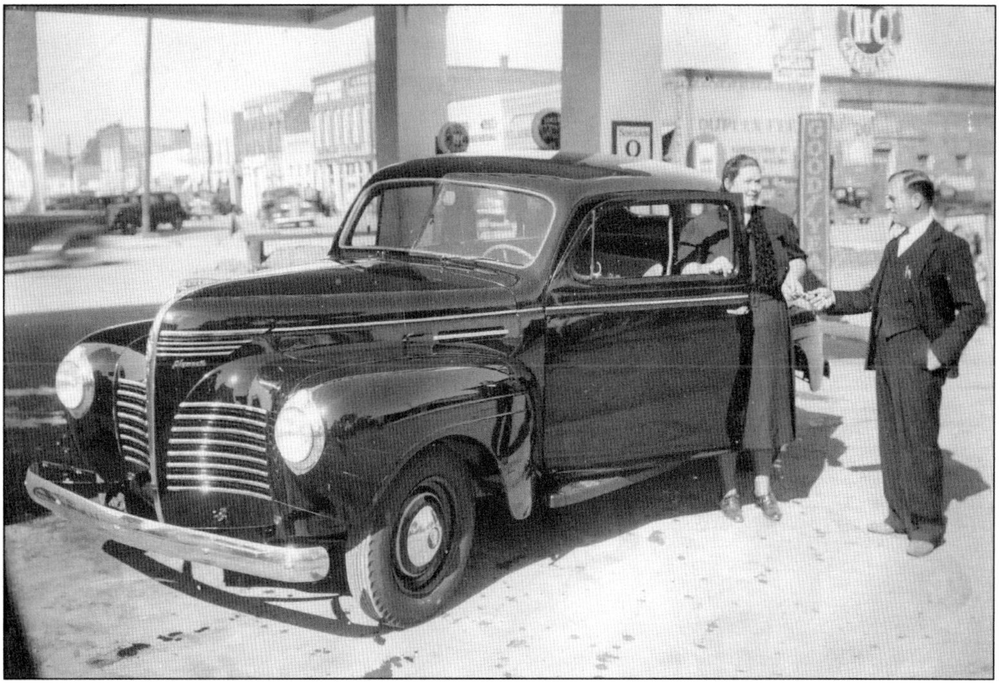

Sam Albert Way Jr., like his father, was a gifted businessman and an active promoter of Hawkinsville's development. In this picture, he delivers the keys to a new automobile to a Mrs. Cobb at Way Brothers' second location in Hawkinsville. (Courtesy of the Way family.)

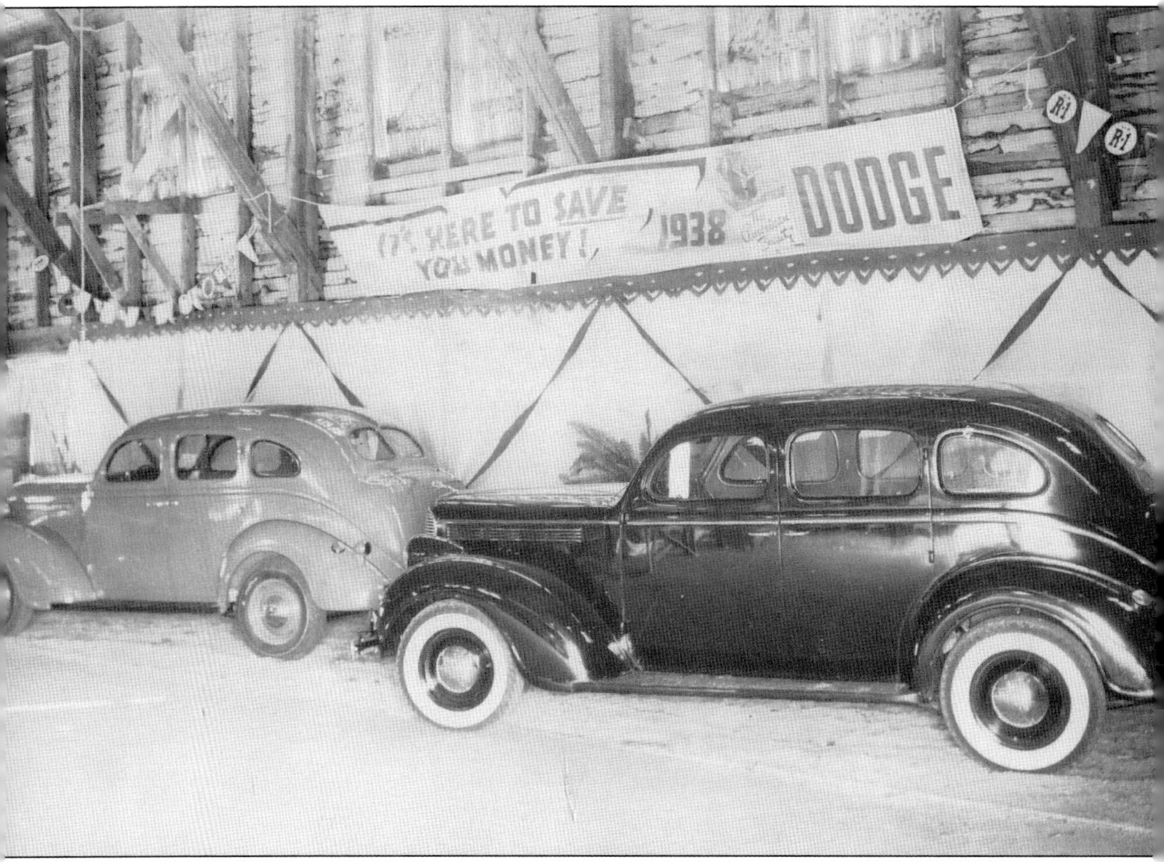

Sam Way and the members of his firm participated each year in a fair held at the city harness racing track. The fair featured a large pavilion for exhibits like these new automobiles from Way Brothers. (Courtesy of the Way family.)

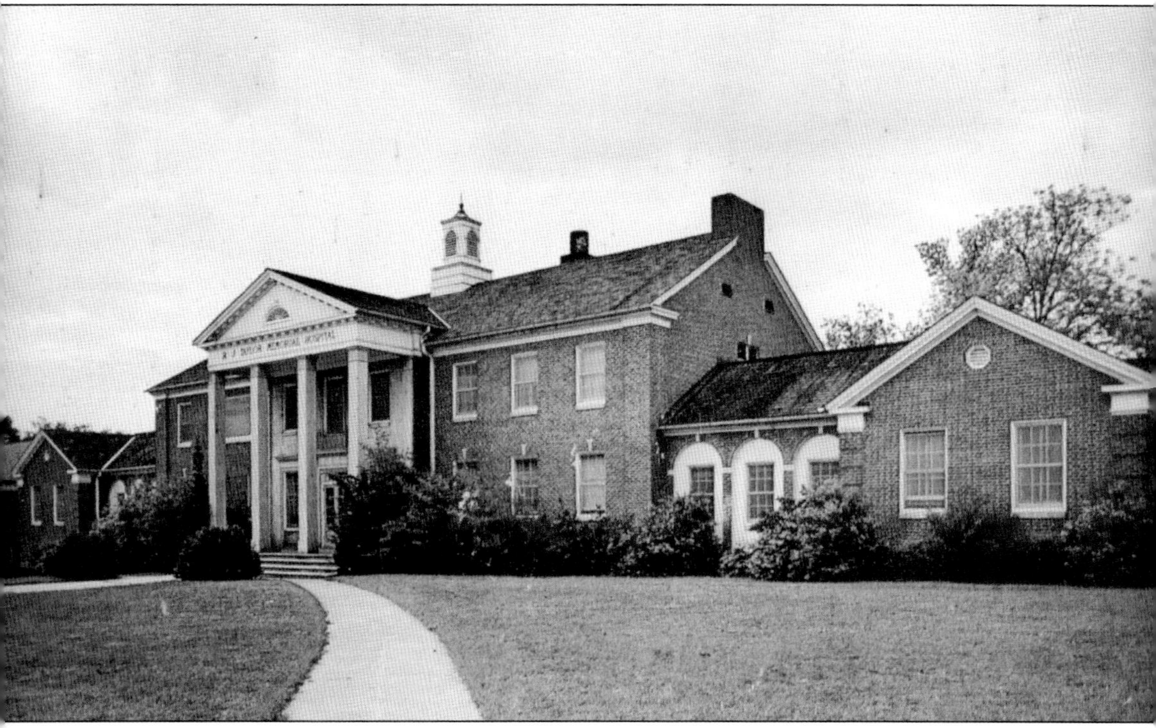

Taylor Memorial Hospital, located on Commerce Street, was dedicated in 1938. Money for the project was donated by Robert Jenks Taylor in memory of his father, E. H. Taylor, and grandfather Robert N. Taylor, both prominent doctors in the area. Taylor Memorial was a regional hospital serving Hawkinsville, Pulaski County, and surrounding areas. (Courtesy of Phillip A. Gibbs.)

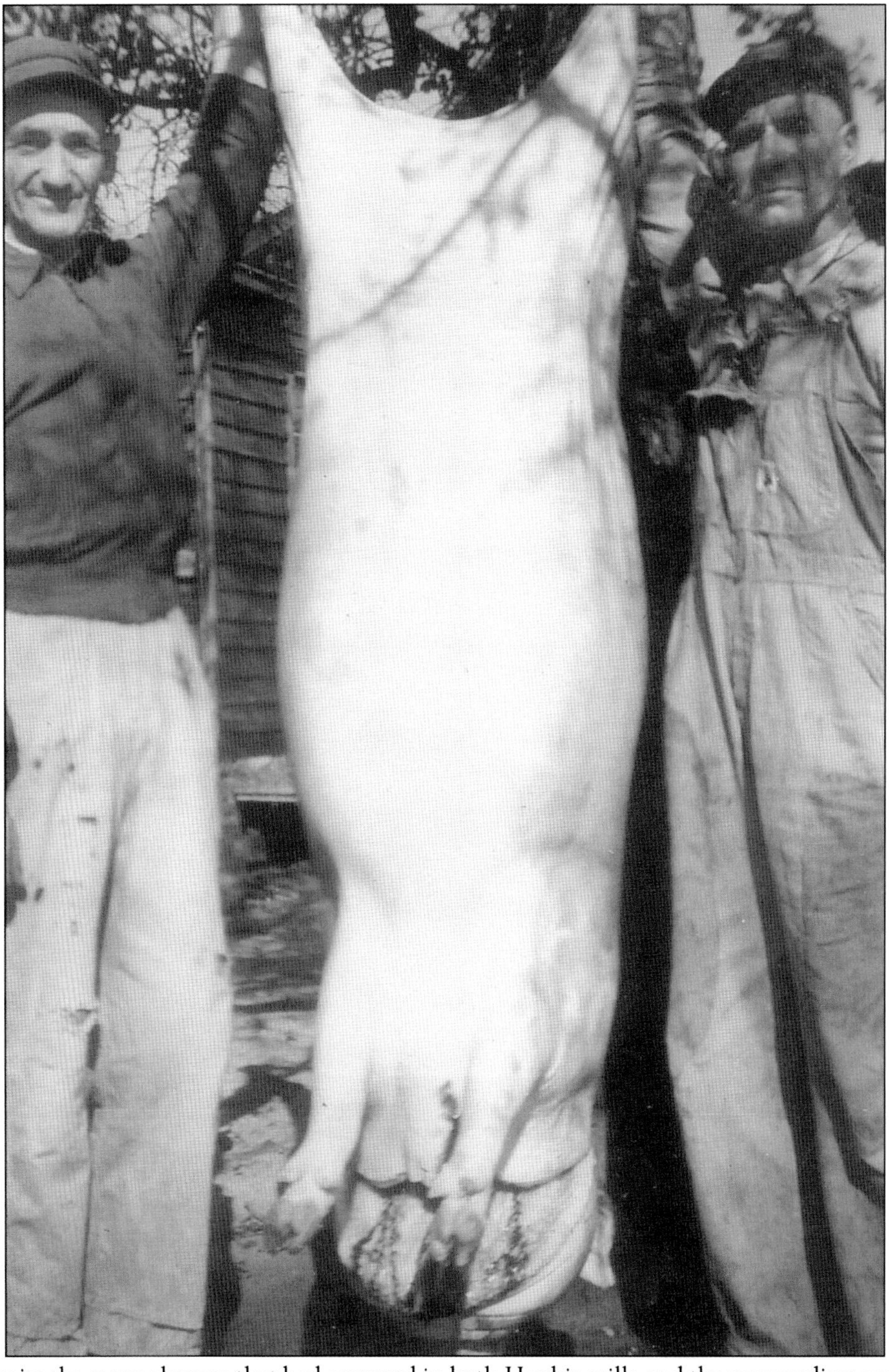

Despite the many changes that had occurred in both Hawkinsville and the surrounding county during the early 20th century, many traditions continued. Each winter, farmers like Richard Cromer (left) and Horace Russ (right) killed and scaled hogs. The hams and shoulders were prepared for the smokehouse. The remaining parts were ground and stuffed into sausage casings. (Courtesy of Troy Sullivan.)

A proud day for any up-and coming farmer in Pulaski County in thc mid-20th century was the purchase of his first tractor. Here Horace Russ gives his new tractor a test run while his daughter Martha looks on. (Courtesy of Troy Sullivan.)

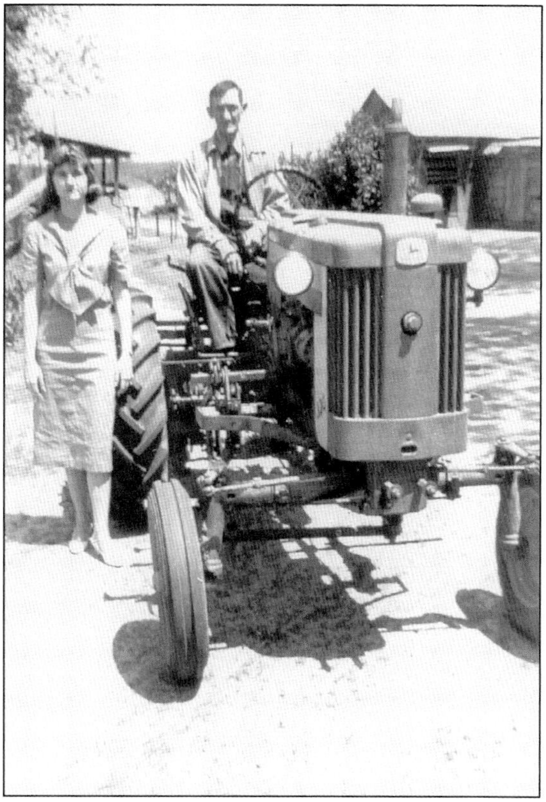

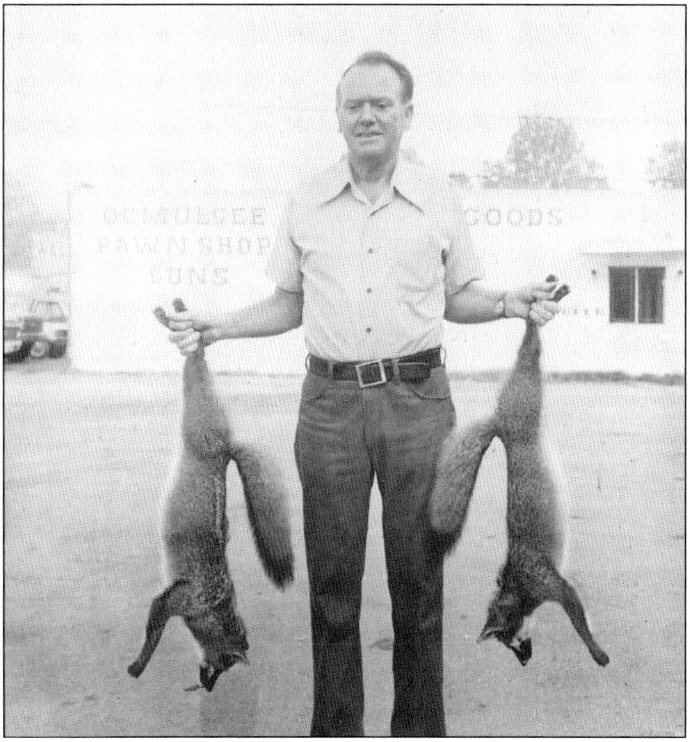

Even though Hawkinsville's citizens enjoyed the amenities of their modern city, they never abandoned the traditions of their ancestors. Foxes were considered a nuisance not only by farmers, but also by many members of the community. Bounties were often given for each fox killed. (Courtesy of Georgia Archives, Vanishing Georgia, pul 055.)

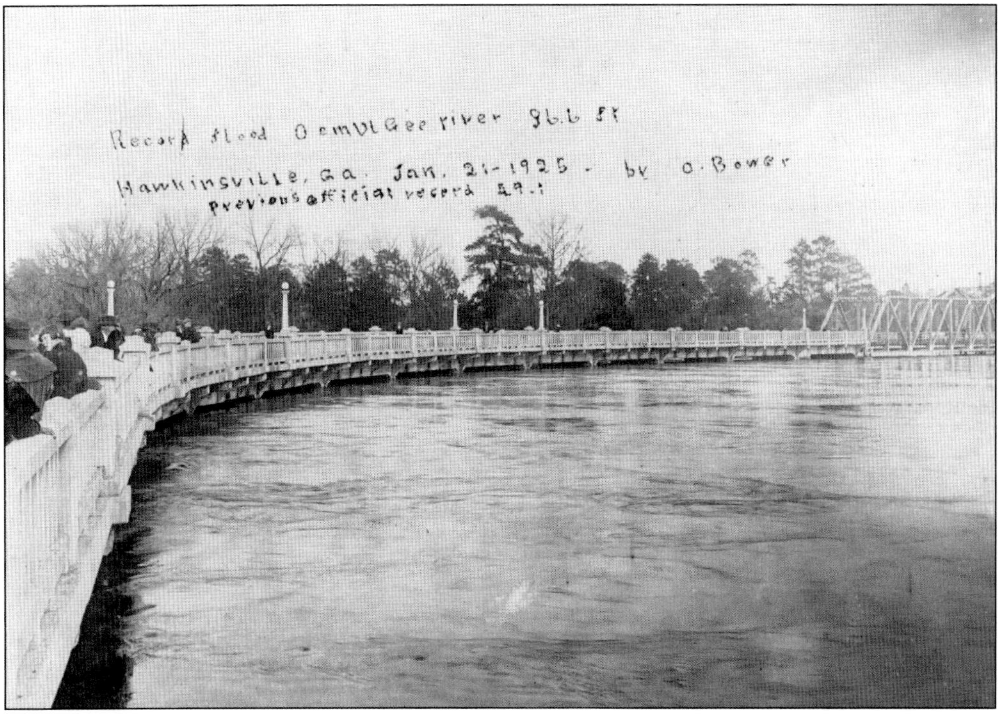

Hawkinsville's bridges are shown here. The river, the roads, and the rail have long combined to make Hawkinsville the "Hub City." (Courtesy of Georgia Archives, Vanishing Georgia, 065.)

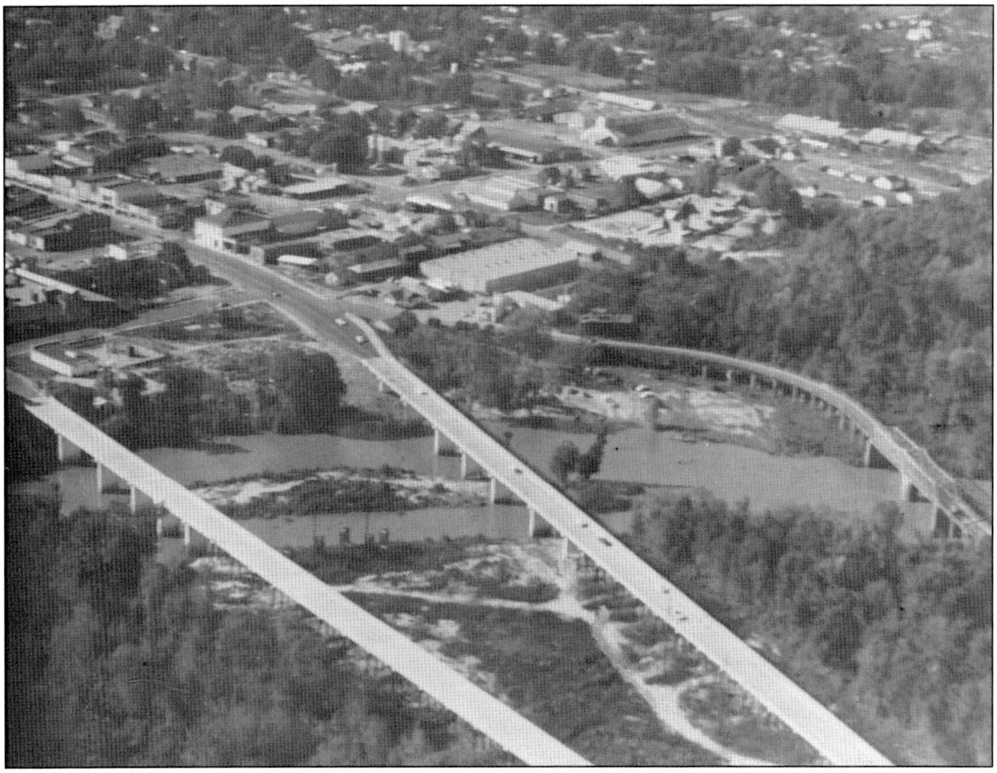

Five

LAST REPOSE

For the people of 19th- and early-20th-century Hawkinsville, life was fleeting. The practice of medicine during much of this period was still, when compared to modern standards, quite primitive. An examination of the death records of the town's citizens during this period reveals that they died from typhoid, cholera, smallpox, measles, seizures, influenza, kidney ailments, and a host of other diseases that are treatable today. Violence also took the lives of young and old alike. From the early years of the 19th century to the 1920s, Hawkinsville men fought and died in the Seminole Wars, the Mexican-American War, the Civil War, the Spanish-American War, and World War I.

Disease, war, and hardship, therefore, were ever present and often sent men and women to an early grave. But the area's ministers reminded citizens that death need not be feared. On the contrary, death was not an end but a beginning. With this in mind, cemeteries during the 19th century were designed in much the same way as parks; they were intended to be places not of dread but of hope, beauty, and reflection. The angels, urns, pedestals, obelisks, and grave markers found in Hawkinsville's Orange Hill and Pine Bloom Cemeteries are fraught with symbolism. They tell us much about how the town's citizens saw themselves and the world around them.

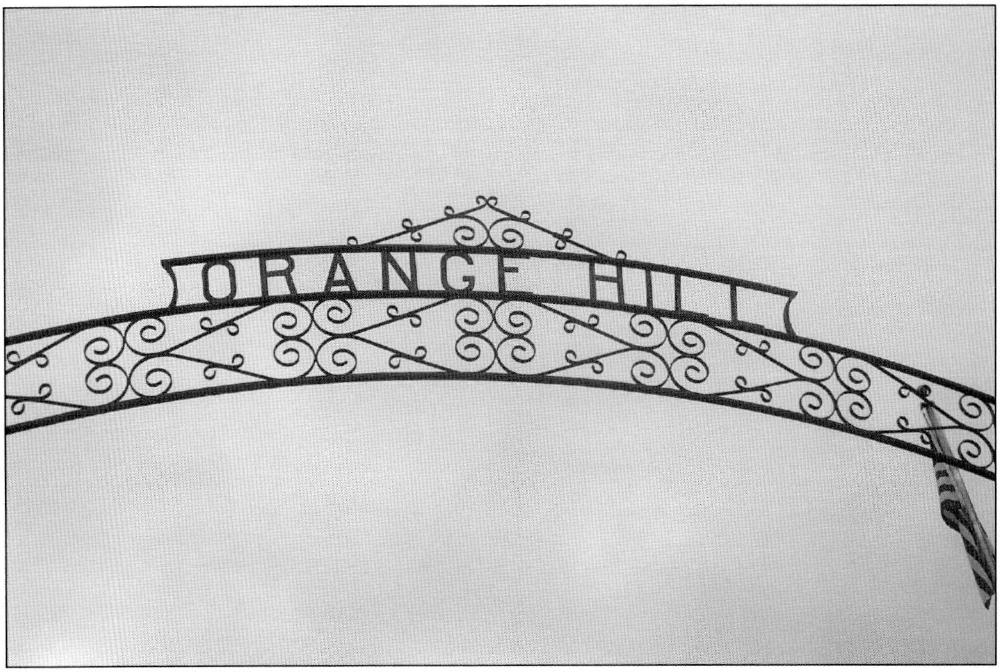

Records indicate that Orange Hill Cemetery was established sometime in the 1830s. A number of planters and merchants donated the land for what they believed would be a proper and fitting place for the town's citizens to be buried. (Courtesy of Phillip A. Gibbs.)

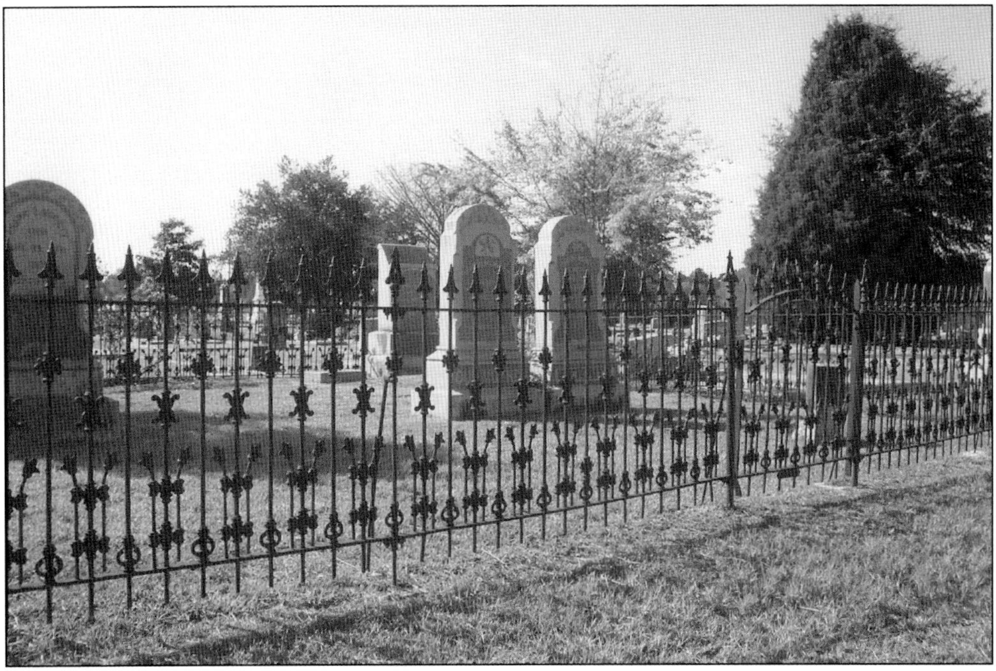

From its inception, Orange Hill was a place of beauty. Cypress, live oak, and magnolia trees stand among the graves of the city's most prominent citizens. Many of these same citizens spared no expense when it came to their family members' last resting place. A number of families placed ornate iron fences around their burial plots. (Courtesy of Phillip A. Gibbs.)

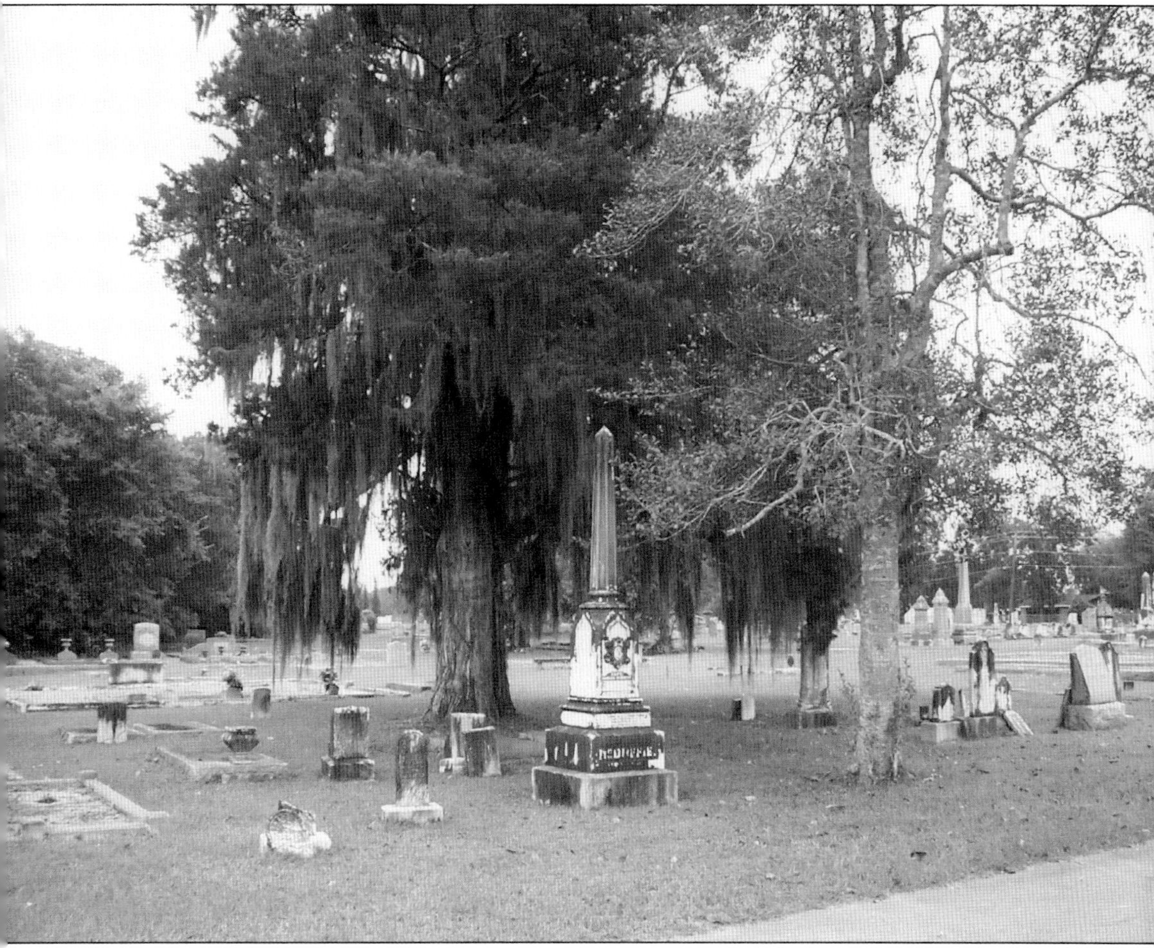

Framed by Spanish moss, Norman McDuffie's monument is a testament to his prominence in the community as well as his service to the state as a Confederate officer during the Civil War. Like many members of the planter-merchant elite, McDuffie was a Mason, as evidenced by the square and compass on his monument. (Courtesy of Phillip A. Gibbs.)

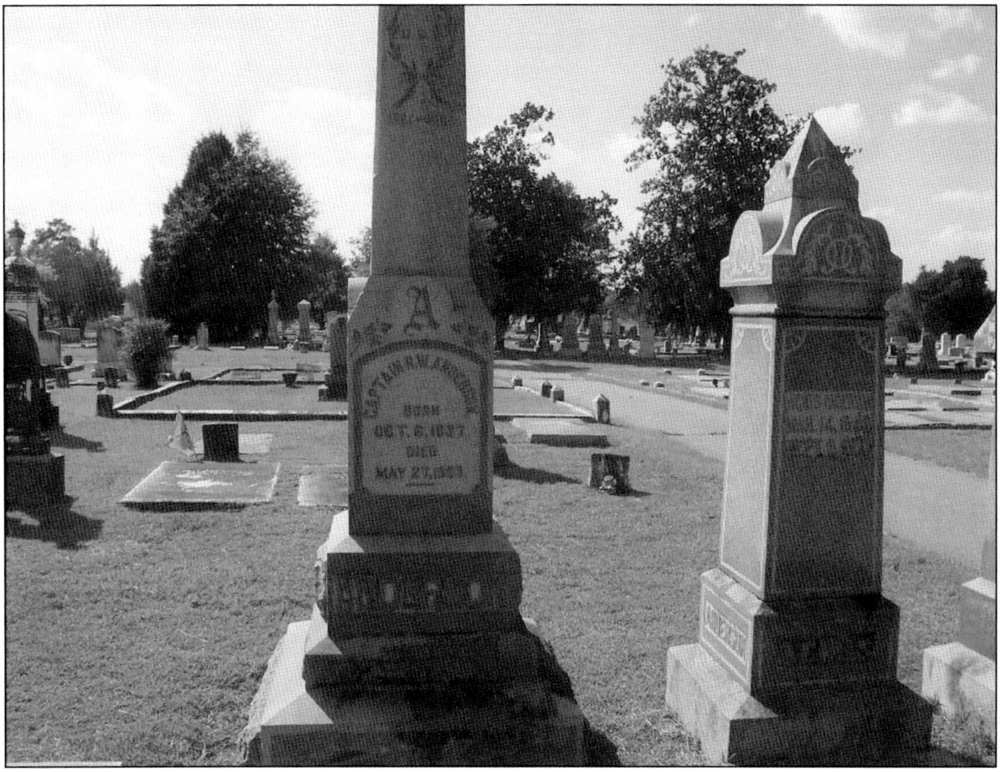

Ruel W. Anderson organized a company of artillery from Hawkinsville and Pulaski County at the beginning of the Civil War. Known as Anderson's Battery, Captain Anderson and his men fought in numerous battles, including Chickamauga and Griswoldville. (Courtesy of Phillip A. Gibbs.)

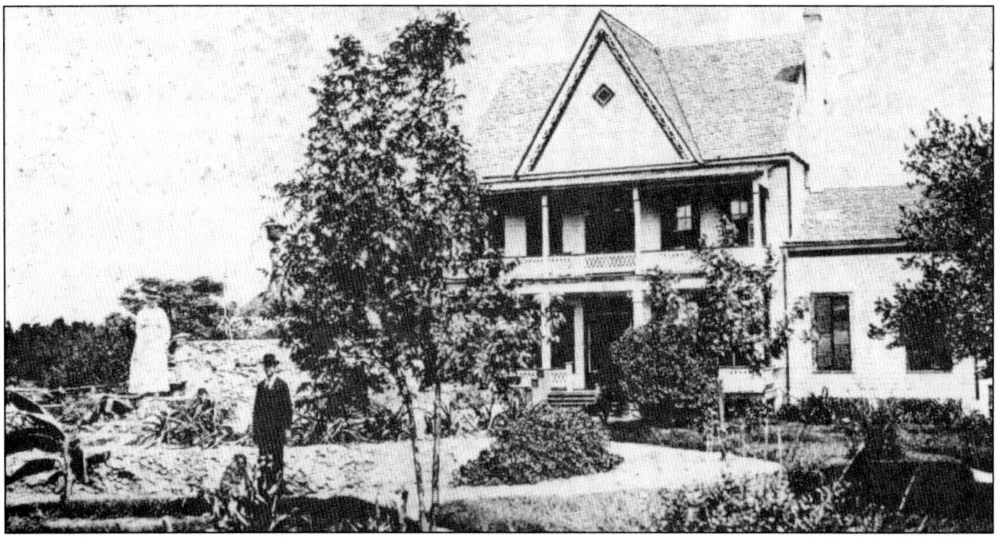

A planter of considerable means before the Civil War, Capt. Ruel W. Anderson returned to Hawkinsville and built the home pictured here. By the time of his death in 1903, he had become a prominent merchant, banker, and state legislator. (Courtesy of the Hawkinsville Chapter of the Daughters of the American Revolution.)

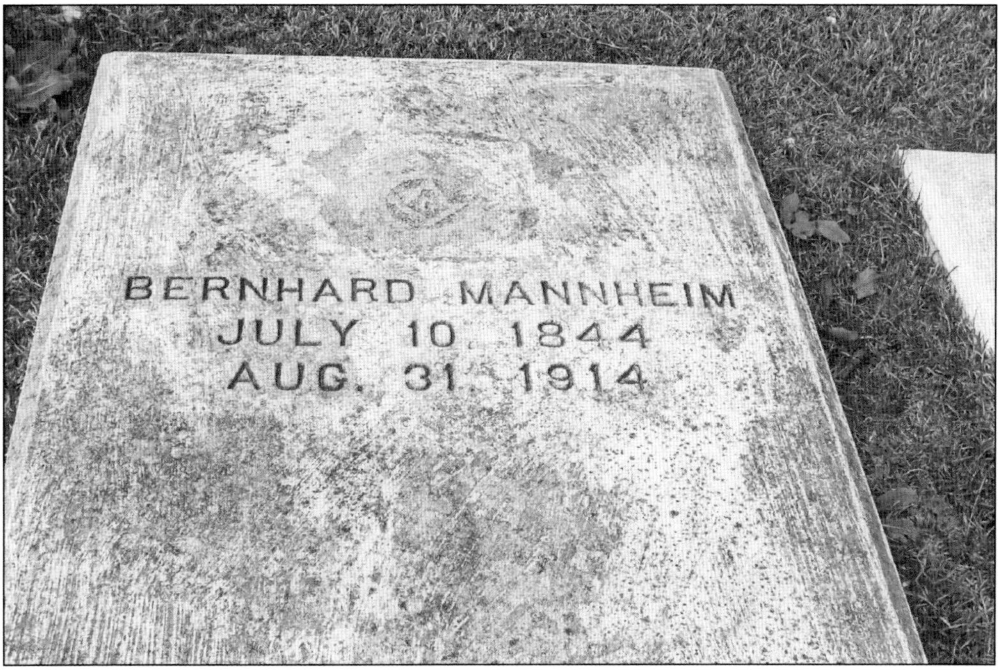

Not far from Capt. Ruel W. Anderson's grave is the last resting place of Bernhardt Mannheim, a German native who settled in Hawkinsville in 1870. Although Mannheim established several businesses in the area and served as a city alderman, he traveled widely and spoke a variety of languages. (Courtesy of Phillip Gibbs.)

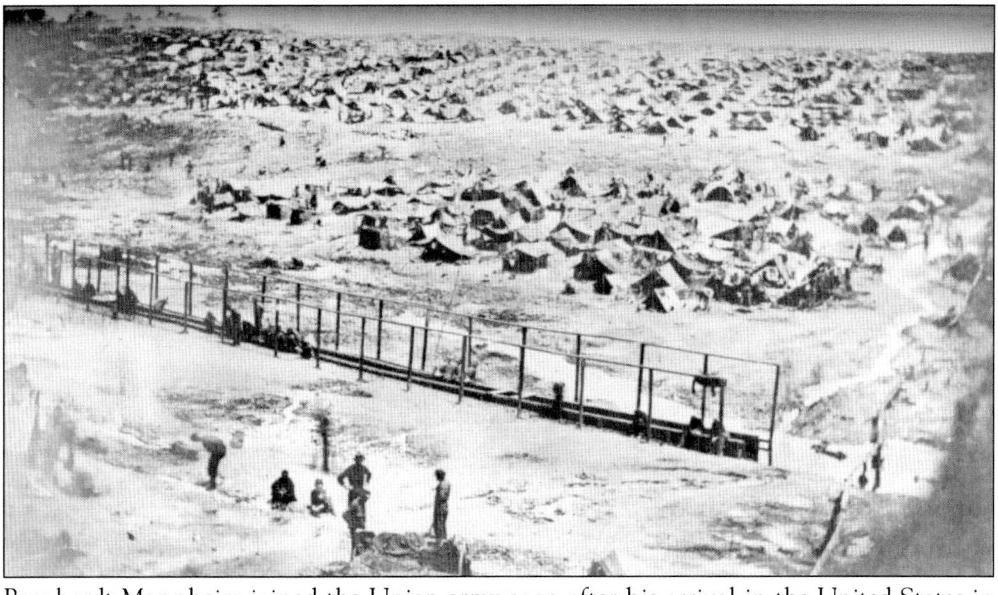

Bernhardt Mannheim joined the Union army soon after his arrival in the United States in 1860. Late in the Civil War, however, he was captured in battle and sent to Andersonville, the Confederacy's most infamous prison. Despite the prison's wretched conditions, Mannheim survived and made friends with a number of the Hawkinsville and Pulaski men who served as his guards. He apparently was so taken with his new friends and the area that he decided to settle in Hawkinsville after the war. (Courtesy of Library of Congress.)

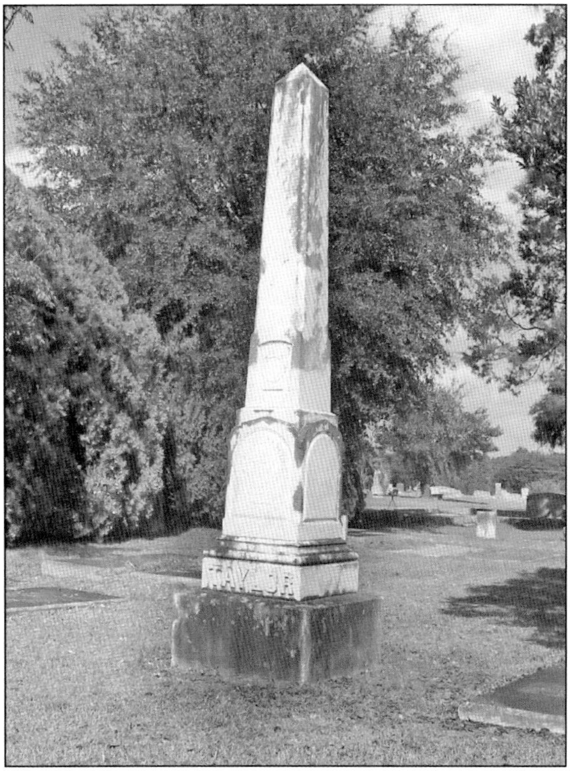

Prominent men of the community during the 19th century frequently chose obelisks and draped urns as fitting monuments to their lives. Obelisks, which date back to ancient Egypt, were adopted by the Romans as symbols of honor, virtue, and integrity. Such monuments also suggested virility and manhood. (Courtesy of Phillip A. Gibbs.)

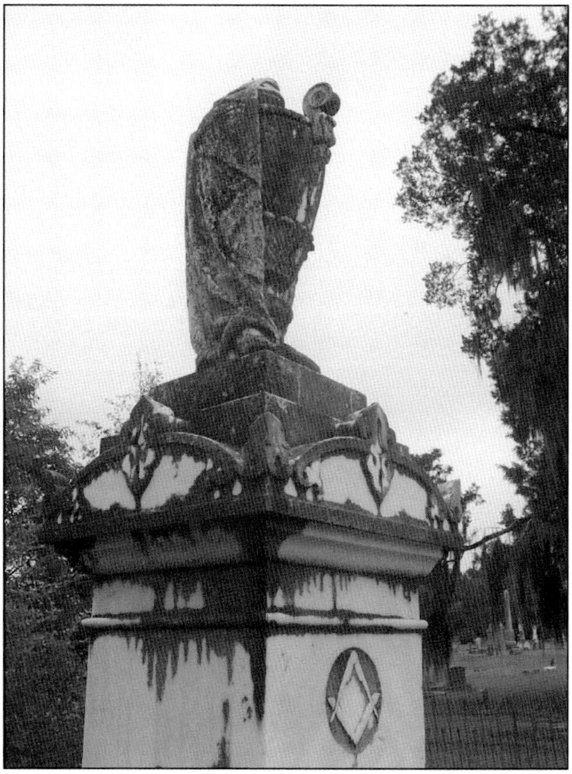

The draped urn that rests upon the pillar marking Gen. O. C. Horne's grave symbolizes immortality. Urns were used in Egypt for the storage and preservation of the deceased's internal organs. (Courtesy of Phillip A. Gibbs.)

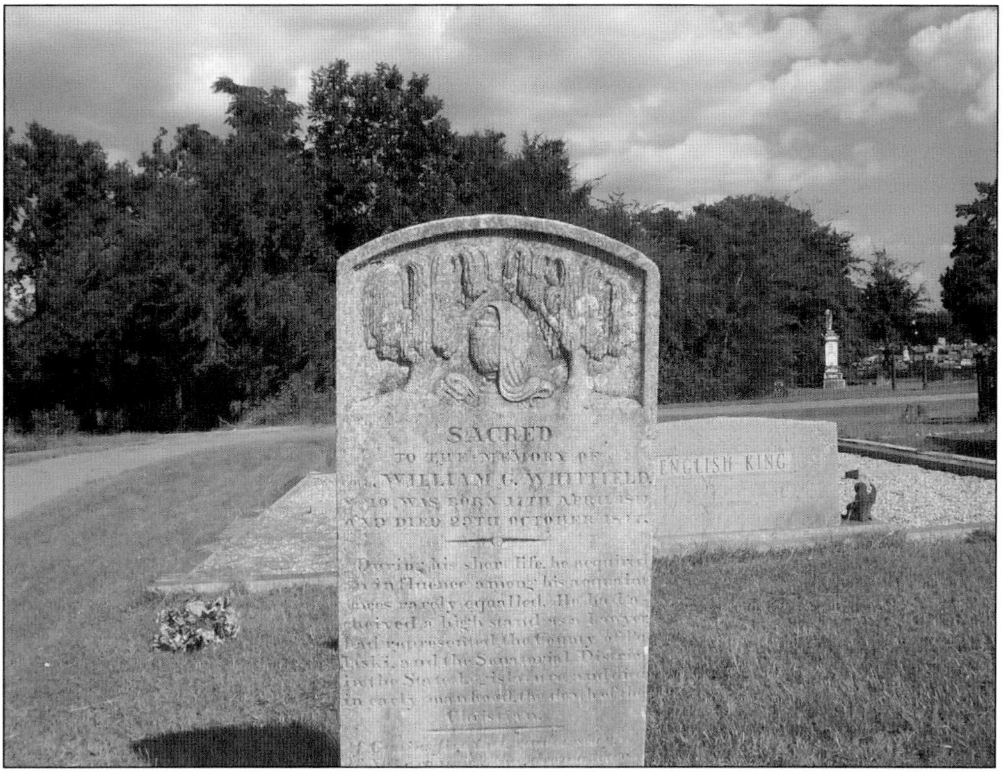

One common form of funerary art found in many cemeteries, particularly in the South, is the weeping willow tree. The willow tree, usually with one of its branches cut, symbolizes the sadness caused by the deceased's passing. (Courtesy of Phillip A. Gibbs.)

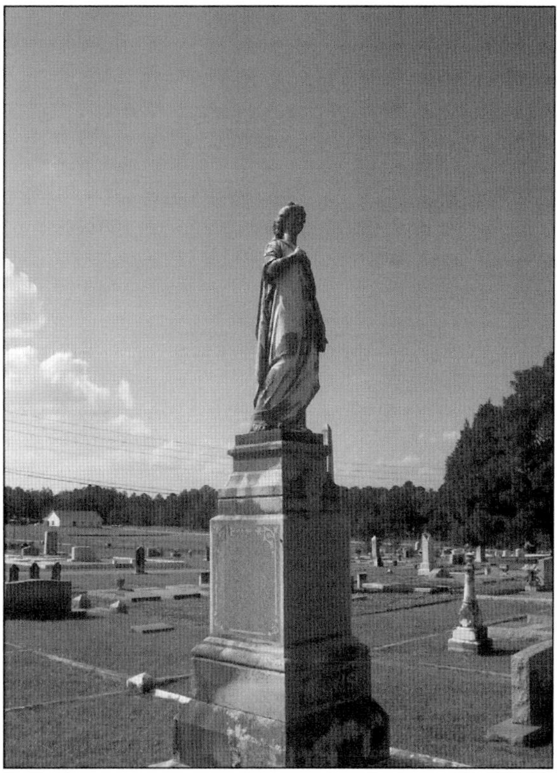

Angels such this one are often found in 19th-century cemeteries like Orange Hill. Such statues were intended to symbolize Christ's return. (Courtesy of Phillip A. Gibbs.)

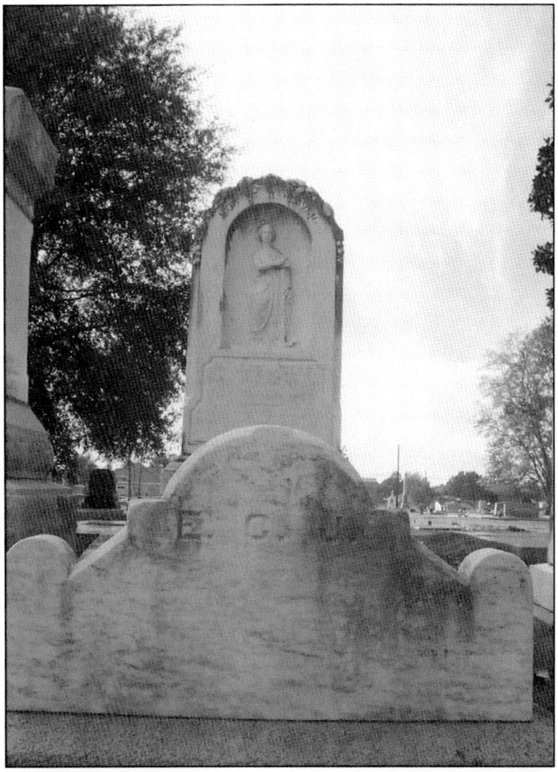

Standing inside this niche is a lady holding a large anchor. The anchor more than likely symbolizes her unwavering commitment to her faith and family. (Courtesy of Phillip A. Gibbs.)

During the 19th century, it was not uncommon for families to lose one or two children to the many diseases and ailments that afflicted the young and old during the period. To symbolize innocence, lambs were often placed upon the child's grave marker. (Courtesy of Phillip A. Gibbs.)

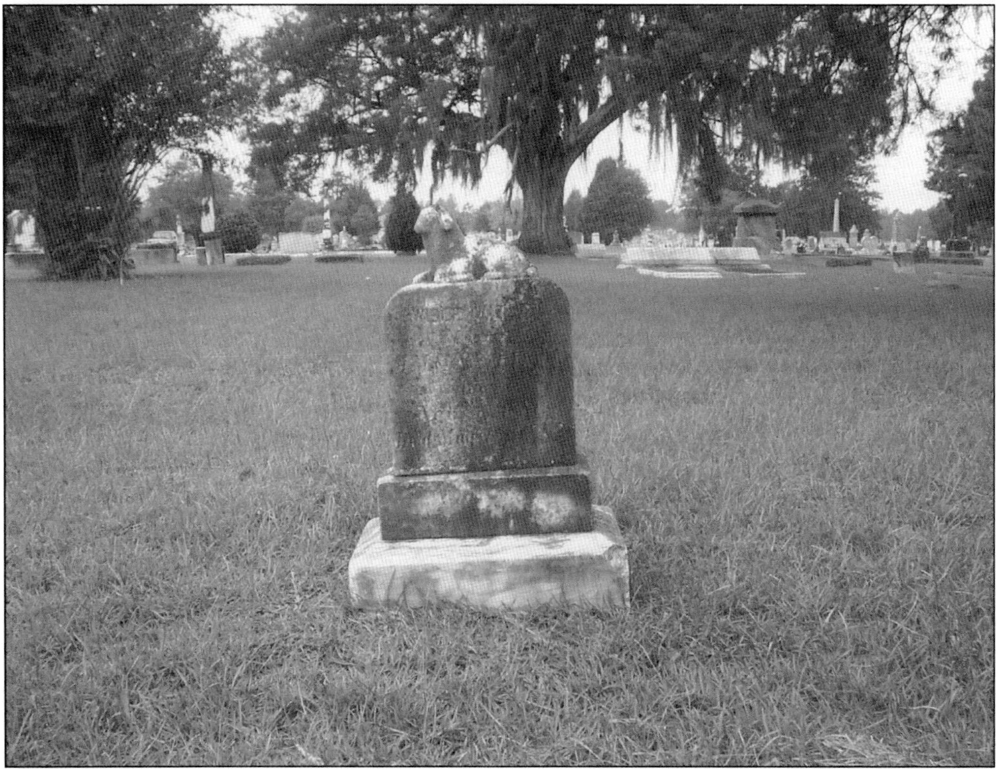

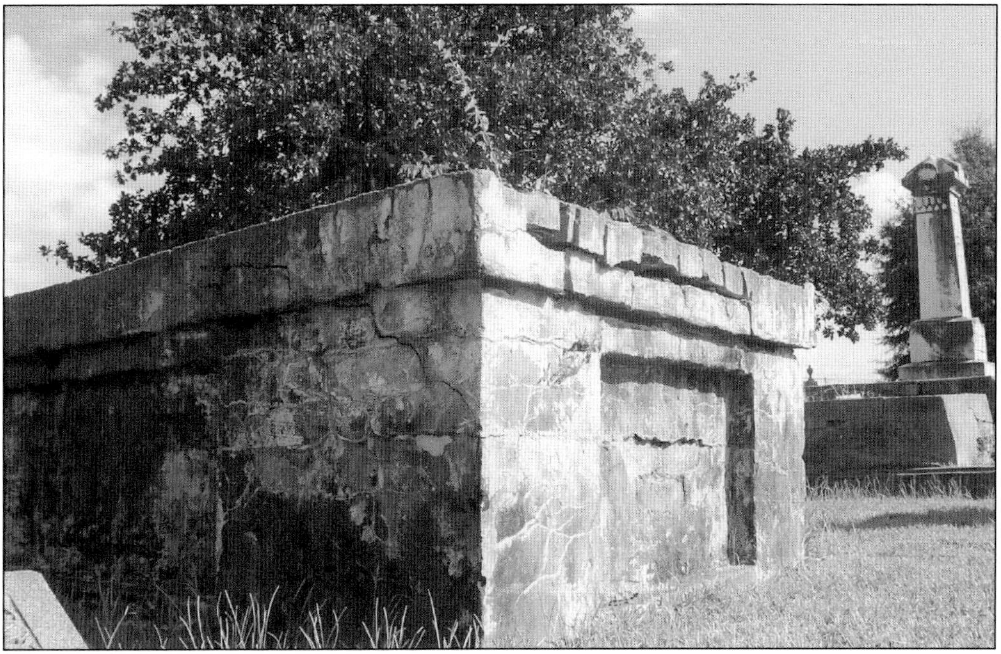

Some families chose to build crypts for their loved ones. Such crypts or vaults generally contained two to four bodies. In some cases, they could be entered so that the last remains of the deceased could be gathered and stored in urns to make room for other family members. (Courtesy of Phillip A. Gibbs.)

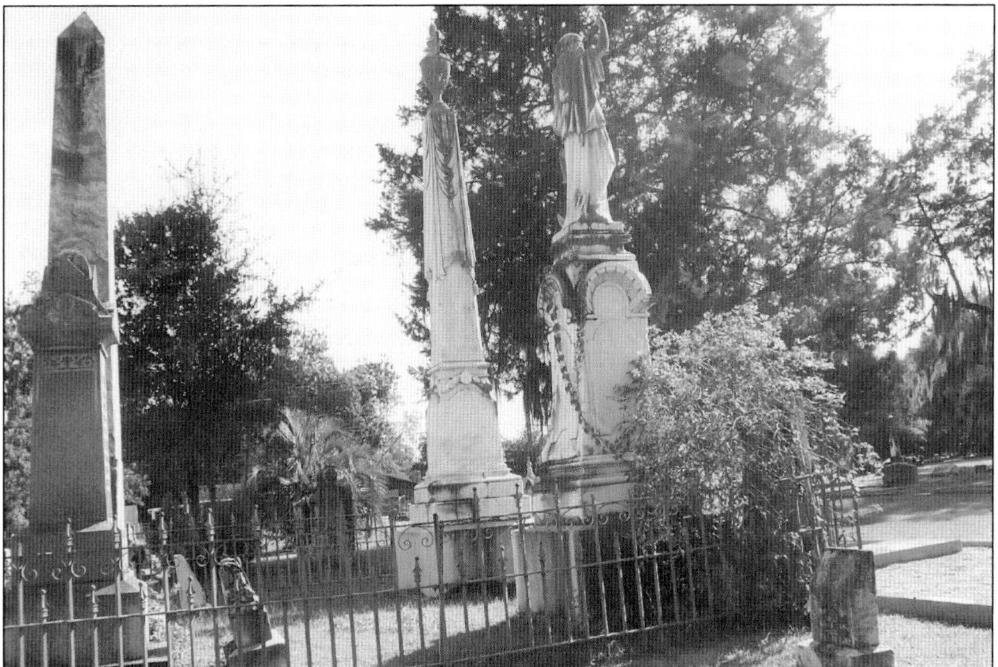

In this beautiful setting are three excellent examples of 19th-century funerary art: the angel (right), an urn resting on top of a draped pedestal (center), and an obelisk (left). (Courtesy of Phillip A. Gibbs.)

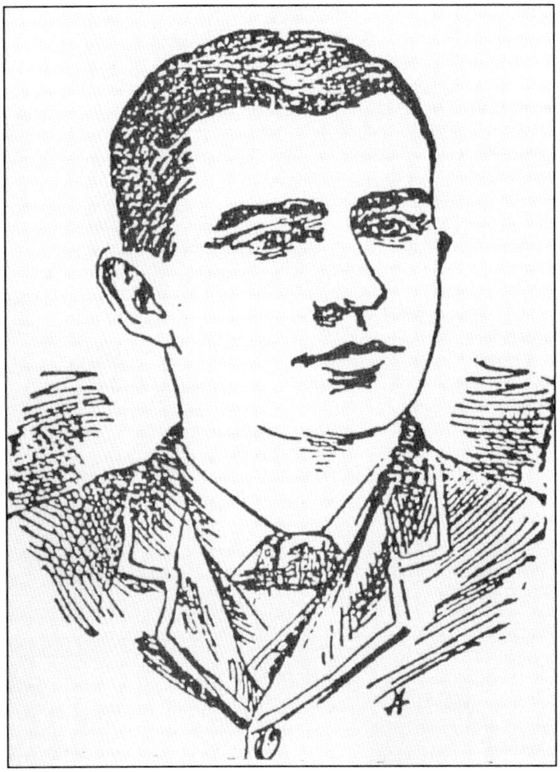

Among the monuments celebrating the lives of Hawkinsville's esteemed citizens is the grave of one of Georgia's most infamous murderers. On October 29, 1890, before a crowd of 10,000 people in Perry, Georgia, Thomas Woolfolk was hanged for the murder of nine members of his family. It was, according to many local and national newspapers, the most heinous crime of the century. The victims, three adults and six children, had been struck repeatedly with an ax. Although Tom maintained his innocence to the very end, the evidence seemed to point irrefutably to his guilt. After the hanging, Tom's sister Flo Edwards, a resident of Hawkinsville, requested that his body be brought back to the city for burial. (Courtesy of Washington Library, Macon, Georgia.)

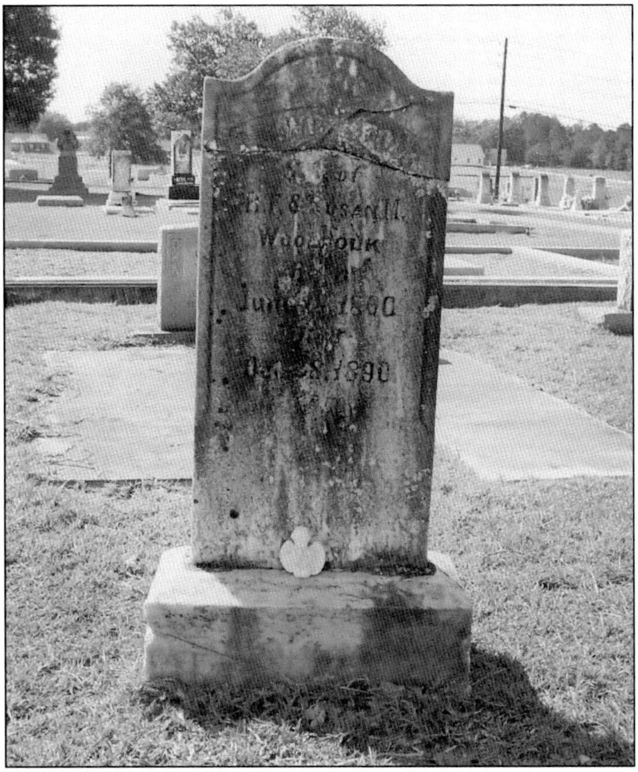

Today Tom Woolfolk lies next to his sister in Orange Hill Cemetery. The nine family members whom he allegedly killed are buried in Rose Hill Cemetery in Macon. (Courtesy of Phillip A. Gibbs.)

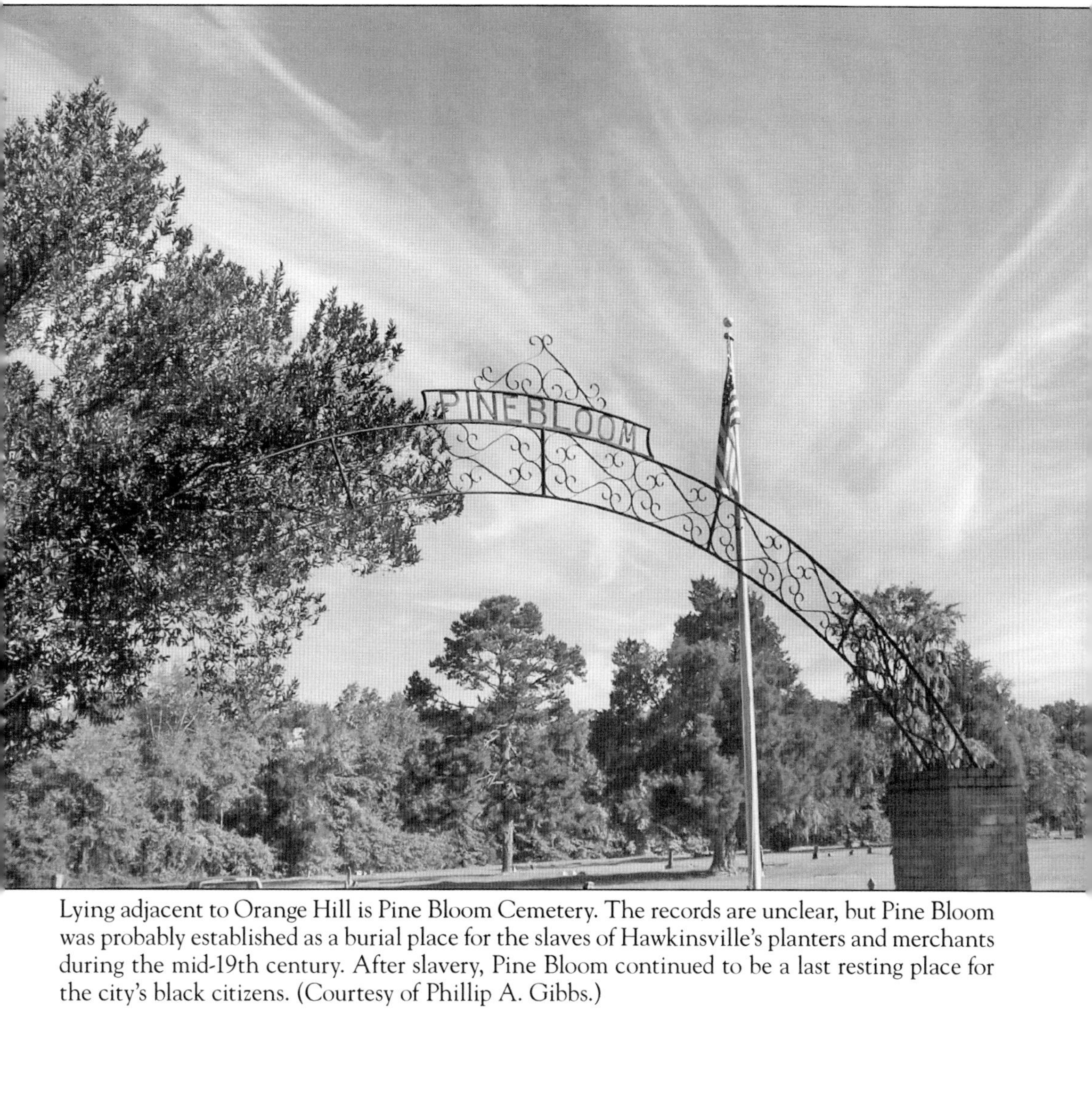

Lying adjacent to Orange Hill is Pine Bloom Cemetery. The records are unclear, but Pine Bloom was probably established as a burial place for the slaves of Hawkinsville's planters and merchants during the mid-19th century. After slavery, Pine Bloom continued to be a last resting place for the city's black citizens. (Courtesy of Phillip A. Gibbs.)

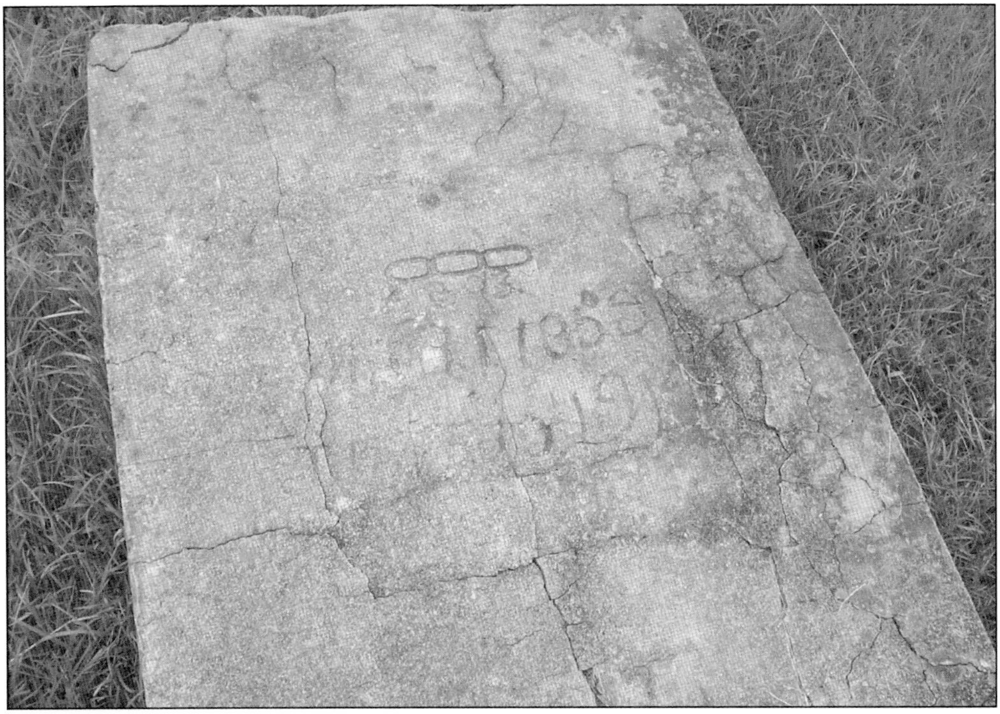

The name of the deceased is no longer legible, but it is apparent from the chain links in the stone and the birth date that he or she was born a slave. (Courtesy of Phillip A. Gibbs.)

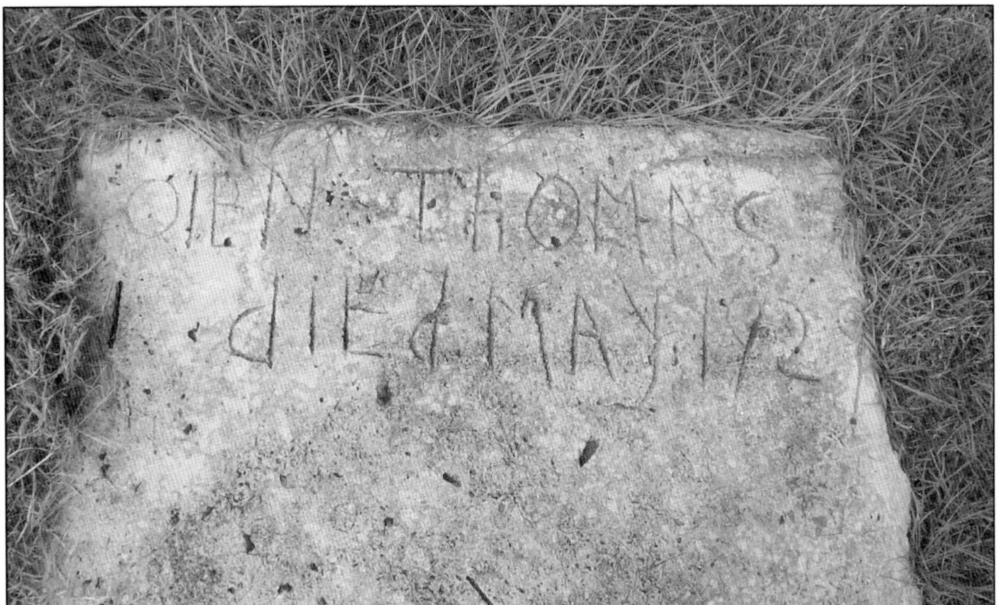

Many of Hawkinsville's black citizens were woefully under-prepared for the challenges of making their way in the world. Not surprisingly, they had little or no money to spend on grave markers or monuments. Moreover, prior to Emancipation, it was a crime to teach a slave to read and write. With only rudimentary writing skills, former slaves did the best that they could for their loved ones. (Courtesy of Phillip A. Gibbs.)

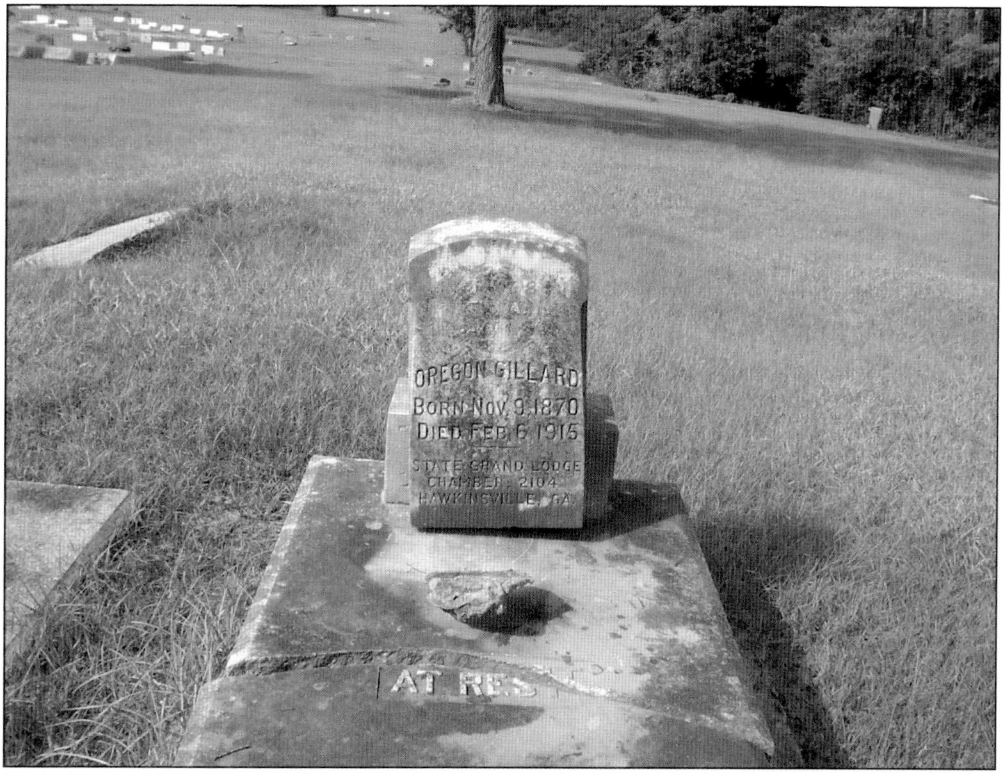

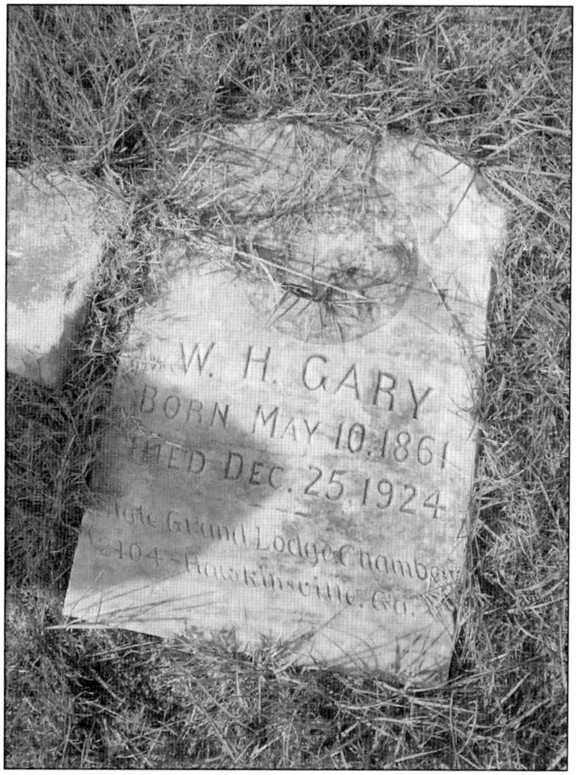

Many black citizens attended industrial schools, purchased land, and started their own businesses. They also joined social clubs, secret societies, and fraternal orders. Some, like Oregon Gillard and W. H. Gary, belonged to one of the Odd Fellows or Masonic Lodges established for black men during the late 19th century. Lodges like the Odd Fellows and Masons gave black men a sense of self worth and belonging. Such organizations also provided insurance plans and financial assistance for their members' families. (Both, courtesy of Phillip A. Gibbs.)

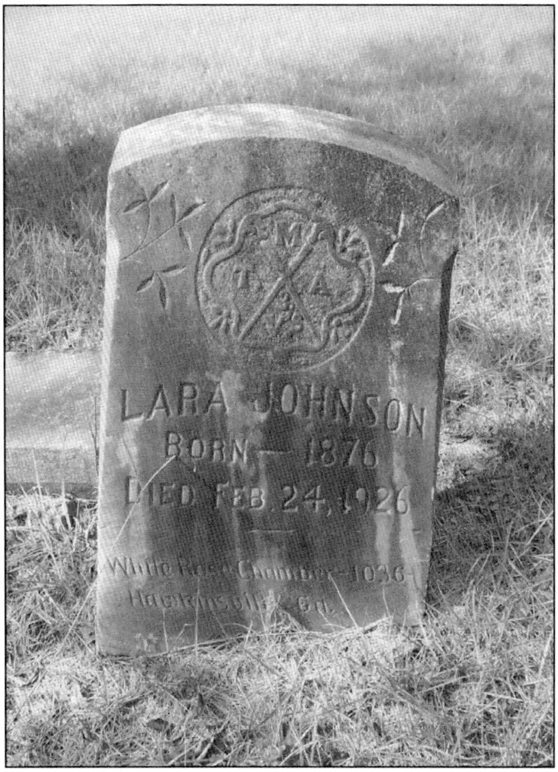

Hawkinsville women such as Lara Johnson and Fannie Way also belonged to civic organizations. Many such groups were auxiliaries of the Odd Fellows and the Masons. Two such organizations were the Daughters of Ruth and the White Rose Chamber. (Both, courtesy of Phillip Gibbs.)

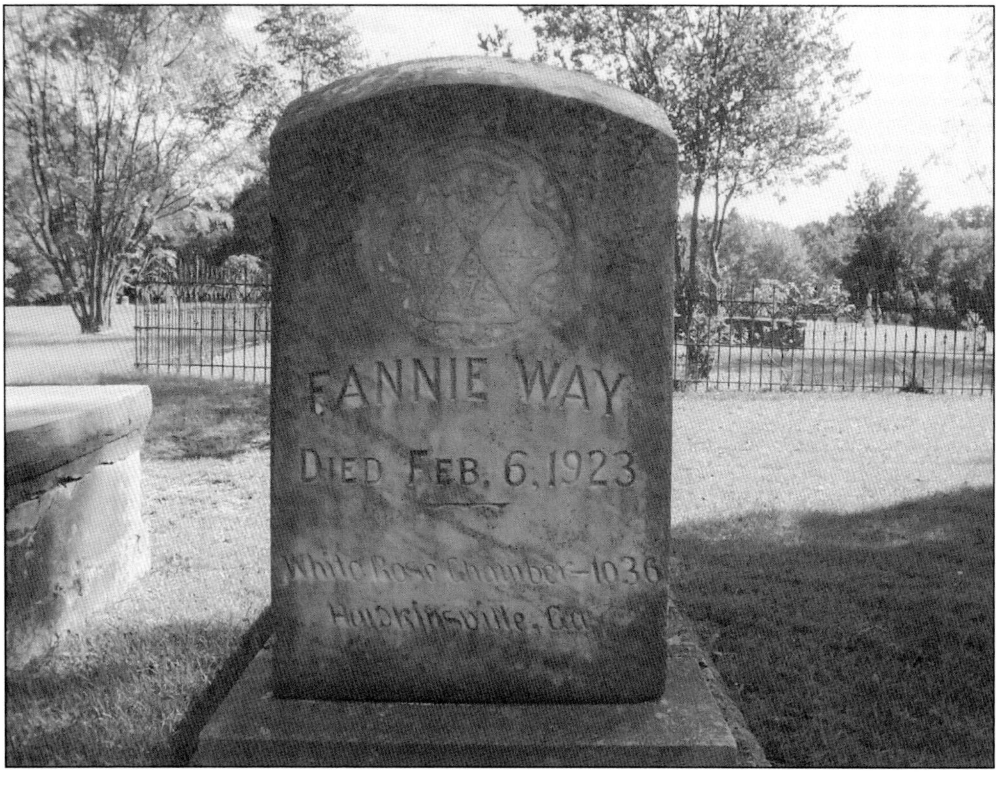

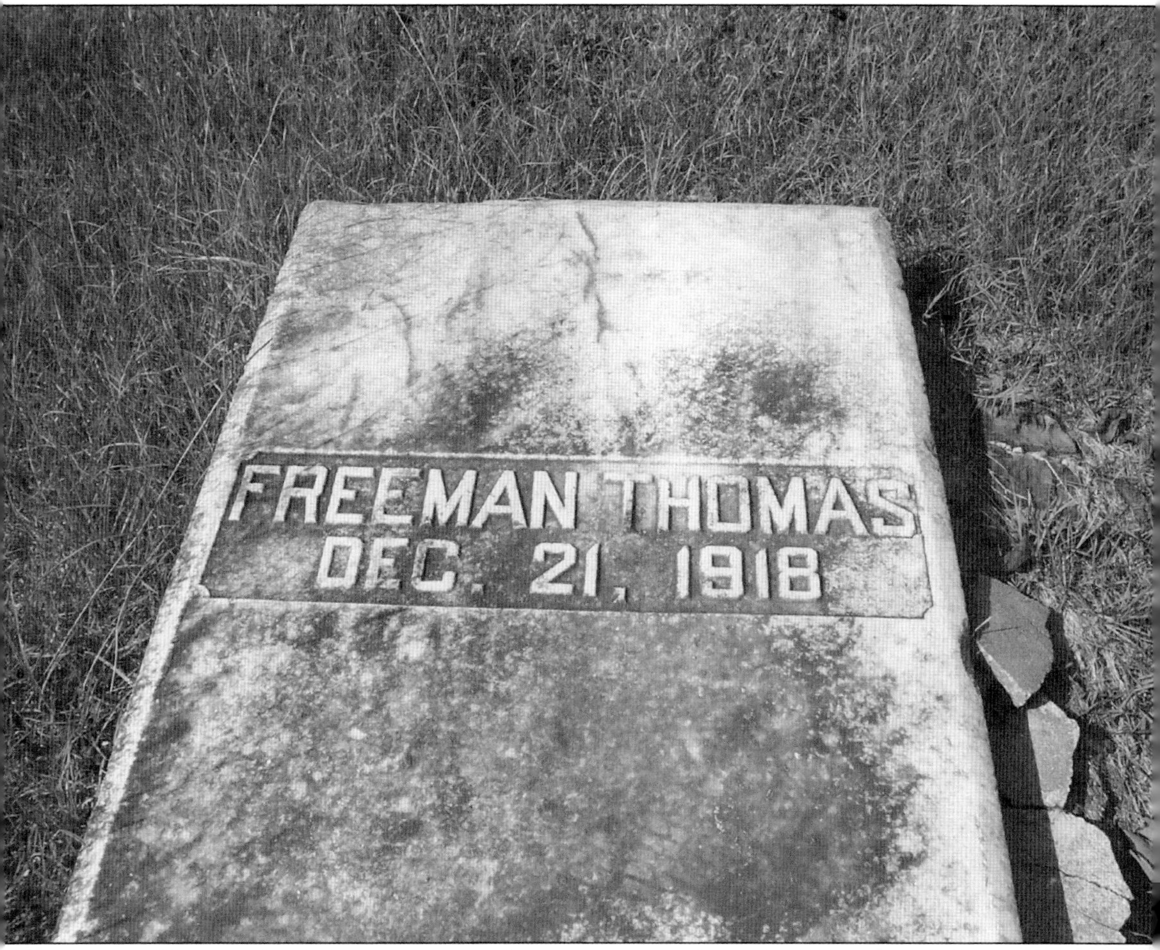

Freeman Thomas's birth date is not given, but one suspects that either Thomas took this name to celebrate his emancipation from slavery or his parents gave him the name to commemorate their own. (Courtesy of Phillip A. Gibbs.)

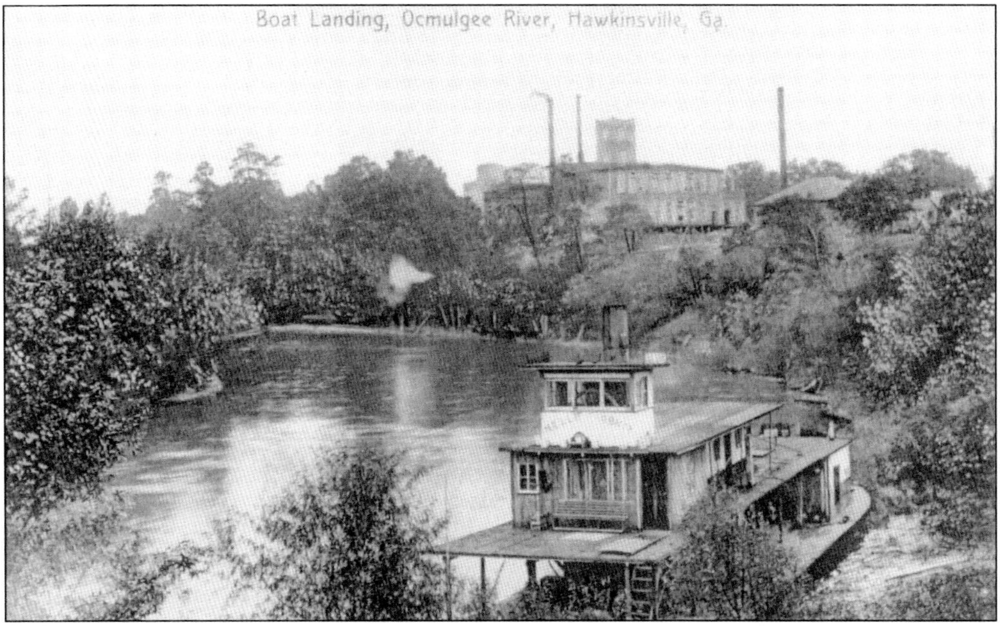

Hawkinsville's first 100 years saw the city rise from a small village on the banks of the Ocmulgee River to a thriving and vital center of transportation, commerce, industry, and agriculture. (Courtesy of Hawkinsville *Dispatch and News*.)

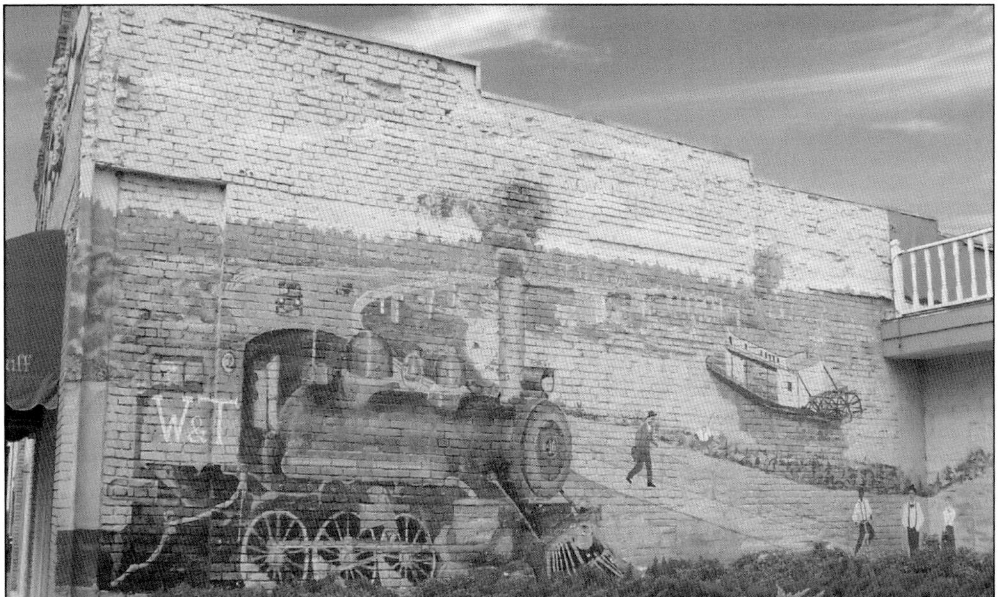

Drawing people from distant lands and all walks of life, Hawkinsville, as this Commerce Street mural suggests, flourished and became a hub of transportation by the early 20th century. And while it may never become a bustling metropolis like its neighbors to the north, it has managed to blend the best of the Old and New South. Rich in tradition, yet brimming with entrepreneurial spirit, Hawkinsville has always looked to the future without losing sight of its past. It remains in the hearts and minds of its citizens the "Queen City of the Wiregrass." (Courtesy of Phillip A. Gibbs.)

SELECTED BIBLIOGRAPHY

Coleman, Kenneth. *A History of Georgia*. Athens, GA: University of Georgia Press, 1991.

Dittmer, John. *Black Georgia in the Progressive Era, 1900–1920*. Urbana, IL: University of Chicago Press, 1977.

Daughters of the American Revolution. *History of Pulaski County, Georgia, 1808–1935*. Mansfield, OH: Book Masters, 2002.

Harris, Wallace. *History of Pulaski and Bleckley Counties, Georgia, 1808–1956*. Macon, GA: J. W. Burke Company, 1957.

Hawkinsville *Dispatch and News*.

Loftin, Bernadette Kuehn. *The Cochran Community: Development, Continuity, and Challenge*. Macon, GA: Uchee Trail Publishers, 1999.

Memoirs of Georgia. Atlanta: Southern Historical Association, 1895.

Miles, Jim. *Civil War Sites in Georgia*. Nashville, TN: Rutledge Hill Press, 1996.

Morrison, Carlton A. *Running the River: Poleboats, Steamboats, and Timber Rafts on the Altamaha, Ocmulgee, Oconee & Ohoopee*. St. Simons, GA: Saltmarsh Press, 2003.

Reidy, Joseph P. *From Slavery to Agrarian Capitalism in the Cotton Plantation South, Central Georgia, 1800–1880*. Chapel Hill, NC: University of North Carolina Press, 1992.

Remini, Robert V. *Andrew Jackson and the Course of American Empire, 1767–1821*. New York: Harper and Row, 1977.

Wetherington, Mark V. *Plain Folk's Fight: The Civil War and Reconstruction in Piney Woods, Georgia*. Chapel Hill, NC: University of North Carolina Press, 2005.

———. *The New South Comes to Wiregrass Georgia, 1860–1910*. Knoxville, TN: University of Tennessee Press, 1994.